Corporate Governance,
Market Structure and Innovation

Corporate Governance, Market Structure and Innovation

Edited by

Mario Calderini
Professor of Economics and Management, Politecnico di Torino, Italy

Paola Garrone
Professor of Economics, Politecnico di Milano, Italy

Maurizio Sobrero
Professor of Management, Università di Bologna, Italy

Edward Elgar
Cheltenham, UK • Northampton, MA, USA

Published by
Edward Elgar Publishing Limited
Glensanda House
Montpellier Parade
Cheltenham
Glos GL50 1UA
UK

Edward Elgar Publishing, Inc.
136 West Street
Suite 202
Northampton
Massachusetts 01060
USA

A catalogue record for this book
is available from the British Library

Library of Congress Cataloguing in Publication Data
Corporate governance, market structure, and innovation / edited by Mario Calderini, Paola Garrone, Maurizio Sobrero.
    p. cm.
Includes bibliographical references and index.
1. Corporate governance. 2. Technological innovations—Economic aspects. I. Calderini, Mario. II. Garrone, Paola, 1962– III. Sobrero, Maurizio, 1967–

HD2741 .C7765 2003
338—dc21   2002037944

ISBN 1 84064 876 7
Printed and bound in Great Britain by MPG Books Ltd, Bodmin, Cornwall

Contents

Figures

Tables

Contributors

Mario Calderini
Professor of Economics and Management, Politecnico di Torino, Italy

Paola Garrone
Professor of Economics, Politecnico di Milano, Italy

Giancarlo Giudici
Research Fellow, Department of Engineering, Università di Bergamo, Italy

Federico Munari
Research Fellow, Department of Management, Università di Bologna, Italy

Raffaele Oriani
Research Fellow, Department of Management, Università di Bologna, Italy

Stefano Paleari
Professor of Management and Finance, Università di Bergamo, Italy

Giuseppe Scellato
Research Fellow, Department of Production Economics, Politecnico di Torino, Italy

Maurizio Sobrero
Professor of Management, Università di Bologna, Italy

Preface

The purpose of this book is to investigate the relationship between corporate governance, market structure and research and development (R&D) performance. The motivation for our attempt is the observation that a number of radical mutations are occurring in industries that have played a crucial role in sustaining and fostering the pace of technological progress. Specifically, we refer to three classes of institutional discontinuities: privatization processes, the increase of mergers and acquisitions (M&As) and market liberalization.

In different countries, under different political regimes and governments, several state-owned activities in numerous manufacturing and service industries have recently been restructured and offered to private investors. Between 1977 and 1997, privatizations worldwide generated $520 billion revenues, from a total of 1 013 operations promoted largely in Europe and in South America. According to recent estimates, the number of firms to be privatized in the future is still around 1 500 and likely to generate revenues of $750 billion (Siniscalco et al., 1999). Governments' divestment of state-owned enterprises is usually accompanied by regulatory reforms of internal markets, aimed at both promoting widespread competition and attracting potential foreign and domestic investments in the companies to be sold.

In 1993 the mergers and acquisition activity gained new momentum, starting the so-called 'fifth wave'; by the end of the 1990s, the corporate combination process resulted in a yearly number of deals that more than doubled the 1993 level. Such a wave showed a strongly rising trend in high-value crossborder mergers, with a significant participation of European firms in the global M&A market. It can therefore be considered as the first truly international takeover wave. The most striking example was Vodafone's $180 billion acquisition of Mannesman in telecommunications, while the Daimler–Chrysler merger created one of the largest automotive groups in the world. At the same time, a number of acquisitions have targeted smaller domestic and foreign technology-based firms, especially in information and communication technologies and in bio-technologies.

Finally, over the last decade, many public utilities markets in the European Union have started their processes of liberalization. The old monopolies have been replaced by liberalized markets, where domestic and foreign investors are striving hard to establish and consolidate their market positions. The magnitude of the institutional change was particularly great in the telecom and energy markets; the most visible consequence of regulatory reforms induced by European directives is a striking downward trend of retail service prices. From 1997 to 2000, across the European Union countries, household prices for national calls, electricity, and natural gas experienced a yearly decrease rate equal to, respectively, 12 per cent, 15 per cent and 23 per cent (net of gas import prices).

It should be noted that the three processes are intimately intertwined. On the one hand, in most countries and in many sectors, governments wishing to expose industries to market discipline have jointly pursued privatization and liberalization programmes. On the other hand, the liberalization of final markets has in several cases spurred a phase of horizontal M&As and upward acquisitions through the *filière*, with privatized companies actively involved in corporate restructuring strategies.

Such institutional changes, both at the corporate and the industry levels, are usually deemed to produce virtuous effects in terms of static efficiency. Privatization processes, for example, allow governments to access new capital sources to structurally reduce operating deficits and to increase the independence of industry, to promote entrepreneurship and efficiency, and thereby enhance competitiveness and growth.

In contrast, the effects exerted on dynamic efficiency, and in particular on the incentives of the firms and of industry as a whole to sustaining an appropriate rate of innovative activity are largely unexplored by academics, and rarely acknowledged by institutional decision makers. Yet, numerous studies on R&D investments show that tomorrow's growth will strongly depend on today's innovation strategies.

Our goal is to show that an array of specific and new typologies of market failures may arise as a consequence of these discontinuities in corporate and product markets, along with the well-documented beneficial effects as far as allocative and productive efficiency are concerned. Such market failures may seriously affect the market value of the firm in the short run, and the performance of the national system of innovation as a whole in the medium/long run. For this reason, we argue that this issue should occupy a high position not only in managers' agenda but also in policy makers' lists of priorities.

We shall discuss and summarize the predictions made by theoretical studies about the likely implications of the institutional changes mentioned above on firms' innovation activities. However, our research programme stems from the view that these effects can be better understood through a set of coordinated yet specific empirical investigations. The privatization programme, regulatory reform and M&A wave that took place through the 1990s shaped a highly differentiated industrial landscape, by sectors and countries. More importantly, the three processes triggered a number of patterns of change that overlap and interact within individual companies.

When analysed empirically, the innovation process turns out to be affected by each of the considered institutional changes along different lines of argument. In particular, we investigate the effects of such events along three main dimensions: the change in R&D efforts (input), the R&D performance (output), and the organizational setting of the firm. The analysis of the first two dimensions (input and output) will be decomposed in order to allow us to account for two different characteristics of the firm's R&D portfolio, namely the intensity and the composition of its investments. In fact, both these characteristics are crucial in determining the performance of the single firm and of the national system of innovation as a whole. An articulated picture emerges from the comparison between theoretical predictions and empirical evidence, where corporate and product markets are shown to succeed in stimulating certain innovation activities and to fail in supporting others. Despite such a diversity, we believe that our empirical findings will eventually help to set out a coherent representation of the changes occurring in R&D activities at firm, industry and country levels, to validate a few theoretical hypotheses, and to raise new research questions.

From a methodological perspective, the reader will find in the different chapters a variety of research designs, analytical techniques and empirical approaches. We understand that such variance could lead to several negative comments. It could be disconcerting, as the book is not clearly following a specific discipline-based expected path. It could read as confusing, when different chapters are compared. It could weaken the final conclusions by building on different research perspectives that too often pursue similar interests without turning aside from the well-worn track.

We believe that these very same weaknesses are the strengths of our collective efforts, for several reasons. First, as showed at the beginning of the book, the research agenda we are interested in lies at the intersection of several disciplines. A multidisciplinary–multimethod approach is therefore necessary if we do not want to oversimplify a fairly complex picture. Second, the specific problems we are discussing are hardly modelled in simple terms, and necessarily require a systemic perspective, which could not fruitfully be applied within a single study, though it could benefit tremendously by coordinating the efforts of several studies sharing several important commonalities. Finally, while there are many differences, there are also many similarities, and these similarities are related to what we believe is fundamental, from a methodological perspective.

The most important point shared by all the different studies presented in the book is our view of the economic actors as boundedly rational and operating in a world of imperfect information, be they firms, managers or policy makers. Second, rather than applying more normative cause-and-effect models, or phenomenological approaches, we all share the belief that the nature of our research problem can best be understood and investigated by relying on the Weberian notion of adequate causation, where the focus is not only on the issue of interest, but also in the simultaneous occurrences of different conditions in the external environment. While this approach is highly considered and applied in other disciplines, such as macro-sociology or political science, we believe that it is particularly appropriate to consider a problem so complex and articulated as the one characterizing the relationships among corporate governance, market structure and innovation. Finally, all studies used the same unit of analysis, namely the firm. This is not a research book about countries, technological and innovation systems, groups of individuals or individual behaviour. This is a book about firm behaviours and their relationships with the related institutions, product markets and financial markets, always carefully analysed and taken into consideration, but never taking any primacy. We hope that we shall convince the reader throughout the book that our intuitions are not a sign of arrogance, but rather an attempt to practice a multidisciplinary approach coherently.

The book is structured in three parts, followed by a concluding chapter. Each chapter, in its conclusions, together with the merits of the single study also presents the specific limitations and some suggestions on how to go beyond such limitations. The first part of the book outlines the theoretical setting, which constitutes the background for the empirical analyses developed and illustrated in the second and third parts. In Chapter 1, Munari and Sobrero analyse several aspects of corporate governance structuring decisions and their effects on innovation activities. They examine to what extent the tension between ownership and control, the role and characteristics of the shareholders, and the role and the characteristics of the board influence the decision to invest in innovation. Building on the most recent results presented by research in economics, strategy and organization theory, the chapter offers the reader a systematic rationalization of usually dispersed evidence and introduces formally the research questions which will be further elaborated in the rest of the book. In Chapter 2, Calderini and Garrone present a selective review of the literature on market structure and innovation; they survey the most recent contributions from a particular viewpoint, the so-called 'short-termism' debate. The main insights of this stream of studies are mediated from the traditional context of financial markets into the field of end-product markets, in order to analyse the relationship between a changing market structure and the composition of R&D portfolios (in terms of basic/long-term and applied/short-term activities). Finally, in Chapter 3 Calderini and Garrone survey the predicted effects of acquisitions on the post-acquisition innovation performance of the acquired firm. The review considers four major drivers, which are deemed to affect the innovation performance of the acquired company: the change in the ownership and financial structure; the change in corporate structure; the change in size; and the change in organization.

The second part of the book illustrates the results of the empirical analysis. We present four different contributions. In Chapter 4, Munari and Sobrero analyse the effects of privatization processes on R&D investments and productivity. They compare the pre- and post-privatization R&D efforts of 35 companies from nine European countries that were fully or partially privatized through public share offering between 1980 and 1997. Their results show that, after controlling for inter-industry differences, privatization processes negatively affect different measures of R&D commitment. Moreover, they suggest that, the higher is the transfer of control from the state to private shareholders, the higher is the change in the investment horizons of the companies. The R&D output, as measured by overall patenting activity as well as by the value of the patents registered (measured by citation intensity), however, improves after the privatization period.

In Chapter 5, Calderini and Garrone analyse the effect of an exogenous change in market structure (the liberalization process) on the intensity and composition of R&D activities at the firm level. They present an empirical model set to demonstrate that basic and applied activities respond to growing competitive pressure in opposite ways: the former decreases, whereas the latter increases. As a consequence, market turmoil is likely to provide firms with short-term incentives, shifting the allocation of resources towards applied and development activities. The model is tested on an original data set drawn from the telecom sector, including innovation measures from the incumbent national monopolies of 17 European countries between 1980 and 1999. They demonstrate that concurrent with (or in anticipation of) the liberalization date, firms tend to change the composition of their R&D portfolio, allocating more resources to development activities and reducing their efforts towards basic research tasks.

In Chapter 6 Calderini, Garrone and Scellato use data from the US stock market in order to empirically assess the effect of acquisitions on the innovation performance of the acquired companies. They study the companies that went public on one of the US stock markets during the years 1989–92 and belonging to the information and communication technology (ICT) industry. Through the analysis of a sample of 115 firms they show that target companies tend to significantly reduce their patenting activity immediately after the acquisition is completed.

Finally, in Chapter 7 Munari examines the impact of privatization on the R&D internal organizational structures and processes. By using a multiple case-study approach, he examines the evolution of corporate R&D units within privatized companies, focusing on four primary areas of intervention in the management of technology and innovation: the aim of R&D units; the size of R&D units; the composition and funding of the R&D portfolio; and the valorization of research outcomes. The analysis of the experiences of the corporate R&D units of Telecom Italia, Ilva and Enel in Italy, and of France Télécom, Usinor and Renault in France, documents and discusses how privatization exerts a relevant influence on the way R&D activities are organized along different critical dimensions, consistent with the new role emerging for R&D in a changed institutional and competitive environment.

In the third part of the book we shall be highlighting the impact of innovation and R&D on a firm's market value and finance, and getting a better understanding of how market and corporate governance structure mediate such a relationship.

In Chapter 8 Oriani and Sobrero present a meta-analysis of the empirical literature linking R&D investments and firms' performance and assess the magnitude of the reported coefficients against three potential moderating factors: the time window used in the study, the reliability of the independent variable and the reliability of the dependent variable. Applying Hunter and Schmidt correction procedures on all the published studies using hedonic models to estimate the impact of different corporate assets on the market value of the firm, the relationship is shown to be consistently positive. Significant differences in the size of the effect emerge, however, depending on the period of observation, while the concerns commonly raised on empirical indicators such as Tobin's q or R&D investment measures find no empirical support.

In Chapter 9, Munari and Oriani examine the relationship between privatization, R&D investments and the market value of the firm, using data from a sample of 40 firms – including 19 privatized firms that were matched, at both country and industry levels, with 19 publicly-held firms Their findings show that, during the first two years after the initial public offering (IPO), firms reduce the level of their R&D investments, while their market valuation, expressed by Tobin's q, rises. Moreover, they show that the first year after IPO there is a gap between the R&D investments of privatized and matched firms, which tends to disappear from year two onward.

In Chapter 10, Giudici and Paleari focus on R&D and innovation financing, and on how small innovative firms may raise capital on stock markets to finance their growth through innovative investments. They focus in particular on stock exchanges designed for technology-based and innovative firms. The analysis, based on a sample of firms recently listed on pan-European stock markets (Easdaq and Euro-NM), allows the authors to determine the value drivers recognized by the market both in the short and long runs.

We conclude by summarizing the results obtained on both the theoretical and the empirical sides, trying to set our conclusions in a comprehensive scenario (Chapter 11) to offer our readers some reflections on the strategy and policy implications arising from the analysis of this crucial set of interrelated topics.

Mario Calderini, Paola Garrone, Maurizio Sobrero

Acknowledgements

We would like to thank many colleagues and friends who have criticized and supported our research efforts over the years. We are particularly grateful to Cristiano Antonelli (University of Turin), Luigi Buzzacchi (Polytechnic University of Turin), Franco Fontana (LUISS Guido Carli, Rome) Alessandro Grandi (University of Bologna), Gianni Lorenzoni (University of Bologna), Bronwyn Hall (University of California, Berkeley), Sergio Mariotti (Polytechnic University of Milan), Stan Metcalfe (University of Manchester), Edward B. Roberts (Massachusetts Institute of Technology), Sergio Rossetto (Polytechnic University of Turin), Peter Swann (Manchester Business School), Thierry Weil (Ecole des Mines de Paris) and Andrea Zanoni (University of Bologna).

Mario Calderini also owes a particular debt to the people at CRIC (University of Manchester), where he found a stimulating and creative research environment, and in particular to John Cantwell (University of Reading) and Jeremy Howells (University of Manchester), for their sharp and valued comments on his PhD dissertation at the University of Manchester.

Most of the studies included in this volume were presented at different conferences all over the world, and we are indebted to all the people who on those occasions provided useful comments and criticisms. Among these, we remember with particular gratitude the ones organized at the Fondazione Giovanni Agnelli by Dr Marco Demarie, who has constantly supported our research activities.

We were also lucky, over this period, to have worked with a great number of clever and committed students, whose research work contributed significantly to the realization of this book. In particular, we wish to mention Chiara Laudanna (Polytechnic University of Turin), Antonio Pugliafico (Polytechnic University of Milan), Lorenzo Trapani (University of Bergamo) and the students of the Dottorato in Economia e Management della Tecnologia at the Polytechnic University of Turin and University of Bergamo and of the Dottorato in Direzione Aziendale at the University of Bologna.

Finally, we owe a special thank you to Dr Barbara Sancin whose invaluable editorial work and patience was greatly appreciated.

The research work presented in this volume was carried on within the project 'Ricerca Industriale e Innovazione Tecnologica: privatizzazione, apertura dei mercati, assetti economico-finanziari' (COFIN 2001, prot. 2001097179-003) funded by the Ministero dell'Istruzione, Università e Ricerca (MIUR), whose crucial support is gratefully acknowledged.

PART I

Market Structure,
Corporate Governance and Innovation

1. Corporate Governance and Innovation

Federico Munari and Maurizio Sobrero

1. INTRODUCTION

This chapter reviews the theoretical contributions and the empirical studies linking corporate governance structures and innovation. Both concepts have attracted the attention of a vast community of scholars coming from different disciplinary perspectives. It is therefore important to clearly assess at the beginning of this chapter the boundaries of discussion with respect to the assumptions made on both issues.

Corporate governance refers to the set of internal and external control mechanisms that reduce the conflicts of interest between managers and shareholders deriving from the separation of ownership and control (Berle and Means, 1932; Fama and Jensen, 1983; Shleifer and Vishny, 1986). A possible approach to the corporate governance problem emphasizes the role of external institutions and organizations in alleviating the agency costs arising from the specialization of management and finance, as in the case of the legal protection given to investors from the risks of expropriation by managers (Shleifer and Vishny, 1986). However, in this chapter we shall explicitly focus on the core internal relationships between managers and shareholders and refer to some critical characteristics in a company's governance system, such as large individual shareholders, institutional investors, the role of the government within state enterprises, and the board of directors. Moreover, we shall emphasize the implications of the theoretical arguments discussed not only for the relationship between managers and shareholders, but also, within management, between decision makers and executors.

We interpret innovation activities as a set of interwoven processes, starting with the generation of new knowledge targeted to the discovery of new products and processes, and ending with their commercial exploitation. These processes are multiple, overlapping and performed by a multitude of different actors inside and outside companies, with a distribution of actions and decision making at different organizational levels, which is often difficult to observe and monitor. As a consequence, innovation activities are related both

3

to higher-level structural organizational arrangements, and to lower-level microbehavioural attainments.

The different dimensions of corporate governance structures and instruments cross all these levels and, as we shall see throughout this chapter, create a set of conditions that can profoundly affect the nature and the direction of innovative activities. Economic approaches rooted in transaction cost theory and in agency theory rely on the high level of uncertainty characterizing innovation activities, the presence of asymmetric information between researchers and decision makers, and the high level of asset specificity generated by dedicated R&D investments, to link governance structures and innovation.

The increasing strategic importance of innovation and the concurrent wide-spread diffusion of several reforms, both in the international capital markets and in the regulatory frameworks of all major industrialized countries, require a deeper analysis of the empirical consistency of these theoretical predictions. Such analysis should also discriminate among the different aspects of innovation activities, as well as among the different elements of corporate governance structuring decisions.

Starting from a threefold distinction of the latter, in the following sections we analyse to what extent the tension between ownership and control, the role and characteristics of the shareholders, and those of the board influence the decision to invest in innovation. Building on the most recent results presented by research in economics, strategy and organization theory, we offer to the reader a systematic rationalization of usually dispersed evidence and introduce formally the research questions which will be further elaborated in Chapters 2 and 3, to be investigated empirically in the following chapters.

2.   THE TENSION BETWEEN OWNERSHIP AND CONTROL

The theoretical underpinnings of the separation of ownership and control rests upon the assumption of the benefits of a functional division of roles between capital holders and managers. On the one hand, investors can benefit from the potential gains of entrepreneurial ventures without necessarily possessing managerial skills or any in-depth knowledge of the businesses they invested in. On the other hand, managers can leverage on their competencies and focus on profitable business opportunities even when lacking the personal resources or collaterals needed to secure debt financing.

This functional distribution of roles within the organization generates the well-known distinction between those who invest (the principals) and those who make use of the resources invested (the agents); besides, it generates the costs associated with the monitoring of the agents by the principal (the agency costs). Agency costs arise out of a structural misalignment between the principal's and the agents' incentives. On the one hand, the principal expects his/her agents to maximize the returns of his/her investments. On the other hand, agents 'have an incentive to consume excessive leisure, perquisites and in general be less dedicated to the goal of wealth maximization than they would if they were not simply agents' (Jensen and Meckling, 1976, p. 509). Monitoring efforts, therefore, become an inherent condition of the way public organizations are directed and controlled, and account for a significant portion of agency costs, together with the costs incurred in aligning the management's incentives to the shareholders' and to impose sanctions on inefficient behaviours.

Since the seminal work published by Berle and Means in 1932 as a response to the increasing diffusion of a distributed stock-ownership structure in the US economy, the general framework of the agency theory briefly sketched above has been extensively used, either to devise optimal agents' compensation schemes, or to identify the costs and effectiveness of different monitoring mechanisms, and also to compare the effects of alternative governance structures on management decisions and market reactions. Within the extremely broad and qualified set of studies related to all these issues, for our purposes it is important to focus on those that have directly considered innovative activities, either in their empirical analysis or in their theoretical models.

In particular, in the following subsection we shall start by revising the market efficiency assumption and the so-called 'short-termism' criticism as a possible explanation of the unresolved inefficiencies in the allocation of resources to innovative investments.[1] We shall then focus on how differences in the level of concentration of the ownership structure might affect the characteristics of the investments in R&D activities. Finally, we shall move to the analysis of the different mechanisms used to control management's decisions and actions, and try to assess how these mechanisms can influence the amount and kind of the innovative activities pursued.

2.1 The Short-termism Criticism

Capital market myopia in the evaluation of long-term investments is proposed by research on corporate restructuring as the determinant of lower levels of investments in innovation. The argument is simple and strictly related to the agency theory approach to the analysis of corporate governance structure. While shareholders might benefit from the high-risk/high-return strategies associated with aggressive R&D investments, thanks to their ability to distribute investment variance throughout their portfolio, managers' risk is inherently firm specific and cannot be diversified. Managers are, therefore, naturally risk averse and prefer to emphasize short-term gains through efficiency-seeking strategies, which might, however, hamper long-term returns. The increased amount of capital invested in the stock markets, the fragmentation of the shareholding base within each individual company, the increased importance of individual investors and the increased reliance of internal control systems on financial performance indicators, all combine to strengthen the rationality of managerial risk aversion, with the overall effect of depressing innovation-related investments.

Evidence on the early 1980s in the US showed that expected or realized changes in the shareholder base of 24 of the top 200 R&D spenders resulted in a decline of R&D investments of 5.3 per cent, while the other 176 top spenders increased theirs by 5.4 per cent (Pollak, 1989). Similarly, using more aggregate data, the decrease in US R&D spending at the beginning of the 1980s has also been linked to an increased occurrence of mergers and takeovers. Meulbroek et al. (1990) report that firms having successfully avoided takeover bids, afterwards tend to decrease their R&D spending, almost as if this was a direct signal of increased managerial attention to the principals' interests.

More recently, Roberts (2001) compared the changes and the evolution of strategic management of technology of large R&D investing firms in North America, Europe and Japan during the 1990s. Focusing on about 250 firms with an annual budget of at least 100 million current US dollars, he showed that, even after controlling for industry-specific effects, both corporate and business unit long-term R&D allocation decreased significantly (from 42 per cent to 32 per cent and from 13 per cent to 10 per cent of the available budget, respectively), while development projects, and even nearer-term product and process technical support, were assigned an increasing amount of resources and importance.

Advocates of capital market efficiency replied by showing different results and claiming that restructuring occurs to cut back unproductive investments and eliminate unprofitable projects. The timing of expected positive returns would only affect the option chosen to leverage financial sources, while the profitability of the investments will determine market evaluation (Hall, 1990a). In her review of the studies on this subject, for example, Hall (1994) showed that restructuring pressures and the decline in long-term investments such as R&D expenses were concentrated in mature industries and were perfectly rational, considering the high interest rates and a tax system favouring debt over equity.

Several scholars analysed the relationship between R&D spending and end-of-the-year market value of the firm, showing a positive effect of appropriable innovation in industries characterized by higher expected technological changes. Event analyses documented positive share price responses following long-term investment that included R&D changes (McConnell and Muscarella, 1985; Woolridge and Snow, 1990; Bajo et al., 1998). Chan et al. (1990) showed, in a sample of 95 announcements of increase in R&D spending, that the share value increased immediately after the day of the announcement, but only for high-tech firms and not for low-tech ones. They concluded that markets are efficiently evaluating not merely capital allocation, but more importantly expected returns, which in industries that are technologically mature might not justify an intensification of R&D efforts.

Similarly, building on Fazzari et al.'s (1988) results, showing that liquidity and corporate value affect investments, Cho (1998) provided a direct test of whether ownership structure affects investments by building endogeneity into his model, and concluding that investments in R&D affect the corporate value, which in turn affects the ownership structure. More recent research also showed high levels of inter-temporal and inter-industry variability in the shadow value of R&D investment on firms' market value (Chan et al., 1999). Such volatility points to the need to open up the 'black box' of firm's effect to analyse the role, if any, of reputation, learning, and technological or market uncertainty. At the same time, however, it also raises a number of issues related to the characteristics of the governance structure and the innovation-related investment behaviours.

For example, all studies agree that, under capital rationalization pressures, investments in R&D are more likely to decrease, due to both the high relevance of information asymmetries between insiders and outsiders, and the imperfection of current accounting systems (Lev and Zarowin, 1999). Moreover, while markets can efficiently react to the appropriate signals, investors options might be limited, due to some imperfections associated with the governance systems in place. To fully explore the debate raised by the short-termism criticism it is therefore necessary to open the 'black box' of corporate governance systems and to highlight some specific issues related to several of its composing elements. In the next subsection we shall, therefore, start from the characteristics of the ownership structure.

2.2 Diffused versus Concentrated Ownership Structure

The relevance of the distribution of ownership is a controversial issue raised by the agency theory framework. In principle, in fact, inefficient management practices are sanctioned by the market of corporate control through hostile takeovers and the replacement of the older management team, regardless of the distribution of shareholders. In a world of perfect information and trivial coordination costs it is in the best interest of shareholders to 'exit' investments performing below expectations, by diluting or completely selling their current holdings to outside bidders, whatever the amount of share they possessed.

In one of the few empirical studies on this subject, Demsetz and Lehn (1985) used data on the ownership structure of large US firms collected by the Corporate Data Exchange database on stockholdings. They found no relationship between the degree of ownership concentration (measured by a Herfindal index of stock distribution) and return on assets. They therefore concluded that firm performance is not influenced by ownership structure.

Several elements exist, however, to question the full validity of the theoretical assumptions lying behind the complete efficiency of the market for corporate control argument. First, monitoring managerial behaviour in practice requires setting up control mechanisms generating fixed costs, which might discourage small shareholders from pursuing such activities and leave managers leeway to maximize their own utility function. Second, the 'exit' option itself can be costly, if coalitions among small shareholders must be organized to remove managers or stimulate takeover bids. Based on anecdotal evidence, for example, Cowan (1988) calculated that in the late 1980s the costs of a so-called 'proxy battle' were about $1.7 million, de facto limiting its use to coalitions of large and powerful shareholders. More formally, Shleifer and Vishny (1986) demonstrated that the higher the proportion of firm share held by the largest shareholder, the more likely the takeover bid. Moreover, an increase in the legal and administrative costs of takeovers reduces the welfare of the small shareholders, despite an increase in takeover premia.

These potential critical aspects in the monitoring and investment liquidation practices must also be considered together with the characteristics of the institutional environment where the firm's activities occur. Political economy scholars, for example, have long compared the different structural characteristics of the US and UK markets to those of Germany and Japan, showing that, while in the former there are a relatively large number of publicly-owned quoted companies, with liquid markets for corporate control and few inter-corporate equity holdings, in the latter we observe the opposite on all these dimensions. Without challenging the conceptual integrity of the theoretical expectations rooted in the agency theory framework, therefore, there are a number of factors hampering a full empirical confirmation of the irrelevance of the role of ownership concentration in influencing managerial decisions and, hence, firm performance.

Hill and Snell (1989) presented an empirical study testing whether, and to what extent, concentration in the ownership structure influences corporate productivity, either directly or indirectly, through the mediating effect of diversification, R&D investments and the level of capital intensity. Conceptually, while they agree with the agency theory assumption of divergence between management's and shareholders' interests, they claim that 'the efficiency of the capital market as a disciplinary device varies systematically across firms depending on the level of stock concentration' (p. 26). Information asymmetries between managers and stockholders and the costs of activating the market for corporate controls determine the importance of ownership concentration. The higher the stockholding concentration, the easier and the less costly for the individual stockholders to coordinate the collection and diffusion of relevant information, or to signal credible threats of retaliation to reluctant management teams, or to engineer takeover bids.

Among the different managerial decisions, those related to R&D investments are particularly indicative of the divergence between management's and shareholders' interests, and of how ownership concentration might limit managerial discretion. R&D investments are usually considered inherently risky, due to the low rate of success of the associated projects. Such high levels of risk, however, are also coupled with extremely high potential returns, which make R&D investments particularly attractive for shareholders, who can diversify their risk through their portfolio of investments. In contrast, managers' wealth is directly and uniquely linked to the success or the failure of a firm's specific projects and cannot be diversified. *Ceteris paribus*, therefore, managers will prefer committing the firm's resources to low-risk R&D activities targeted to 'me-too' projects, or unrelated diversification options, increasing the firm's size and, as a consequence, their own power, status and personal wealth, trading efficiency for lower risk (Amit and Livnat, 1988).

Using a cross-sectional set of 81 Fortune 500 firms reporting R&D expenses between 1979 and 1981 and the same data on the ownership structure of large US firms collected by the Corporate Data Exchange database used by Demsetz and Lehn (1985), Hill and Snell (1989) found support for their arguments, showing that stock concentration influences positively the R&D expenditure per employee, which in turn positively influences firm productivity. Moreover, they also found that stock concentration influences negatively the degree of unrelated diversification, which in turn negatively influences firm productivity.

Building on these results, Baysinger et al. (1991) studied a sample of 176 Fortune 500 firms from 1981 until 1983, regressing the corporate R&D spending per employee on the level of stock concentration among individual and institutional investors and the percentage of insiders on the company's board of directors. Controlling for the level of industry-specific R&D intensity, the degree of company diversification and size, they found evidence, through a cross-sectional regression analysis, of a statistically robust positive association between R&D spending and the level of stock concentration among institutional investors, but not between R&D spending and the level of stock concentration among individual investors.

Stock concentration can represent a necessary but not sufficient condition for monitoring managerial action and steering strategic decision-making towards higher investments in R&D activities. Yet, even if we accept the results of the few studies conducted on this stimulating subject, that cannot be considered a sufficient condition. We therefore move, in the next subsection, to the analysis of the role and influence of different management control mechanisms on management's propensity to innovate.

2.3   Strategic Control versus Financial Control

Principals can use several monitoring mechanisms to control agents' actions. The characteristics and composition of the ruling bodies of the firm (for example, the board of directors, the executive committee, the general assembly), as well as the specific regulatory framework defined in the statute of incorporation, are usually identified as the main areas of attention to lay down the foundations of an effective alignment between management and ownership objectives. Complementarily, compensation schemes and remuneration plans are another critical area for shareholders to consider in order to steer *ex ante* management actions towards their objective of returns maximization.

Regardless of the institutional arrangements chosen, however, shareholders must also select the indicators to be used to evaluate management's actions, and prompt the intervention of the market for corporate control when under-performance is detected. This choice, however, could in principle determine where managers will concentrate their attention and what type of strategies they will pursue. Research examining internal control theory relies on the type of information being collected and processed by corporate-level managers and the board in order to anticipate the firm's investment strategy and its propensity to innovate (Johnson et al., 1993; Hoskisson and Hitt, 1988; Baysinger and Hoskisson, 1989, 1990). According to Eisenhardt (1985, p. 137), in fact, control-system measures and rewards not only motivate behaviours, but also alter risk-sharing patterns.

In particular, Hoskisson and Hitt (1988) proposed distinguishing two basic types of control systems, depending on the characteristics of the indicators used. The first type, which they call 'strategic control system', requires a deep knowledge of the business where the firm is operating and is largely based on long-term indicators of performance, usually highly influenced by subjective evaluation of the multiple contingencies that are typically faced by any organization. Clearly, the use of strategic control indicators requires high levels of communication between managers and shareholders, both to give the latter the opportunity to increase their familiarity with the evolution of the business, and to facilitate critical strategic decision making. The long-term orientation and the criticality of business-specific information characterizing strategic control indicators generate high opportunities for the rise of information asymmetries between managers and shareholders, especially if they cannot commit enough resources to follow the firm's activity closely. At the same time, however, if managers know that they will be evaluated on neither short-term commitments nor immediately measurable achievements, they could have higher incentives to leverage their tacit knowledge of internal entrepreneurial resources and support longer-term development plans (Zahra, 1996).

Financial control systems, in contrast, are based on objective criteria widely used and easily understood by a variety of subjects, regardless of their knowledge of the business. Indicators like ROI (return on investment), ROE (return on equity) or ROA (return on assets) are commonly used by financial analysts all over the world and, together with other, more sophisticated, forms of accounting measures normally reported quarterly by all public companies, offer a clear benchmark to evaluate managers' performance. Financial indicators, while offering a reassuring realm of objectivity, suffer from several problems, too. First, they are by nature short-term oriented and, therefore, more prone to push managers towards low-risk strategies, emphasizing efficiency, but potentially hampering growth and long-term returns. Second, their use tends to reduce information-processing needs at different levels of the organization, with emphasis shifting from communication and understanding to reporting, thus potentially devaluing, both symbolically and practically, business-related knowledge. Third, the more the core activities of the firm are incorporated in intangible assets, the more difficult it becomes for standard financial and accounting measures to exhaustively represent the economic value of the decisions taken.

Hoskisson and Hitt (1988) used survey data on 124 industrial firms taken from the Fortune 1000 list to study whether the degree of diversification and the type of control systems adopted ultimately impact on the level of R&D investments. Data were analysed through analysis of variance and correlation analysis, and their results showed that shareholders tend to value R&D expenditures more highly when strategic controls are in place, while the emphasis on financial controls is generally associated with a lower market evaluation of R&D investments.

Hitt et al. (1996) presented an integrated theoretical model explaining how acquisitions and divestitures (taken as examples of strategies to participate in the market for corporate control) affect internal control mechanisms and, in turn, affect internal and external innovations. Using structural equation modelling on a sample of 250 firms operating in the US and reporting R&D data each year between 1985 and 1991, they found that the use of financial control systems affects internal innovation negatively, but external innovation positively. In contrast, strategic control systems affect internal innovation positively.

Munari et al. (2002) compared and contrasted management's decisions on R&D activities before and after the announcements of privatization plans by the government, using evidence extracted from case studies selected in different industries and different countries. Under the rationalization pressure posed by the forthcoming public offering and the need to increase the companies' value in order to maximize the amount of resources realized by the state, managers faced economic, political and cognitive pressure for reducing the amount of resources dedicated to long-term, risky and not easily evaluated projects and investments. R&D activities, therefore, become a natural target, showing a marked overall decline, a shift towards more applied and development-related activities, and a decreased sensibility for external collaborations. Similar patterns are presented and discussed in Chapter 7.

Taken together, the different studies presented suggest the criticality for firm performance of a contingency fit between control strategies and the firm's strategic context. Subjective information on the external and internal environment based on strategic controls is often more complete than quantitative information generated by financial controls, and seems more apt to technologically turbulent environments requiring high-risk strategies and high levels of R&D expenditures. In contrast, more formal and objective controls related to financial indicators emerge as more appropriate solutions for stable industries, where business-specific knowledge is less critical, and short-term efficiency-seeking strategies through low-risk process innovations are more likely to increase the firm's value. Such a distinction, however, risks underscoring the role that might be played by different kinds of principals. While more orthodox approaches assume an even distribution of competencies and resources among investors, there are several theoretically sound arguments and empirical results that need to be discussed to counter such an assumption. Therefore, in the next section, we shall turn our attention to the relationship between the nature of the principal and innovation activities.

3.   THE NATURE OF THE PRINCIPAL

Principal–agent models of corporate governance present the existing arrangements as the outcome of a bargaining process, where different subjects freely entered, at some point in time, to maximize individual expected payoffs (Jensen and Meckling, 1976). Capital and labour markets, together with the market for corporate control, provide the most effective restraints on managerial discretion, and the residual voting rights controlled by shareholders commit internal resources to value-maximizing needs (Hart, 1995). More recently, this perspective has been challenged on the grounds that the maximization of shareholder welfare by the maximization of the company value underestimates the expectations of a larger pool of stakeholders interested in the activities performed within the company (Keasey et al., 1997). Rather than focusing on direct control of capital through share ownership, therefore, the goal is to identify all those subjects having some kind of stake in the company, under the form of a long-term interest or association with its economic activities. Despite the apparent differences, however, both models suggest focusing on the expected payoffs of a relevant group of actors who design and structure the activities to be performed.

Studies on the relationship between ownership structure and organizational actions are generally confined to a macroperspective on firm activities, looking at aggregate economic and financial quantities such as the amount and degree of investments as indicators to evaluate the coherence of managerial decisions with principals' interests, as we have seen in Section 2.2. Often, however, there is a lack of deeper analysis on the different areas of activities that those decisions affect. Innovation development activities is one such area, where differences in the principals' characteristics can be used to discriminate among alternative choices. In the following subsections we shall therefore discuss how differences in the characteristics of the principal can affect innovation-related investment decisions, focusing first on the role of large individual shareholders, then on the influence of institutional shareholders, and finally on the specificities of having the government as the sole or dominant shareholder.

3.1 The Role of Large and Institutional Shareholders

Anecdotally, several factors characterizing the US economic landscape during the 1980s attracted the researchers' attention to the role, if any, of large shareholders in influencing firms' innovative activities. First, the stagnation of US productivity and the emergence of Japanese firms as serious competitors even in the internal market was accompanied by several observations of a diminished effort of US firms on R&D investments. Second, in the same period institutional investors such as pension funds and insurance companies steadily increased their stockholdings in publicly traded firms, and ended up controlling, according to recent estimates, over 50 per cent of outstanding equity (Gompers and Metrick, 2001). Third, and partly as a consequence of the introduction of the Bayh–Dole Act and of the Sherman Act, even within universities and public laboratories the proportion of basic R&D contracted at the expense of more applied projects. Understanding whether and why large institutional investors could hamper long-term competitiveness by shifting resources from riskier long-term innovative project to efficiency-maximizing ones, therefore, became a matter of interest not only for theoretical economists, but also for investors and the economic community at large.

As we have seen in greater detail in the previous sections, the decision to carry on R&D activities inherently involves high agency costs, since R&D projects are typically risky, unpredictable, long-term oriented and multistage, labour intensive and idiosyncratic (Holmstrom, 1989). Innovation is, therefore, a potential arena of acute conflicts of interest between executives and shareholders, whose characteristics may influence the management's decision whether to pursue risky R&D projects. One such characteristic is the investor's power within the company, expressed as the amount of shares he or she holds. Another characteristic is whether the investor is risking his or her own money, or employing somebody else's capital.

Different empirical studies (see Section 2.2) document a positive relation between stock-ownership concentration and R&D spending (Hill and Snell, 1989; Baysinger et al., 1991), suggesting that large stockholders are more effective at closely controlling management decisions and at reducing their potential risk aversion. Studies on the association between institutional ownership and innovation, however, offer conflicting evidence, some reporting a positive relationship (Baysinger et al., 1991; Hansen and Hill, 1991) and others reporting a negative one (Graves, 1988).

In the first empirical study on this subject, Jarrel et al. (1985) analysed the relationship between institutional ownership and level of R&D spending in 324 companies, operating in 19 industries between 1980 and 1983. Their ordinary least squares (OLS) estimates on the pooled data showed a positive association between the level of institutional ownership and the amount of R&D expenses expressed as a percentage of total sales. Later, Graves (1988) proposed extending their study on two grounds. First, between 1980 and 1983 both the increase in stockholding participation by large institutional investors and the decrease in R&D spending were at a very early stage, thus posing some possible problems in the detection of their true effect. Second, the uneven distribution of R&D spending among the different industries might have further complicated the estimates, especially for a low level of magnitude of the expected association. He therefore decided to focus only on the computer industry, collecting data on 22 companies between 1976 and 1985, and regressing R&D intensity, measured both as constant dollar R&D expenditure per employee and as R&D over sales ratio, on level of institutional ownership, controlling for firms' profit and market share, their level of interest rates, and a generically specified secular trend, expressed by a yearly dummy variable. His pooled OLS estimates on 112 lagged observations show strong and negative association between the level of R&D spending and the level of institutional ownership.

Hansen and Hill (1991) heavily criticized both these studies for their statistical weaknesses. On the one hand, Jarrel et al. had failed to control for confounding effects by limiting the right-hand variables in their equation to the industry dummies and the institutional investors indicator. On the other hand, Graves had operated on a very small sample, not including lagged R&D spending as an additional control variable, and using OLS techniques leading to potentially serious serial correlation biases. Hansen and Hill therefore collected data for 129 firms in the aerospace, chemicals, pharmaceuticals and computer industries between 1977 and 1987, using Generalized List Squares (GLS) cross-sectionally heteroscedastic and time-wise autoregressive estimators in 1290 observations to control for the autocorrelation and heteroscedacity biases. After controlling for the level of firm-specific cash resources, its leverage, size and past R&D expenses, the industry, and the year of observation and level of insiders' holdings, their result showed a weak positive association between R&D intensity and institutional ownership. They interpreted their results more as a rejection of the market myopia argument, than as a confirmation of efficient market perspectives (Hansen and Hill, 1991, p. 9).

In the study examined in Section 2.2, Baysinger et al. (1991) found a statistically robust positive association between R&D spending and the level of stock concentration among institutional investors, but not between R&D spending and the level of stock concentration among *individual* investors, and offered several possible explanations for their results in comparison to previous studies. First, they suggested that, rather than focusing on ownership distribution, what matters is a deeper analysis of who are the main investors. In terms of measurement, the use of a cumulative measure of stock concentration, which weighs equally the effects of all stockholders and of a Herfindal index assigning greater importance to larger stockholders, seems critical to control for the fact that, typically, the largest stockholders are individuals, rather than institutions. Moreover, while conventional wisdom depicts institutional managers as short-term oriented, by managing widely diversified portfolios, they can increase their overall returns, spreading the risk of R&D investments more effectively than individual investors.

Finally, Hill and Snell (1988) explored the relationship between the major elements of the corporate governance system, corporate strategy and firm performance within research-intensive environments. Using the Fortune 500 listing for 1980, they selected a sample of 94 large firms operating in five research-intensive industries (chemicals, electrical and electronics, computers, industrial and farm equipment, and pharmaceuticals). Their stepwise regression analysis showed that stockholders' power, measured by stock concentration, is positively related to R&D expenditures, thus suggesting that stockholders favour a strategic emphasis on innovation in such dynamic contexts.

Institutional investors, however, are heterogeneous in terms of investment horizons and behaviour, as a consequence of differences in their goals and objectives. Zahra (1996) found that those institutional investors with long-term horizons, such as mutual, pension and retirement funds, are more likely to promote innovation and venturing, whereas short-term institutional owners, such as investment banks and private funds, seem to discourage executives from investing in activities with a long pay-off period. Similar results were found by Kochnar and David (1996), who categorized institutional owners by their ability to influence the firms where they have an ownership stake. Their findings suggested that pressure-resistant institutions (that is, public pension funds, mutual funds, foundations) have a more positive influence on firm innovation than pressure-sensitive institutions (that is, banks or insurance companies).

Theoretically, all these results support what Heiner (1983) called the competence–difficulty gap and rests on Simon's notion of bounded rationality (Simon, 1957) and on Kahneman and Tversky's (1979) prospect theory. Within efficient markets all actors are not alike. In principle all actors are intentionally rational. However, the correlation between intentions and outcomes is a function of information-processing capabilities. Since institutions and large shareholders have greater resources and more competencies at elaborating information, their choices are the product of a more complete information set and can therefore evaluate long-term investments more consistently. This line of reasoning, as we shall see in Chapter 10, is particularly interesting in examining the different investment behaviour of institutional and private investors, and certainly poses several questions as to the characteristics and functioning of the so-called 'high-tech' stock markets.

3.2   The Government as Principal

Traditional public administration models resist extending an objective function-maximization logic to the public sector, claiming that public organizations are created by governments for primarily collectivist or political purposes and are ultimately accountable to the political representatives, whether the services are provided by the private sector, by an agency, or within the public sector (Farnham and Horton, 1989). Public organizations should consider the equity in the distribution of their services of primary importance, as well as the indiscriminate access to those services and their availability to the population at large. The so-called 'nationalization programmes of utilities' were used in several countries to align these objectives in offering to the population the same opportunities to access water, electricity, transportation and sometimes also telecommunication services.

Even in these cases, however, one might claim that the governance issues faced by the organizations identified to implement the institutional agenda are isomorphic to the world of private enterprise. The separation between management and control is still strongly present and visible, and the group of principals is even more fragmented and less stable than in public enterprises, as belonging to a political constituency, not necessarily elected by the majority of the voters and free to change its agenda during its mandate.

State-owned enterprises are set up – or nationalized – to achieve a wider set of objectives, targeted to the maximization of social welfare through the control of possible market asymmetries that would generate inequality in the distribution of or access to both the revenues coming from the activities controlled, and their physical or non-physical output. Generally speaking, therefore, the attitude towards R&D activities within companies controlled by the government is likely to be more permissive with regard to R&D's

possible contributions to public goods, favouring not only business-specific objectives, but also broader national goals.

More precisely, Munari et al. (2002) characterized this general attitude by analysing the goal structure of R&D investments, their expected pay-off structure, and the corresponding behavioural attainments. Considering the goal structure, we can distinguish three separate but interrelated targets. First of all, R&D investments ought to be directed to meeting specific business objectives, as in any other economic environment, in order to guarantee the achievement of a stronghold in the area occupied by the company. This is particularly important when there is a direct government intervention in such industries and areas of activities where the country is weak for some reason (for example, demand or offer size, level of technology and so on) with respect to foreign competition, or where it is considered as a strategic priority to secure an international lead.

Especially in these cases, however, the inability to stand competitively in international markets, or even to offer efficient and effective services and products in the national context, is likely to depend on a more widespread lack of correlated assets, competencies and services. To achieve its first goal, therefore, R&D could also be leveraged to a second objective: the more general strengthening of the nation's scientific and human infrastructure, either directly, by initiating and leading multipartner projects, or indirectly, by creating a demand for qualified resources and products. At a yet more general level, however, all these efforts could be fruitless, in the absence of an adequately installed base of research activities, focused on more upstream stages and able to generate the necessary spillovers on more applied projects. A third goal for R&D activities, therefore, becomes a wider and less definite effort to participate in the production of the public goods of basic research, generating somehow related/somehow relevant knowledge advancements that might later funnel into business-related activities and directly contribute to qualifying and steering the national levels of investments in R&D. Cooperative ventures with other national firms or universities are therefore not only encouraged, but also directly used as a practical way to achieve this objective. To this purpose, it is important to highlight that the public benefits obtained from government-promoted or -funded basic research can assume different and mutually supporting forms, and that new, useful knowledge is just one type of benefit, and not necessarily the most important one. Other public pay-offs include the development of new instrumentation, methodologies and skills, the possibility of accessing national or international networks of experts and information, the ability to confront and solve complex technological problems, and the creation of new spin-off companies (Salter and Martin, 2001). All these different and interrelated pay-offs consistently impact on the rate and direction of the national technological and economic competitiveness and therefore can further encourage the support given by state-owned enterprises to basic research activities.

The rationale for these different goals is to be found in the pay-off structure of the related investments with respect to the institutional investor utility function. First of all, the timing of direct returns for a significant portion of the investments, if not of their entire amount, can be deferred longer than in privately-owned firms. By operating outside the so-called 'discipline of the market', state-owned enterprises are rarely called to justify how and with what returns taxpayers' money is being used, under the assumption that their possible below-average or even negative returns are compensated by their subsidizing their products and services to the larger public. The longer time span used is therefore complemented by the source of returns, where the direct component represents the less significant fraction of the total, especially whenever the more general goals of public spillover and basic research efforts are considered. The larger the expected return from indirect sources, the longer the time span tolerated for the projects, and the fewer the demands for specific returns from single projects.

These attitudes and expectancies are reflected in the characteristics and structure of R&D activities. The nature of the goals favours a centralized structure responsible for the R&D mission and integrating both long- and short-term projects in order to achieve some internal economies of scale, perhaps decentralizing local support to more applied internal needs, even if possible duplications might emerge. Internal evaluation systems should consequently map the emphasis on knowledge production and diffusion, favouring and promoting publication and the establishment of a peer culture at the technical level, nurturing the creation of a community of reference in different fields. Smaller attention to control mechanisms against information leakage and know-how spillover is therefore justified and can be not only less strict, but also not even codified. Funding becomes an almost exclusively internal issue in terms of sourcing and allocation, centrally controlled and assigned to projects not necessarily by promoting inter-project competition, especially in the absence of precise elements to benchmark proposals and results. The nature of the goals also affects the characteristics of the promotion and reward system, which, on the one hand, cannot be completely homogeneous to that of the scientific community, and on the other hand cannot emphasize the more managerial and market-oriented attitude typical of privately-owned enterprises.

Overall, the presence of an institutional investor such as the government in companies engaged in R&D activity is likely to generate profound differences not only at the macrolevel of investments, but also at the microlevel of structures, processes and employee attitudes. Given the peculiarities of this type of principal, expectations or manifestations of changes in its role and presence in the company could determine profound adjustments or reformulation of the agents' mandate and, as a consequence, of the organization goals and processes. This is the focus of the empirical research presented in Chapters 4, 7 and 9.

4.   THE ROLE AND CHARACTERISTICS OF THE BOARD

One of the most important corporate governance internal mechanisms intended to reduce the agency problem between managers and shareholders is represented by the board of directors. As the legal representatives of corporate stockholders, directors have the formal authority to ratify managers' decisions, to monitor executives' behaviour and performance, and to evaluate and reward them. As Baysinger and Hoskisson (1990) effectively summarized: 'Placing the responsibility for decision control with a board precludes managers from being the sole evaluators of their own performance and, thus, provides a safeguard to invested capital' (p. 76).

In line with organizational control theory (Eisenhardt, 1985; Ouchi, 1979), since directors are responsible for controlling, evaluating and rewarding the management performance, their characteristics and behaviour may be expected to consistently impact on managers' strategic decision-making processes and therefore on the overall performance of the firm. There is a rich and diversified literature assessing the relationship between the different characteristics of the board and the firm's financial performance, focusing for instance on the board composition in terms of inside versus outside directors, board size, demography and leadership structure (see Daily and Dalton, 1992; Daily et al., 1998; Zahra and Pearce, 1989, for comprehensive reviews on these topics). However, those findings generally provide very little support for a systematic relationship between the two variables.

With specific regard to the case of innovation, different studies highlighted the potential impact of some characteristics of the board on the firm's propensity to engage in R&D activities and to promote corporate entrepreneurship and strategic change and renewal (Hill and Snell, 1988; Baysinger and Hoskisson, 1990; Johnson et al., 1993; Zahra, 1996). In the following subsections we shall recall the main theoretical contributions and empirical findings of this stream of literature, focusing first on the composition of the board of directors, then on the influence of board demography, and finally on the impact of the social network of ties of the board directors with external organizations.

4.1   Inside versus Outside Directors

The composition of the board of directors, particularly the presence of outside directors and their proportion to inside directors, has often been identified as an important element to realign shareholders' and managers' interests and alleviate the agency problem. Consistent with agency theory (Eisenhardt, 1989; Jensen and Meckling, 1976), in order to effectively control management behaviour and to safeguard shareholders' interests, the board should operate as an active and independent entity, a situation that may be facilitated by a high involvement of outside directors (Daily and Dalton, 1992; Zahra and Pearce, 1989). In fact, their presence fosters the independence of the board from the firm's management, leads to a stronger and more objective control of the chief executive officer's (CEO's) decisions, expands the expertise and the knowledge base of the board, and strengthens the network of relationships with external firms and institutions (Zahra and Pearce, 1989; Daily and Dalton, 1992; Baysinger and Hoskisson, 1990). One potential drawback resides in the fact that outside directors may lack the necessary specific knowledge and experience of the firms'capabilities and processes, and of the environment in which they compete. In contrast, inside directors, who actively participate in the operations of the company, are more and better informed and, consequently, should be more competent in assessing the strategic desiderability of decisions and their potential consequences in the short or in the long run (Baysinger and Hoskisson, 1990; Baysinger et al., 1991; Hill and Snell, 1988; Zahra, 1996).

Moreover, since outside directors usually spend only a limited amount of time at the company serving on the board, and lack the necessary information to understand the business in depth, it is also likely that they favour objective financial criteria in evaluating and rewarding top management decisions. On the other hand, inside directors should be more willing to adopt strategic control strategies in their evaluation, on the basis of more open, subjective and qualitative criteria (Baysinger and Hoskisson, 1990).

From the above-mentioned considerations, it follows that the balance between inside and outside directors within the board becomes particularly important within firms facing high levels of uncertainty and dynamism, such as R&D-intensive firms. Indeed, by definition R&D and innovative projects are inherently risky, since their potential consequences are not only difficult to predict, but also require a long period to manifest. In this sense, insider-dominated boards are likely to be better informed about the sources of uncertainty and the potential returns stemming from innovative projects, and therefore they are more qualified in promoting and assessing their undertaking. As a consequence, many authors have argued that a higher insider to outsider ratio within the board should enhance R&D investments and corporate entrepreneurship, an expectation largely supported by empirical evidence (Hill and Snell, 1988; Baysinger and Hoskisson, 1990; Baysinger et al., 1991; Zahra, 1996).

In the previously quoted study by Hill and Snell (1988), the insider/outsider ratio emerged as a significant predictor of strategic decision making regarding innovation and diversification activities. In this study, the presence of outsiders in the board was associated with lower R&D investments, greater scope of diversification and a lower concentration of diversification on related areas. In their study on 176 Fortune 500 companies, Baysinger et al. (1991) found the proportion of inside directors to be positively related to the level of R&D investments and, based on that, they argued that top executives may be more willing to invest in risky innovative projects when they are less dependent on the evaluation of external directors.

The findings reported by Zahra (1996) further confirm the view that insiders may be better positioned for evaluating and promoting entrepreneurial and innovative projects. In this study, the proportion of outsiders in the board is negatively and significantly associated with different measures of corporate entrepreneurship, including innovation through research and new product development, venturing and strategic renewal. Interestingly enough, these findings also suggest that when outsiders hold ownership interests in the company, they become more willing to encourage entrepreneurial risk taking, consistently with the criticism that outside directors, having limited stakes in the company they control, have little incentive to strictly monitor managerial actions and promote entrepreneurship (Kosnik, 1990).

All these findings provide strong support for the idea that insider-dominated boards may be more effective in fostering innovation. To this purpose, a particular kind of insider who can be expected to provide an important contribution to strategic decision making within companies operating in the high-technology industry is the chief technology officer (CTO). In R&D-intensive companies, the CTO typically oversees all areas of technology and, together with the CEO, is the most critical position in order to achieve a strong and effective linkage between the corporate technology strategy and the overall corporate strategy (Roberts, 1995).

In this sense, it is interesting to recall the findings of the global survey on the strategic management of technology conducted in 1999 under the supervision of Ed Roberts on 209 companies accounting for about 80 per cent of the R&D expenditure in Europe, Japan and the US (Roberts, 2001). The study, undertaken in 1999 and updating a prior similar survey of 1992, showed that about 90 per cent of the Japanese major R&D spenders have their CTO serving on the board of directors, whereas the percentage greatly declines for European and North American firms, respectively to 35 per cent and 8 per cent. The percentage improves when considering the companies whose CTOs are involved in the senior management committee, with Japan showing once again the highest value (respectively about 90 per cent, 70 per cent and 70 per cent for Japanese, European and North American companies). These findings showed how the practice to include CTOs within the board of directors varies greatly around countries, and highlighted a surprisingly low representation of

CTOs serving on the board in the case of North American firms, especially when considering that the survey included the largest R&D spenders in the most technologically advanced sectors. However, empirical analysis showed no statistically significant correlation between the presence of the CTO on the board and various measures of corporate-level performance, a result that seems counterintuitive and deserves further inquiry.

4.2   Board Demographics and Innovation

Different studies tried to establish a direct link between the demographic characteristics of the board of directors – such as age or tenure heterogeneity of its members or board tenure itself – and firm performance (Daily and Dalton, 1992; Johnson et al., 1993). The underlying logic assumed that demography can be considered as 'a causal variable that affects a number of intervening variables and processes and, through them, a number of organizational outcomes' (Pfeffer, 1983, p. 35). Under this assumption, the study of such intervening processes may not be necessary since they can be directly inferred by the demographic variables.

However, in a comprehensive review of the literature on board composition and performance, Johnson et al. (1996) concluded that demography does not seem to exert a significant influence on board performance. This conclusion highlights the importance for researchers to consider in more depth the processes that mediate the relationship between board demography and firm performance (Forbes and Milliken, 1999), in line with the more general criticism of the 'black box' view of organizational demography (Lawrence, 1997). For our purpose, it is interesting to focus on those team characteristics that may be expected to proactively influence the board of director involvement in promoting strategic change and innovation, such as receptivity to change, willingness to take risk, diversity of information sources and creativity and innovativeness in decision making (Wiersema and Bantel, 1992).

For instance, the homogeneity of tenure on the job and of age was positively related to higher social integration (O'Reilly et al., 1989), by increasing both the opportunities for interactions and the attractiveness of members to one another, as a consequence of the similarity of their experiences and understanding of events. However, as cohesiveness is also related to conformity, routinization and greater adherence to group norms (Goodman et al., 1987), the creative predisposition of the group and its propensity to change could be frustrated. Moreover, research in the field of the management of innovation has also associated group heterogeneity with high levels of creativity and innovative performance, in particular in the context of R&D teams (Ancona and Caldwell, 1992).

It is possible to extend these considerations to the specific case of the board of directors, and expect that the tenure heterogeneity among its members should reduce the possibility of groupthink and inertia, thus enhancing the board propensity to foster strategic renewal and experimentation (Johnson et al., 1993).

Another dimension of board demography that can be expected to impact on firms' propensity to innovate is board tenure: some authors argued that boards having served together for a long period are likely to become increasingly resistant to change (Johnson et al., 1993; Forbes and Milliken, 1999). This expectation is consistent with the studies on the so-called 'not invented here' (NIH) syndrome, which showed how a group of stable composition progressively tends to develop homogeneity of perspective, to believe it possesses a monopoly of knowledge and to become increasingly isolated from outside sources of relevant information and new ideas (Pelz and Andrews, 1966; Katz and Allen, 1982).

With respect to top management teams, Tushman and Romanelli (1985) and Keck and Tushman (1993) showed how, all through the period of environmental stability, they tend to be characterized by higher stability and homogeneity, which in turn leads to further inertia and incremental change. In contrast, organizations facing greater technical or institutional discontinuities are more likely to present higher heterogeneity and change in executive teams, which in turn are more likely to promote strategic reorientation and organizational renewal. In a study based on 87 firms randomly selected from the Fortune 500 list, Wiersema and Bantel (1992) analysed the relationship between the demography of top management teams and corporate strategic change, measured by the absolute percentage change in diversification strategy over the 1980–83 period. Their OLS regression estimates showed that the firms most likely to undertake changes in strategic direction had top management teams characterized by a lower average age, shorter organizational tenure and higher team tenure, whereas very little support for the heterogeneity argument emerged. In this case, contrarily to the authors' expectations, high top management team tenure was associated with changes in strategy. Their additional analysis, however, supported the existence of an inverse curvilinear relationship between the two variables, similarly to the study on the NIH syndrome: firms with very short team tenure presented the least amount of strategic change, whereas further increases beyond the average level of team tenure did not influence the group ability to promote changes in corporate strategy.

The theoretical considerations and empirical findings summarized above suggest that age and tenure homogeneity among board members, and prolonged board tenure could constrain risk taking and entrepreneurial decision making. However, the empirical evidence on this topic is rather scarce and controversial, and requires further and deeper inquiry. Johnson et al. (1993) studied how board and top management characteristics influence the participation of the board of directors in strategic changes such as restructuring decisions. Using survey data on a sample of 92 firms that had undertaken voluntary restructuring from 1985 to 1990, they found no significant relationship between board tenure and board tenure heterogeneity with the board's involvement in restructuring decisions. The authors provided different explanations for such evidence, arguing that it might be inappropriate to extend the properties and dynamics of top management teams to the board of directors, since these two kinds of groups function in different ways. The most important difference is that the former meet and interact on a regular basis, whereas the latter meet only a few times a year, so that power and political processes may have a weaker influence on board behaviour (Johnson et al., 1993).

4.3   Interlocking Directorates and Imitation

The use of social network analysis provides the opportunity to analyse innovation processes as the result of individual actions embedded in a larger set, in which ties with other subjects are established in order to access new knowledge and complement the internal base of competencies (Bijker et al., 1987; Arora and Gambardella, 1991; Rappa and Debackere, 1992). Turning to external partners is viewed as an important source of variance and complementary knowledge, challenging an internally integrated view of innovative processes. This search is made not only through predetermined formal channels, but it often becomes more effective through more indirect and informal contacts (Granovetter, 1973; Schrader, 1991).

Under the social network embeddedness perspective, interlocking directorates may be seen as an important mechanism through which information is spread and innovative practices are diffused among firms (Davies, 1991; Palmer, 1993; Westphal and Zajac, 1997). The participation in multiple boards may provide directors with direct strategic experience and access to new information, and therefore influence their ability to contribute effectively to strategy (Mizruchi, 1996).

For instance, the work by Davies (1991) examined the relationship between a firm's interlocking network and its tendency to adopt 'poison pill' anti-takeover actions. His results showed how firms centrally located in an interlocking network and interlocked with other firms having already experienced such practices were more likely to adopt them. According to the author, in these cases interlocking ties facilitated the exchange of information through the network and contributed to clarifying the value and potential effectiveness of this innovative mechanism. Similarly, Palmer (1993) studied the adoption of the multidivisional form in a sample of large US firms in the 1960s, and found that those firms linked through non-officer ties with firms that had already adopted the multidivisional form were more likely to adopt this organizational form than firms without such ties.

However, the literature suggests that social network ties not only facilitate the transfer of information, but also channel social influence and conformism

(Burt, 1992; Carpenter and Westphal, 2001). Institutional theory holds that organizations tend to adopt goals, processes and structures in order to conform to extra-organizational norms rewarding similarity (Powell and Di Maggio, 1991). In this sense, firms are forced to imitate the business practices adopted by others, in a search for legitimacy. The sharing of interlocking ties among different firms may thus reinforce imitative behaviours: managers serving on the board of a company adopting a certain business practice experience a model that they may try to replicate in other interlocked firms.

Haunschild (1993) adopted a neo-institutional perspective to explain how strategic decisions related to corporate acquisitions are significantly influenced by the interlocking relationships of board members with firms that have previously made acquisitions. Her sample included all the medium and large-size firms (over $35 million in assets) listed in the 1981–90 Compustat databases for four industries. A Tobit estimation model was adopted to study the relationship between the number of acquisitions promoted by the focal firm and the number of prior acquisitions by 'tied-to firms' (firms having on their board an inside director of the focal firm), controlling for size, free cash flow, past performance, previous acquisition activity, industry and macroeconomic conditions. Her results support the imitation argument by showing a positive relation between a firm's acquisition activity and the number of prior acquisitions completed by the interlocked firms.

More recent research (Carpenter and Westphal, 2001; Gulati and Westphal, 1999) has also suggested that, in order to understand how the interlocking network influences corporate behaviour, it is important to consider not only the overall size of the network (the simple number of directors appointed to other boards), but also the composition of the relational set (the heterogeneity of the firms to which the directors of the focal firm are tied) and its articulation (the mediating effect of indirect ties).

Indeed, a wider and more diversified distribution of social ties, including board interlocking ties, decreases the cohesiveness of the established exchange structure and favours a higher variance in the information processed, creating better conditions for overcoming cognitive and competency rigidities (Arora and Gambardella, 1991; Badaracco, 1991). For instance, in turbulent and highly dynamic environments, characterized by high uncertainty and volatility, a board composed of directors serving in companies operating in different businesses and following a wide variety of strategies may become more exposed to and better informed about the range of strategic options and their potential consequences. Thus, boards tied to a heterogeneous mix of companies, both strategically similar and dissimilar ones, may be more willing to promote change in the strategic orientation of the firm. Carpenter and Westphal (2001) used survey data from 228 CEOs and 492 outside directors of the Forbes 1000 index of US industrial and service companies to test this argument. Their results support the idea that, in highly dynamic environments, strategically heterogeneous board ties increase the involvement of directors in the strategic decision-making process. In contrast, in relatively stable environments directors make a better contribution to strategy when they are tied to firms that are strategically similar to the focal one.

In addition to the size and the scope of the interlocking network, a third dimension to be considered is its articulation. Exchanges occur not only through direct contacts, but they often flow indirectly via normally overlooked channels (Granovetter, 1973). In this sense, dyadic interlocking ties between firms can also be mediated by third-party external ties. In their study examining the influence of the social network of board interlocks on strategic alliance formation, Gulati and Westphal (1999) demonstrated that the presence of third-party ties (through the appointment on external boards) between a CEO and his or her board members may significantly influence the trusting/distrusting relationship between them. Ultimately this helps to predict alliance formation between the focal firm and the firms of outside directors.

All the above-mentioned considerations suggest that the different dimensions of the interlocking network can also be considered as predictors of the innovative behaviour of firms, and that such a perspective may open up fruitful avenues of new research.

5.   CONCLUSIONS

In this chapter we offered an articulated review of the theoretical premises and the empirical studies linking corporate governance and innovation. Building on a multidisciplinary approach, we combined studies rooted in the economic, strategic and organizational theory traditions to highlight the complex and systemic nature of the research problem lying at the core of this book.

To move further and focus on the empirical analysis of some of the issues raised, however, some more steps must be taken. First, we did not discuss the role of market structure as a key moderator, or primary covariate, which has to be considered to fully model innovation decisions and actions within different governance structures. Second, we did not discuss at length the role and impact on innovation activities of a set of corporate restructuring activities such as mergers and acquisitions or alliances. Their widespread use in several industries, their continuous relevance over different time frames, and their pervasive geographic diffusion, however, suggest the need for a specific treatment of these issues.

In the next two chapters we shall attempt to fill these voids, before approaching the original empirical contributions presented in the following chapters and before exploring a set of specific research hypotheses directly linked to the theoretical arguments developed in this first part of the book. As stressed in our introduction, we hope to have started persuading our reader that the characteristics of our research topic could vastly benefit from a multidisciplinary perspective, respectful of the possible differences in the original epistemological approaches, but also rigorous in suggesting how different fields could offer complementary contributions leading to a better understanding of complex phenomena. This effort will continue throughout the rest of the book.

NOTE

1.   An additional analysis of the short-termism criticism in the context of market structure is presented in Chapter 2, Section 5.

2. Market Structure and the Balance of R&D Investments

Mario Calderini and Paola Garrone

1.   THE RESEARCH PROBLEM

Chapter 1 surveyed a wide number of studies addressing the relationship between corporate governance structures and innovation decisions. In this chapter we want to challenge another classic issue in innovation studies, namely the relationship between market structure and innovation. Although this is among the most popular issues in industrial economics, we shall analyse the problem from a rather unusual perspective, in order to understand whether dealing separately with the two fundamental components of research activities, research and development, may contribute to shedding more light on a very complex and controversial theoretical and empirical issue. The intuition is that, when we consider the different stages of a generic knowledge production function, from basic research activities to development, the economic nature of the goods which are produced all through the process varies greatly; any attempt to treat the intermediate goods produced in the different stages aggregately will result in unclear and controversial results. Our claim is, therefore, that both the theoretical arguments and the empirical tests can be specified in a much clearer way when we study separately the basic research–market structure relationship and the applied research–market structure relationship.

In this chapter, we shall critically review the literature on market structure and innovation in order to outline the ideas that are relevant to understand the relationship between market structure and the *composition* of R&D activities. In this sense we depart from the classical market structure–R&D intensity stream of literature.

In the following, we set out to define the theoretical background that may help to understand the empirical results presented in Chapter 5 of this book; such results demonstrate that dealing separately with the two components of R&D may indeed provide new insights into the problem.

The remainder of this chapter is organized as follows. In Section 2 we review some of the basic concepts that will be used throughout the book in relation to the economic nature of R&D activities. In Section 3, we present a critical survey of the contributions of several authors who have investigated the complex relationship between market structure and innovation, within the broad class of endogenous growth models and the industrial organization (IO) literature. We do so paying special attention to all those aspects that are relevant to our specific research problem. Finally, we try to integrate the main findings of this stream of literature with some interesting approaches derived from corporate finance literature, namely the contributions on short-termism.

2.   THE ECONOMIC NATURE OF R&D

The most simple representation of research and development activities is the so-called 'linear model', according to which basic research (BR) creates the knowledge that is used by applied research (AR), which in turns creates the intermediate output to be used by development activities (D).

The basic components of this sequential process, according to the National Science Foundation (NSF), can be defined as follows: BR includes the set of tasks that represent original contributions to the progress of scientific research and that are not oriented to specific commercial objectives; AR is defined as the set of research activities aimed at fulfilling new commercial needs through the creation of new technological knowledge; finally, D is the set of technical and engineering activities focused on the problems that are systematically encountered when we try to apply technological knowledge to either specific products or processes.

Such representation, although general and comprehensive, presents major limitations. First, the very complex bundle of connections and mutual relationships makes the linear picture sketched above fairly reductive. Second, experts seem to share the view that at least one intermediate category of R&D has to be introduced when we are dealing with certain types of economic activities, the mission-oriented applied research. The definition is deemed to include all those activities that are finalized to generic commercial objectives, but whose results cannot be predicted and planned, either in terms of quality or in terms of expected release time (Rosenberg, 1994).

Whatever the number of different categories and their distinction, the point to be emphasized is that R&D should be represented as a continuum of activities, linked by complex feedback loops and exerting reciprocal externalities at different levels.

A prolific starting point, when we are trying to assess the different nature of basic and applied research activities, is the one proposed by Pavitt (1991), based on the classification of the output of the different phases of R&D. He proposed drawing the line between basic research on one side and applied research and development on the other according to the different kind of knowledge that they produce. Both use researchers and engineers to study and investigate a natural phenomenon, but the former creates knowledge in the form of generalized, explicit, formalized notions, while the latter creates tacit, specific and idiosyncratic knowledge, which will not be reproduced easily for application to different specific objectives. Such definition underpins an important characteristic of the two activities: the different appropriability regimes that their respective outputs are subject to.

Mainstream analysis tends to consider the output of basic research as a pure public good. Moreover, the standard hypotheses describe the output as hardly appropriable, given the specific nature of its codified results; conversely, results from applied research and development can, by their own nature, be easily appropriated by innovators, guaranteeing sound incentives to invest in R&D. As we shall see in the following, many authors criticized that definition, and in particular the idea that the product of basic research can be univocally classified as a pure public good.

In fact, Rosenberg (1994) questioned this definition. He argued that the results expected by the vast majority of firms from long-term basic research activities are just marginally leapfrog advances in their own scientific knowledge base; rather, there are indirect effects, such as gaining prospection on technological opportunities, absorptive capacity, researcher selection and training, access to the scientific community, reputation signalling and many other indirect returns.

Those considerations underline the complex bundle of relationships that tie up applied and basic research, which can never be interpreted as two distinct and independent phases of the same process. The argument is twofold: in many sectors, important results are achieved unintentionally, through applied research and development; conversely, some basic research activities are fruitful only in contexts where important applied research is carried on. Basic research produces indirect input to applied innovative activities that, given their specificity and their tacit nature, can be internalized only if both such activities are brought forward in-house. This is to say that basic research, rather than simply feeding engineering research, co-evolves with it, creating the belief that private basic research has peculiarities that are missed in public institutions. Other scholars also questioned the simplistic 'public good' definition and contended that basic research yields appropriable benefits if (and only if) it is performed in-house.

According to David (1991) and Dasgupta and David (1994), the participation of industrial researchers in the scientific community yields private returns since it allows access, transfer and the acquisition of basic knowledge through the sharing, evaluation and control of the results, on the one side, and through learning and training on the other. Furthermore, many basic technological and scientific results present specificities that may be fully understood only by the firms that are directly committed to the production of their own knowledge stock (Cohen and Levinthal, 1989). These aspects are typically referred to as the 'absorptive capacity'.

Furthermore, David et al. (1994) argued that the in-house knowledge base provides industrial researchers with valuable pieces of information about the actual distribution of innovation's success probabilities; therefore, carrying on in-house basic research reduces uncertainty and the risks of applied research efforts. In other words, basic knowledge allows firms to direct their research activity more efficiently and to explore the frontier of technological opportunities with increased probability of success. These aspects are typically referred to as the 'prospection capacity'.

Finally, Rosenberg (1994) emphasized that performing in-house research yields positive reputation effects. He also interpreted private basic research expenses as an entry fee that allows companies to plug in to the international scientific community and to access and internalize the fundamental knowledge produced in universities and in public research institutions.

Putting all these different ideas together, we may come to the conclusion that the indirect outcomes of basic research miss the classic definition of public good completely. On the contrary, these results are highly appropriable, specific and non-tradable.

3. MARKET STRUCTURE AND INNOVATION

Past and recent empirical literature has widely demonstrated that there is no clear indication about the effects of market structure on R&D intensity. Besides the relevant empirical problems that are typical of such research questions, this also reflects the fact that such a relationship incorporates a vast number of different phenomena, all exerting opposite effects on firms' innovation performance. The efforts of the scholars who studied the problem over the years, therefore, were aimed at separating such effects, in order to be able to understand which are bound to prevail, why, and under what conditions. Our claim is that treating the different components of R&D separately may considerably facilitate the task.

Before moving on to analyse the papers that contributed to shedding light on the issue, it should be noted that the literature on market structure and innovation includes two main streams of empirical literature, one dealing with firm size and innovation and the other with measures of market concentration and innovation. We shall focus on the latter, given the nature of the theoretical and empirical problem that will be tackled in this chapter and in Chapter 5.

Although it is beyond the scope of this chapter to extensively review the enormous corpus of literature dealing with the issue, we want to direct the reader's attention to the fact that in this specific field of literature the most striking feature is the lack of a shared view on the expected signs in the concentration–innovation relationship, and the relatively weak support that empirical results were able to provide in the dispute.

The classical IO literature, in general, tends to predict that innovation is bound to decline with increasing competition, since the monopoly rents for new entrants are reduced by a higher degree of competition. The standard references for this class of contributions are, for example, Dasgupta and Stiglitz (1980) or Kamien and Schwartz (1982).

Many other studies, following the classical Arrow paper (Arrow, 1962), hypothesized a positive relationship between competition and innovation.

Empirical evidence is no clearer, as reviewed by Cohen and Levin (1989). This is due to a number of common empirical problems that we shall briefly survey in the following. The most important empirical problem is the endogeneity of concentration. The two-way causal relationship is the main reason that has prevented scholars throughout the years from achieving conclusive evidence. A second relevant problem is related to the industry-specific characteristics that may be correlated with concentration and also affect innovation. For this reason, a number of studies have controlled for appropriability conditions and technological opportunities.

Finally, Symeonides (1996) argued that a further relevant problem lies in the fact that most studies focused on the relationship between market concentration and innovation, while the classical Schumpeterian hypothesis is based on the notion of market *power* rather than concentration. When we consider a framework where market structure is endogenous (Sutton, 1998), it is not obvious that concentration is an efficient proxy for market structure, thus yielding unclear results.

For example, Geroski (1995), Nickell (1996) and Blundell et al. (1999) demonstrated that an increased level of product market competition affects positively the innovation output. On the other hand, starting from the early contribution of Scherer (1967), a great many empirical attempts supported the original Schumpeterian hypothesis, providing evidence for a positive correlation between concentration (market power) and innovation. Finally, recent contributions in the neo-Schumpeterian tradition have adopted a hypothesis that had been proposed from time to time in the literature (Scherer, 1965), according to which the relationship between competition and innovation is basically U-shaped, with competition effects prevailing for low levels of competition and Schumpeterian effects dominating at higher levels of product market competition. A recent robust empirical test of this latter hypothesis was provided by Aghion et al. (2002).

Among such variety and heterogeneity of empirical results, three main results seem to emerge in the standard IO literature (Symeonides, 1996): there is little evidence in support of a positive relationship between R&D intensity and concentration, and there is even less evidence of a positive relationship between market structure and innovative output; finally, industry characteristics and in particular technological opportunity explain much more of the variance in R&D intensity than market structure as such.

A more prolific stream of research seems to be represented by the last generation of Schumpeterian growth models (see Aghion and Howitt, 1998). This is the class of models to which we shall make explicit reference in order to discuss our research hypothesis on the relationship between market structure and R&D composition.

4.   COMPETITION AND INNOVATION IN SCHUMPETERIAN GROWTH MODELS

Similarly to standard IO models, Schumpeterian growth models are also based on the idea that opposite forces are at work in determining the competition–innovation relationship, and there is little chance of foreseeing, *ex ante*, which one is going to prevail. Such forces can be roughly summarized into two broad categories, the so-called 'Schumpeterian effects' and the 'Darwinian effects' (see Aghion and Howitt, 1998, for a review).

The first class of effects, which are referred to as 'Schumpeterian', indicates that there might be a negative correlation between increased levels of competition and the private incentives to perform R&D. On the other side, the latter set of effects, referred to as 'Darwinian', indicates that a positive correlation between R&D intensity and product market competition should be expected. There is no strong reason for predicting, *ex ante*, which of these effects will prevail.

We claim that the question whether increased product market competition will increase R&D intensity or not is ill-posed, if no distinction is made between research and development activities. For the sake of clearness, we shall present a rather trivial picture of R&D: we identify two distinct components, basic research activities and applied research activities. Given the very different nature of these components, the effects mentioned above are likely to operate with different strengths and direction on the two kinds of research activities. Therefore, we claim that, even though nothing can be said about the overall intensity of R&D, a mutation in the *composition* of R&D should be expected. Precisely, we expect the balance between basic research and applied research to shift in favour of applied and commercially directed activities and against basic research.

Before briefly describing the two effects, it is worth recalling the exact terms of the problem. We are dealing with the problem of understanding what happens to the *composition* of R&D activities when market structure changes, and precisely how the balance between basic and applied activities is upset by a substantial change in the degree of market competition.

We represent (see the previous section) R&D investments as consisting of two broad components: basic research activities and applied research activities. Basic activities include research aimed at exploring new scientific principles and at creating the knowledge stock that will be used as an input to applied research activities. Such efforts are not directed to any specific commercial application, are very loosely appropriable and typically yield long-term returns. Applied activities, on the contrary, include the efforts directed to transforming generic scientific and technological knowledge into specific marketable applications. These latter are highly appropriable and typically yield short-term returns.

We can now describe in some detail the nature of the two classes of effects. The 'Schumpeterian effects' relate strictly to the appropriability problem. The prospect of appropriating future monopoly rents and the availability of present monopoly rents motivates firms to perform a larger amount of R&D. The basic idea is that research yields returns in the medium/long term. The higher the degree of competition, the higher the chance that such returns are appropriated by competitors.

A direct implication of this approach is the fact that the current level of research will be negatively correlated to the expectations regarding the future level of innovation. When firms expect higher research after the next innovation, they are discouraged from performing their own research by the prospect of rapid obsolescence. Furthermore, the appropriability issue is obviously strictly related to the free-riding problem. Given the quasi-public good nature of basic research, the private subject incentive to perform its own research is weakened by the increasing number of competitors, or by the prospect of new entrants in the product market competition. Given these characteristics, we expect the appropriability effect to be strongly present as far as basic research activities are concerned, whereas it can be assumed that it operates with weaker intensity on applied research activities.

'Darwinian effects' are based on the hypothesis that neck-to-neck competition motivates firms to invest more in R&D for two basic reasons: the disciplining market effect for non-profit-maximizing firms and the need to take a lead on rivals in order to avoid tough price competition.

Let us start with the former issue. The idea is that product market competition may force the managers of firms subject to agency problems between owners and managers to speed up technological innovation, in order to avoid bankruptcy. The argument that is at the core of this class of models can be formulated in the following terms: market discipline encourages managers to perform more R&D. Let us examine the extent to which this argument can be applied to basic and applied research separately. The first element that we need to address is the fact that there is a different degree of asymmetric information between ownership and control as far as the two activities are concerned. Applied activities signal the performance of managers efficiently and rapidly, whereas research activities yield deferred and ambiguous returns, which are hardly interpreted as good performance indicators (see Lev, 1999, and Lev and Sougiannis, 1996). Therefore, it is likely that managers suddenly faced with market control will concentrate on those activities whereby they can signal their performance very clearly to shareholders. In this respect, the corporate finance literature on short-termism might provide an interesting insight into the problem. In particular, our hypothesis is that short-termism makes the agency effect very weak for basic research activities, but rather stronger as far as applied activities are concerned.

For the sake of exposition we present here very briefly the issues at the core of the short-termism debate that are relevant to our argument, leaving an in-depth review of the subject to the following section.

The key is that, in specific circumstances, managerially controlled firms tend to shorten the time horizon of their investment decisions. We follow Laverty's (1996) exhaustive review of short-termism. He grouped the various approaches into the following main categories: the diffusion of managerial practices, the emergence of different organizational arrangements, managerial opportunism, stock market myopia, and takeover threat. The last three issues are central to our problem.

The 'managerial opportunism' stream of literature builds on the notion that managers' personal intertemporal choices are suboptimal for the organization as a whole. The structure of this interpretation is the classic moral hazard one, where information asymmetry and incentive disalignment let an inefficient time horizon emerge in the firms' decisional process. Specifically, managers tend to undertake short-term projects with rapid returns in order to build up their reputations, on which their earnings are based. Actually, an inclination to rapidly increase their own reputation might lead managers to pursue projects that would emerge as 'bad' in the long run; however, the opposite argument (managers tend to prefer projects with shorter-term rewards in order to enhance their reputations) seems to have attracted more attention, and was originally deployed in Narayanan (1985) and Holmstrom and Ricart i Costa (1986).

The issue of 'stock market myopia' is centred on the idea that the stock market undervalues investments that will pay off only in the long run. Managers have no way of conveying to shareholders the benefits of long-term strategies and therefore maximize their rewards by choosing short-term objectives. In other words, by pursuing stock price maximization, managers destroy long-run value. They divest long-term assets (basic knowledge, in this case) in order to increase the current price of the stock (Stein, 1989).

The last issue along this line of interpretation is the 'takeover threat' hypothesis. The idea (Stein, 1988) is that takeover pressure forces managers to sacrifice profitable long-term investments in favour of smaller, but immediate returns. In other words, the threat of takeover encourages myopic behaviour on the managers' side.

The implications of these arguments with respect to our specific problem are straightforward. The crucial question is whether market discipline operates with the same direction and intensity on the two distinct components of R&D. We claim that the influence exerted by market discipline on the two components of R&D is opposite in sign, because market discipline introduces a substantial level of short-termism in managerial behaviour. The crucial point is that the disciplining effect at work biases the managers' incentives towards applied activities at the expense of basic research, basically because the former are more efficient signalling devices than the latter. Therefore, although we recognize the positive influence of market discipline on applied activities, we argue that the emergence of short-termism prevents market discipline from operating with the same efficacy on basic research. In contrast, the pressure to perform more applied research tends to erode the resources previously allocated to basic research projects.

Finally, we address the second kind of Darwinian effects that are claimed to foster firms' incentives on R&D activities, namely the effects of neck-to-neck competition on R&D. The explanation is based on the existence of tacit knowledge and the resulting possibility that firms below the frontier have to catch up with the technological leader to compete on an equal basis. Then, more product market competition will result in more neck-to-neck competition, this in turn spurring firms to invest more efforts in R&D in order to acquire a lead over their rivals. Such models are based on the idea of replacing leapfrogging assumptions with step-by-step technological progress. The rationale is that firms will invest in R&D trying to acquire a technological lead (or to fill a technological gap), which will last until competitors are able to catch up through new small incremental product innovations. This is, by definition, a process taking place in the short term; therefore, it is highly plausible that the incentive will work very strongly on applied activities (generating step-by-step progress), while it is likely to operate rather loosely on basic activities (generating leapfrogging progress).

In summary, we have pointed to three main forces that let us suppose that a greater degree of competition will modify the incentives of the firms to perform different kinds of research and development activities. We have examined the so-called 'Schumpeterian effects' and we have concluded that, given the different appropriability degree, it is plausible that the negative effect will be stronger in basic research than in applied research. Second, we have explored the two main classes of Darwinian effects. Following literature on short-termism, we have argued that the market discipline effect is likely to operate very weakly on basic research activities, characterized by a large degree of asymmetric information, but more intensely on applied activities. The latter, neck-to-neck competition, is by its own definition related to those activities allowing firms to compete in the short term; therefore, also in this case, applied activities will be favoured.

These considerations point in a conclusive direction: the introduction of a substantial degree of product market competition is bound to unbalance the relative composition of R&D activities, broadening the scope for applied and commercially oriented activities and reducing the incentives to perform basic non-directed research tasks.

Before moving on to the empirical exercise, we need to confront our hypotheses with the findings discussed in Aghion and Howitt (1998), where the authors analysed extensively the relationship between market structure, research and growth. The basic result of their analysis is that product market competition is good for growth, which is somewhat in contrast with our hypotheses. This conclusion, which is opposite to those obtained in most elementary Schumpeterian models, is motivated through three different approaches, which have partly been discussed above. The first one is based on the idea that more market discipline leads non-profit-maximizing firms to accelerate the pace of technological adoption and to speed up technological innovation. The second builds on the notion that neck-to-neck competition encourages firms to invest more resources in R&D, in order to gain temporary monopoly rents or to protect them from excessive product market competition. Finally, they demonstrated that the 'Lucas effect', that is, the fact that an increased adaptability of the workers will enhance growth, can be replicated in their analytical setting by endogenizing the workers' adaptability parameter. The basic idea is that an increased degree of substitutability between new and old products increases competition between them and induces production workers to abandon the old products more rapidly, with the overall effect of increasing the level of research.

Our approach is consistent with the one described above. We make explicit reference to two classes of effects, *Schumpeterian* and *Darwinian*. The latter are directly related to the first two findings of Aghion and Howitt, when they argue that market discipline is an efficient incentive for firms to invest in research and development. Our discussion is basically in line with that result; we simply add that market discipline works more effectively on the applied component, due to short-termism. Specifically, we argue that in the non-profit-maximizing model, product market competition will align managers' incentives to shareholders' short-term objectives. As for the neck-to-neck competition model, in a similar way, we argue that, although the effect on the overall R&D spending may be positive (in line with the finding of Aghion and Howitt), this results from the combination of an increase in applied research and a decrease in basic research.

Finally, the workers' adaptability issue (the 'Lucas effect') is yet to be discussed. We have deliberately kept this matter out of the general hypotheses discussed above, because we interpret our basic/applied dichotomy in a rather radical way, arguing that there is a clear discontinuity between basic activities, based on scientific paradigms, and applied activities, based on the application of technological principles. This derives from the consideration that applied researchers will need high fixed costs in order to upgrade their technological skills to scientific knowledge. We believe that, in this respect, the framework within which we discuss the hypotheses is substantially different from that of Aghion and Howitt, who seem to refer to a less radical dichotomy (research versus development), justifying the existence of a relatively high adaptability parameter. We argue that, in the same firm, basic research is carried on by scientists, whereas applied research is carried on by technologists, even if precious feedbacks from the latter are likely to benefit the former. The implication of this view is that the adaptability parameter, that is, the rate at which workers switch from applied to basic research, is very low.

5.   A DIGRESSION ON SHORT-TERMISM

The debate on short-termism has long been a crucial theme in economic literature. The main argument is that, in specific circumstances, managerially controlled firms tend to shorten the time horizon of their investment decisions. Many arguments were brought forward in favour of or against the hypothesis that, when the course of action that is most desirable in the long term is not necessarily the best one in the short term, firms tend to favour the shorter-term horizon in their decisional process. The debate pivots around the supposed myopia of managerial firms, which some scholars tend to acknowledge, while others firmly deny. The debate was enlivened by the fact that empirical evidence only ambiguously reinforced the theoretical findings, leaving the central question basically unanswered. In this section we shall provide a comprehensive review of the different hypotheses that have been formulated so far, in order to explain the (non) emergence of short-termist behaviours in managerial firms. We shall discuss such theoretical approaches in the light of the findings of empirical literature. Finally, we shall report on some interesting opinions coming from non-academic experts, among which it is possible to discern an almost unanimous consensus about the existence and the economic relevance of short-termism.

We shall start by introducing a definition of short-termism from Schumpeter (1942) as reported in Laverty's (1996) exhaustive review. Schumpeter argued:

> A system that at every given point in time fully utilises its possibilities to the best may yet in the long term be inferior to a system that does so at no point in time. It follows that the course of action that is best in the short term may not be the optimal in long run...

The shift in the trade-off between short- and long-term objectives is at the core of the short-termist diatribe.

Economic theory has addressed the problem from many different angles. The common elements among the various approaches are the emphasis on asymmetric information and the centrality of contestability as a key explanatory factor. We group the various approaches into the following main categories: the diffusion of managerial practices, the emergence of different organizational arrangements, managerial opportunism and stock market myopia.

First, we discuss the impact of investment appraisal techniques on the time horizon that firms tend to consider relevant to their decisional process. Hayes and Abernathy (1980) argued that the diffusion of discounting techniques should be indicated as the primary cause of the tendency of firms to undervalue projects with higher returns in the long run. The idea is that quantitative analytical tools have a natural bias in favour of the short term, where quantitative data are relatively easier to estimate, and against the long term, where quantitative elements are difficult to assess. In other words, formal discounting techniques bias the perception of the managers towards short-term objectives in the sense that such techniques prize analytical detachment and methodological elegance over insight, based on experience. As a result, maximum short-term financial returns have become the overriding criteria for many firms. Hayes and Garvin (1982) addressed the specific problem of basic R&D spending as an indicator of long-term attitude. They argued that the steady decrease in basic research spending should be primarily imputed to the rapid diffusion of discounting techniques.

More in general, Morris (1999) highlighted the role of sunk costs in determining short-termism. He argued that managers tend to underplay the effects of intertemporal externalities (that is, learning by doing, the creation of new investment opportunities, entry deterrence and so forth) of their investment plans, since these are more difficult to assess in quantitative terms. Therefore, they will tend to favour those investments that are stronger in the dimension of creating an excess of revenue in the shorter term, though, possibly, weaker in terms of additional profits deriving by medium/long-term strategic advantage, learning by doing, new opportunities and other intertemporal externalities.

Besides the usual claim that discounting techniques are intrinsically biased towards the short term, an interesting view is also reported, according to which managers tend to deliberately use higher discounting rates in order to protect themselves from unforeseen reductions in cash throw-offs triggered by competitors' actions and unexpected inflationary increases in investment costs. Furthermore, managers tend to use higher discount factors in order to increase motivation by making targets more difficult to achieve.

In addition, we witness the cyclical return in fashion of pay-back techniques, which, by their own definition, are biased towards the short term. It is worth considering, though, that the diffusion of such techniques should be regarded as a consequence rather than as a determinant of short-termism. In fact, an abundant literature testifies that actualization-based discounting techniques are systematically and partially replaced by payback-based methodologies, corresponding to periods of cash shortage – which is, on its own account, a determinant of short-termism.

The diffusion of the multidivisional firm is the second explanation of short-termism that we wish to review briefly. As Chandler (1962) anticipated, the need for corporate headquarters to gain control over the division's managers generates the need to define quantitative performance measures that must be assessed and applied in the short term. This, of course, biases the managers' incentives towards fast returns, and this particular structure of incentives is reflected downward to all the operative segments of the firm. Loescher (1984) contended that the practice of increasing control over the divisions by means of more and more frequent mid-term reports is bound to obscure any kind of medium/long-term perspective in the managers' attitude to investments. Once again, Hayes and Abernathy (1980) illustrated how the increased structural distance between those entrusted with exploiting actual competitive opportunities and those who must judge the quality of their work guarantees reliance on objectively short-term criteria.

In a different perspective, Rao's (2000) analysis of the telecommunication industry demonstrated how a structural change in the industry, reflected by the end of the vertical integration model of organization, results in a vastly different structure of R&D activities, which lose their basic/long-term component and become short-term oriented. The information and communication technology (ICT) sector is an excellent example of such a trend. The relocation of many research activities to independent market-based vendors is progressively and rapidly changing the scope of orientation of the whole industry's research focus.

We now turn to the third dimension of the analysis, namely managerial opportunism. This stream of literature is based on the idea that managers' personal intertemporal choices are not aligned to those of the organization as a whole. Managers tend to boost their reputations, on which their earnings are based, by undertaking projects with fast payback. Besides the contributions of Narayanan (1985) and Holmstrom and Ricart i Costa (1986), Rumelt (1987) pointed to managerial mobility as an important source of short-termism. Within this strand of literature, the model presented by Palley (1997) offered an interesting clue to the understanding of short-termism: if managers' rewards are based on current profitability, and there is some probability of managerial turnover, then maximizing managers will choose projects with an intrinsically lower net present value, but yielding higher returns in the short term.

Garvey et al. (1996) reached a counterintuitive conclusion: when managers are allowed to trade the firm's stocks, and stockholders cannot observe their behaviours, these latter will tend to define compensation schemes that are bound to bias managers' actions towards short-term targets. Empirical evidence about this aspect is not, however, particularly rich. Bizjack et al. (1993) tested the hypothesis that managers with fewer career commitments (such as CEOs close to retirement) would be more prone to long-term investments than managers at an early stage of their career. Unfortunately, they failed to find any conclusive evidence. In contrast, Mannix and Lowestein (1994) concluded that mobility, that is, a shorter time horizon, would determine a short-term-oriented strategy.

Finally, we address the issue of stock market myopia. Under this perspective there are different lines of argument in support of short-termism, which should be examined. The classical one is centred on the existence of asymmetric information in an outsider-control structure in contestable financial markets. Managers find it difficult to make shareholders aware of the benefits of long-term strategies, and therefore tend to choose short-term objectives in order to maximize their utilities.

The core feature of this class of models is, therefore, the signalling problem. With outside control, the incentive is to raise the price of shares by boosting profits through the cutback of long/medium-term expenses. This argument is found in Stein (1989), who also discussed the key counterargument to this hypothesis: why do investors not recognize such a systematic bias and react accordingly? Stein argued that managers are locked in a prisoner's dilemma: although recognizing the problem, they fail to coordinate, thus acting in relation to the short term. Since the problem is strictly related to the amount of information that investors are able to gather about the firm, the problem is bound to be greater, the greater the spread of control.

Empirical evidence is rather puzzling. There is an abundant literature documenting the positive relationship between investments and share prices (Hirschey, 1982; Pakes, 1985). According to Lev (1999), markets consider R&D long-term investments as a significant value-increasing activity. Miles (1993) demonstrated that investors overestimate discounting factors to a degree that is greater, the longer the wait for the cash flow.

Morris (1999) quite rightly found it difficult to interpret that as evidence of short-termism. He noted that the fact that longer-term investments do show positive returns in shares does not necessarily imply that myopic behaviour prevented other long-term investments from being financed.

Under this perspective, several authors (Morris, 1999 and Laverty, 1996) noted that the pressure to act in the short term tends to be more acute in relation to less tangible expenditures, such as product and process research and development. Lev (1999) stressed that R&D evaluation is seriously impeded by the intrinsic intangible nature of the asset, as well as by inadequate accounting rules and insufficient disclosure. These elements yield a degree of asymmetry that should, according to theory, exacerbate stock market myopia. Nevertheless, Lev and Sougiannis (1996) presented interesting evidence according to which there is a significant intertemporal association between firms' R&D capital and their subsequent stock returns. This is to be interpreted either as a systematic mispricing of the shares, or as a compensation for an extra-market risk factor associated with long-term uncertain projects.

Another stream of interpretation along this line of reasoning is the takeover threat hypothesis. Stein (1988) argued that, under a takeover threat, managers tend to drop eventually profitable long-term investments in favour of smaller returns to be cashed in more rapidly. Recent empirical findings have nevertheless weakened Stein's conclusions. Meulbroek et al. (1990) found that anti-takeover provisions and defensive measures exacerbate, rather than mitigate, managerial myopia. There is evidence that R&D intensity declines as defensive measures are taken. Mahoney et al. (1997) demonstrated that the effect of anti-takeover provisions on subsequent long-term investments is negative. The common interpretation of these empirical findings is that managers underinvest in long-term projects when they find themselves less subject to market control through overprotection.

There is an important strand of literature that denies the existence of short-termism. The core argument is that competitive markets ensure that the long run is properly valued. Specifically, Jensen (1986) argued that, though managers may be myopic, markets are not, so guaranteeing the optimal trade-off between short- and long-term objectives. The implication of this view is that any short-termist reaction to boundary conditions should not be regarded as myopic, but as an efficient attempt to maximize the total value of the firm.

Finally, within the broad category of stock market myopia, we consider the so-called 'impatient capital' explanation, as proposed by Porter (1992). According to this view, underinvestment in long-term projects is the result of capital fluidity, that is, the tendency of financial capital to move rapidly among different firms and projects, on the basis of short-term perceptions. As a consequence, managers are forced to invest in short-term activities, in order to overcome cash constraints and to capture as much capital as possible.

Outside academia the debate has been equally intense, though perhaps more univocally oriented. The opinion of managers and commentators seems to converge upon the point that short-termism *does* exist and that it should be given greater consideration than it actually got in the past. A survey of the UK Times 1000 (Collison et al., 1993) highlighted a common managerial perception, according to which investments were evaluated according to profits generated within two years. Most surprisingly, the vast majority of the managers interviewed declared that shareholders would not agree to an increase in R&D expenses that would lower earning growth below capital market expectations, independently of any actualized measure.

A recent survey of American manufacturers found that the overwhelming majority of firms pay too much attention to short-term performance and should be much more oriented to long-term results. In commenting on these results for the US government, Jacobs (1998) emphasized the role of capital costs as affected by central regulation. Jacobs argued that, on a national scale, excessive regulation on banks and financial institutions increases capital costs, thus undermining the willingness of investors to support long-term innovative projects.

Nevertheless, the common understanding is that this conclusion cannot be generalized through the different industries. Exceptions are to be found in specific industries, such as pharmaceuticals. A recent survey showed that capital markets (specifically the City) appraised long-term investment in research and development. The survey suggested that there are two distinct groups of firms, one under strong pressure from the City to act in the short term, another that is, in contrast, rewarded for long-term plans, the discriminating factor between the two groups being the intensity of innovation and the degree of attention paid to communication to shareholders.

This latter view seemed to be legitimated in recent years by the performances of the so-called 'new economy IPOs'(initial public offerings), which have, on average, stunningly increased their stock prices with no (or negative) earnings. As Colvin (1998) reported, Abercrombie and Fitch, Amazon, Netscape and the like are the living proof that stock markets are indeed ready to prize the prospects of future earnings. This argument, though, should be treated with caution. There is a difference between the expectations concerning a whole market and those related to a single firm. The problem here seems to be one of coordination. When the market as a whole does not produce short-term results, investors are willing to consider long-term plans. But, as soon as anyone in the market starts producing short-term results, the prisoner's dilemma is triggered and firms begin to feel a pressure towards short-term solutions.

6.   CONCLUSIONS

In this chapter we have tried to examine one of the most classical research questions in industrial economics: the relationship between competition and innovation, from a relatively unexplored point of view. We focused our attention on the relationship between competition and the *composition* of research activity, that is, the relative share of basic and applied research activities in a company's research portfolio.

Our effort was motivated by the idea that a separate analysis of the effects of competition on basic research and on applied research would allow us to formulate much clearer hypotheses than those that would normally be specified when dealing with R&D intensity as a whole.

In particular we examined the framework provided by Schumpeterian growth models, which are based on the identification of two main classes of effects, Schumpeterian and Darwinian. Under such definitions, there is the notion of different forces operating in opposite directions to determine the relationship between competition and innovation. It is very difficult to foresee, *ex ante*, which are going to prevail, but our claim is that the balance between the two kinds of effect is very different when either basic or applied research is considered. Therefore, we argued that an increase (decrease) in competition will act with different intensity and perhaps in opposite directions on the different components of research and development activities. We came to this conclusion by integrating some of the hypotheses upon which Schumpeterian growth models are based, with ideas derived from the literature on short-termism reviewed in the previous section.

In conclusion, the argument presented in this chapter is that, although we are probably unable to foresee the effects of increased competition on R&D intensity as a whole, we are in a position to specify a consistent hypothesis about the *composition* of the R&D portfolio: an increase in competition is expected to unbalance the relative share of basic and applied activities, in favour of applied research and to the detriment of basic research. This is the research hypothesis we shall try to verify through the empirical exercise presented in Chapter 5.

3. Mergers and Acquisitions and Innovation Strategies

Mario Calderini and Paola Garrone

1. INTRODUCTION

The literature on M&As (mergers and acquisitions) and firm performance is among the widest and most controversial areas of economic analysis. This is due to the multifaceted nature of the problem, which involves many different lines of investigation, ranging from literature on corporate finance to industrial economics and organizational science.

When the analysis is restricted to the innovation performance of the company, the research problem becomes more focused, but in no way simpler.

Scholars of different disciplines have looked at the problem from the most diverse angles, depending on the direction of the relationship (M&A affecting R&D, research and development, or vice versa), the unit of analysis selected (acquiring or target firm), the time considered (pre-merger or post-merger effects, short- versus long-term effects), the nature of the acquisition (technology related or unrelated), the variable monitored (R&D input or output), the type of operation (horizontal or vertical) and many other relevant characteristics. As a consequence, the scope of the results and of the available evidence is fairly broad and difficult to synthesize.

This chapter reviews one specific aspect of the problem, the post-acquisition R&D performance, which is the object of the empirical exercise presented in Chapter 6. Although we consider a rather specific side of the problem, there are still very diverse aspects of the question that should be explored separately.

We believe that a fruitful way of surveying the effects of acquisitions on the innovation performance of the acquired firm is to consider separately four major consequences of M&As: the change in ownership and financial structure, the change in corporate structure, the change in size, and the change in organization.

Within these four categories, we shall try to classify the effects that have been identified and studied by many authors in the recent past. In this respect, we shall anticipate two points. First of all, the survey elaborates on issues put forward in the preceding chapters. In particular, acquisitions have far-reaching implications for the relationship between ownership and control, the control systems, and the nature of principals, and, as discussed in Chapter 1, this cannot but modify the firm's innovation incentives and processes.[1] Second, we shall especially focus on the implications of acquisitive decision and process for R&D output, because the latter, rather than R&D input, is likely to represent innovation performances (see Section 2).

First, M&As are bound to induce relevant changes in the ownership and financial structure of the merged entity, with critical implications for corporate governance. On the one hand, in many cases, acquisitions radically modify the degree of separation between ownership and control in the target company; in particular, this will increase when a privately-owned company is taken over by a public company, and it will decrease when a public company goes private. On the other hand, the debt to equity ratio is very likely to increase in the merged entity, especially in extreme cases, as leveraged buyouts. The conventional view is that the two modifications, in combination, have potentially important implications for R&D investments, because ownership concentration will determine the agency relationship between shareholders and R&D managers, while the financial structure will determine the amount of cash flow available for R&D investments. However, conclusions drawn in the available studies are far from being unanimous, as widely discussed in Chapter 1. The traditional hypothesis of efficient financial markets makes the claim that, regardless of possible rationing in the R&D inputs, there should be no concerns for valuable innovation output, since neither debt nor equity holders will favour a cut of high-return R&D projects. In contrast, several voices dispute the foresight capability of financial markets; according to this alternative view (that of 'myopic' financial markets), acquisitions may easily result in a limitation of the innovation output.

A second set of motives pertains to the increased size of the company, and associated literature explores the R&D productivity effects of integration between the acquiring and the acquired firms. If economies of scale exist, the merged firm will be able to obtain the same R&D output using less R&D input, or else a larger R&D output using the same R&D input. The same result holds if economies of scope are at work: more diverse R&D output will be obtained using the same R&D input. In addition, other beneficial effects may arise from the redeployment of the merged company's technological assets and capabilities within the new context, at least under certain conditions, such as technological relatedness. The effect of the merger would be negative or neutral as far as the input is concerned, but it would be neutral or positive as far as the innovation output (and social welfare) is concerned.

The third important aspect relates to the integration content of a takeover. The argument is twofold. On the one hand, the acquiring company's control replaces the market for innovation and redefines both the target's and the acquirer's incentive to innovate. On the other hand, the merger/acquisition may lead to more complex organizational structures, which in turn may induce more emphasis on financial rather than strategic control, resulting in an undervaluation of longer-term investments and a cut of potentially high-return R&D projects.

One last class of effects regards the micro-organizational level. The managerial literature stresses that the merger of two different companies into a larger and heterogeneous organization is likely to cause a clash between different cultures and to jeopardize the 'innovation champion' process in the merged entity, thus preventing positive synergies from materializing. In addition, acquisitions are likely to negatively affect the R&D personnel's attitude and accomplishments. R&D input being equal, the R&D process will slow down and the innovation output will contract.

Although in the following we shall try to decompose the problem in its different aspects, here it is convenient to report briefly on the results presented by the few authors who tackled the problem of assessing the aggregate post-deal impact of M&As on innovation.

Ravenscraft and Scherer made use of data from nearly 3 000 lines of business across industries to estimate a negative *ex post* effect of M&As on the R&D input, compared to industry averages (Ravenscraft and Scherer, 1987). Hitt et al. (1991), in their study of 191 acquisitions in 29 industries, from 1970 to 1988, showed that neither a greater, nor even the former level of R&D outputs – as measured by patents – is achieved by the merged entity after the deal. In some papers dating back to the early 1990s, Hall was able to estimate, on a sample of 2 500 US manufacturing firms, some negative relationship between M&As and R&D intensity of the industry (Hall, 1990a). Both in that paper and in a following one (Hall, 1994), though, she herself reported that the evidence of negative correlation was very fragile. In a more recent paper (Hall, 1999b), she was able to add further elements to the comprehension of the phenomenon. In particular she demonstrated that firms with a low propensity to acquire other firms tend to reduce R&D after the merger, while firms with a high propensity to acquire increase their R&D after the merger. Once again, Hall recognized that the estimated effects, although significant, were very small, probably due to the high heterogeneity of the operations. According to Hitt et al. (1996), acquisitions negatively affect a factor combining R&D output and input (respectively, new product introduction and R&D intensity), along two paths. Their empirical analysis of 250 R&D-active manufacturing firms demonstrated that acquisitive behaviour significantly weakens strategic control, which is conducive to innovation, and directly erodes innovation capabilities. Ahuja and Katila's recent study analyses the innovation output (that is, the number of successful patent applications) of 72 chemicals firms from different countries in the period from 1980 to 1991 (Ahuja and Katila,

2001): the R&D output is shown to be superadditive with respect to the merged knowledge bases. Finally, a not too recent but exhaustive review of empirical evidence on this topic is to be found in Hall (1994).

Our survey will thus pivot around the previously mentioned four classes of problems (namely: ownership and financial structure; R&D productivity; integration and control; micro-organizational behaviour), with some peculiarities that will be illustrated in Section 2. Section 3 reviews the effects related to changes in ownership and financial structure. Section 4 deals with the consequences of increased company size. Section 5 surveys the effects induced by integration. Section 6 summarizes the implications of organizational modifications. Section 7 concludes.

2.   SCOPE OF THE SURVEY

The next sections will review the theoretical and empirical results concerning the relationship between M&As and innovation. Before going any further, it is worthwhile discussing two unusual elements and one possible limitation of our survey.

A first qualification of the current analysis is that we shall try to emphasize the implications of M&As for the innovation output. Even if both R&D input and output are affected by M&As,[2] we shall consider the empirical problems related to the measurement of a company's innovation performance, and try to disentangle the expected effects of acquisitions on its innovation output. Most of the literature resorted to R&D expenditures, a proxy of R&D input, even if a variation in R&D investments does not necessarily imply a variation in innovation performances. From both a private and a public point of view, it is the R&D output that matters more, regardless, to some extent, of possible changes in R&D investment policies.[3] In this respect, note that the R&D output consists of an articulated set of variables: new products, new patents, new publications, as well as uncodified pieces of knowledge and know-how. A few authors focused on patent counts to estimate the relationship between acquisitions and innovation performances of the firm (Hitt et al., 1991; Hagedoorn and Duysters, 2002b; Ernst and Witt, 2000; Ahuja and Katila, 2001); in Chapter 6, we shall make use of patents as dependent variables, as well. It should be emphasized that patents should be considered a signalling variable (Wang et al., 2001); they may vary, to a certain extent, independently from both R&D efforts and all valuable innovation output. In our survey, we shall try to separate as much as possible the variations in patenting that actually reflect a change in valuable innovation output, from those variations reflecting a change in the patenting strategy on its own account.

A second specific aim of our survey is a better understanding of the changes located at the acquired company. Most works on the topics of innovation and acquisitions consider the whole merged entity, even if a smaller part of the literature addresses the effects on the individual acquired company. Even if we are aware of possible relocation patterns between different R&D units of the merged firm, resulting in no observable effects at the aggregate level, we shall try to single out those changes that occur within the (former) boundaries of the acquired company, for two main reasons. On the one hand, a major aim of this review is to outline the hypotheses relevant to the empirical test presented in Chapter 6, which will address the innovation performance of the target company after the acquisition. On the other hand, the degree to which the R&D undertaken at the target company is affected by the acquisition process has so far received relatively little attention in literature (Bloningen and Taylor, 2000). Nevertheless, the issue is critical for a thorough understanding of the general theme (the relationship between M&As and innovation) and presents interesting policy and strategy implications of its own. In particular, any R&D cutback at the acquired company is likely to slow down the pace of technological change at the local (or national) level. Knowledge transmission is strongly fostered by informal contacts and by geographical and cultural proximity (Maskell and Malmberg, 1999); geographic distance, instead, acts as a barrier to knowledge spillovers (Jaffe and Trajtenberg, 1999; Maruseth and Verspagen, 1998).

As to the possible biases of this analysis, our survey may appear to be elusive on the possible effects of M&As on innovation via market structure. Clearly, a merger may result in non-negligible changes in the market structure, thereby influencing the firm's incentives towards innovation activities. However, despite this causal chain, we prefer to focus on other aspects of the relationship between acquisitions and innovation performance, for three reasons. First of all, industrial organization has traditionally focused on the effects of horizontal mergers in concentrated product markets in order to provide support to antitrust policies. However, the antitrust doctrine on innovation matters is far less established (and legitimated) than the traditional body of theories and practices for product markets; as a consequence, literature is relatively silent on the effects of M&As on R&D via market structure. Moreover, some of the M&A operations to be examined throughout Chapter 6 are horizontal, but they target relatively small firms with little market share in rapidly growing markets. As a consequence, the examined deals are unlikely to permanently modify the market structure.[4] Finally, the relationship between market concentration and innovation is an enormous area of economic investigation. It is now quite widely accepted that there are two broadly defined kinds of effect that may determine the sign of the relationship between concentration and innovation (Aghion and Howitt, 1998), that is, *Schumpeterian* and *Darwinian* (see Chapter 2).[5] These effects are opposite in sign and it is very difficult to predict, *ex ante*, which is bound to prevail.[6] As a consequence, such a complex theoretical framework results in rather controversial empirical patterns (Cohen, 1995). In conclusion, a consistent hypothesis regarding the effect exerted by M&As on innovation by means of a change in the market structure cannot be formulated.

3.   MERGERS AND ACQUISITIONS, FINANCIAL MARKETS AND INNOVATION PERFORMANCE

A first significant effect of acquisitions on innovation is felt through the changes in ownership and financial structure. In its simplest form, the idea that inspires the contributions seeking a relationship between mergers and acquisitions and innovation in this direction is that M&As and R&D may be considered alternative and rival strategies, competing for the same resources. Since M&As often require a very large amount of cash which implies a reduction in internally available funds, then longer-term investments such as R&D are the most likely candidate to be cut off. In this perspective, one would expect a negative correlation between acquisitions and R&D intensity, as far as the merged company is concerned.

However, the argument is multifaceted and rather complex. In particular, before surveying the contributions on these topics, it should be recalled that the question about the effects of a more direct exposure to either equity or debt markets on innovation output simply cannot be given a conclusive answer through an analysis based on R&D inputs.

3.1   Ownership and Control

The first aspect relates to the changing degree of separation between ownership and control of the target company. This is a wide area of economic research, and a number of different authors have already outlined several economically important aspects of the problem. Let us consider a private company acquired by a public company: the innovation investments are now conditioned by managers' capacity to convey their value to equity markets.[7] The relationship between ownership and control and its implications for innovation have already been dealt with in Chapter 1, therefore, here we shall limit ourselves to bringing together different specific elements of the theory that may help us formulate hypotheses that will be tested in Chapter 6.

The first side of the argument is linked to the so-called 'short-termism debate' we reviewed extensively in Chapter 2. This line of argument is based on the existence of asymmetric information in an outsider control structure. Managers are assumed to have a sound knowledge of a company's key variables. Where ownership is dispersed among many shareholders, these latter will have much less detailed information, and typically less incentive to improve the information structure. The simple statement that the value of a company's share reflects the value of its net assets is questioned when an important part of its assets is in the form of intangibles, as most of the output of R&D activities. It is often pointed out that, under the accounting standards that are in operation in the majority of industrial countries, intangible assets are poorly accounted for in financial statements. The information asymmetries due to the complex nature of R&D activities, the limited accountability of R&D expenditures, the high uncertainty linked to highly innovative research projects, and the fact that R&D expenses are treated as current expenses against income rather than capital expenses, all make a proper assessment of R&D investment extremely difficult. As a consequence, many commonly used yardsticks, such as price–earning ratios and market-to-book ratios, may prove unreliable when applied to research-intensive companies. In such circumstances, managers' incentives operate in favour of a cutting back of long-term expenses, among which R&D usually represents a significant item. In other words, the need for signalling in the short term jeopardizes the long-term efficiency of the company (Stein, 1989). However, as Chan et al. interestingly suggested, the distortion might operate in both senses: on the one hand, as commonly tested in the literature, the market is myopic and fails to reward long-term investments; on the other, it might behave overenthusiastically, attaching excessive hopes to long-term, ambitious R&D programmes (Chan et al., 1999).

A second side of the argument runs from empirical evidence demonstrating that markets do not behave myopically. Hall cited a few studies providing econometric evidence for a positive correlation between market-to-book values and R&D capital (Hall, 1990a). In addition, she hinted that these estimates are conservative, in so far as the R&D capital is conventionally depreciated at quite a low rate, while the appropriable portion of the R&D output is likely to lose its value more rapidly. Again, Hall and, more recently, Lev argued that capital markets consider R&D to be a relevant value-increasing activity, and cited several event studies showing that investors react positively to new R&D announcements (Hall, 1990a; Lev, 1999). More radically, objections are made to the alleged superiority of managers' foresight capability, at least in terms of welfare-maximizing investments (Hall, 1994). Studies on initial public offerings (IPOs) are particularly apt to give hints on the ability of equity markets to overcome the information asymmetry on scientific and firms' technological capabilities. A recent work reviewed the signalling power of technological variables and provided new evidence in this regard, by comparing technological and traditional (financial) signals (Wang et al., 2001). Pending patents, patents, R&D expenditures and R&D personnel are reliable factors in explaining the market capitalization of IPOs in univariate regressions, but they are often obscured by traditional signals, like underwriters' reputation and underpricing, when a multivariate regression is run. Interestingly, a measure of the R&D personnel enhances the firm's value significantly, but after a severe downturn of financial markets (as in March 2000) it loses its explanatory strength, while traditional factors are shown to be stable, gaining weight 'after the crash'. The authors of the study did not answer the question whether equity markets are really unable to appreciate R&D activities, or if it is the latter which fail to create sustainable value. They resorted to three alternative explanations. Intangible resources other than R&D, and partly proxied by traditional factors, explain the success of the firm; the longer-term effects of technological resources are not captured by the firm's value; technological signals are less credible than traditional ones, because the latter require managers and entrepreneurs to incur more additional costs.

A paper by Hall is among the most complete analyses of the relationship between M&As and innovation, but it does not explicitly address the role of equity markets (Hall, 1990a). First, Hall studied private acquisitions, and stated that, in principle, ownership concentration should reduce agency costs, and debt may prove a cheap form of financing investments. However, two peculiarities of these operations prevent us from empirically answering the question about the effects of the separation between ownership and control. On the one hand, a major role is found to be played by financial leverage (for this reason it will be discussed in the next subsection, together with leveraged buyouts and 'pure' financial restructuring), which can potentially outweigh any impact of the withdrawal from dispersed ownership. On the other hand, private companies have no obligation to provide public information, and the post-merger effects cannot be estimated. Second, 'pure' financial restructuring and acquisitions involving two public companies are examined, but these results are of no direct use in exploring the role of the separation between ownership and control on innovation activities.

3.2   Financial Leverage

A second aspect is related to the changes in the financial leverage of the merged entity. Acquisitions are likely to cause an increase in the debt–equity ratio, especially in the case of leveraged buyouts and private acquisitions. In such cases, debt interest payments compete with discretionary uses of cash flow; apart from particularly favourable industry and economic contingencies, free cash flow will be unavailable for both ordinary and R&D investments. The potential implications of cash flow rationing for innovation output are at the centre of a lively debate, which we shall try to summarize.

According to the traditional view of financial markets as efficient institutions, constrained cash flows should cause no special concern for the innovation output; equity (and debt) markets are able to evaluate a firm's prospects, and the firm will be able to finance high-return R&D projects, even after the acquisition. More specifically, in this line of reasoning, leveraged takeovers may be beneficial to overall efficiency: long-term debt provides managers with the necessary discipline to cut less promising, or 'bad', R&D projects; the acquisition deal was accepted by former shareholders, exactly because its price embodied expectations for superior managerial efficiency.

However, contrasting voices, supporting the idea of financial markets as (partially) myopic institutions, are also presented in the managerial literature. Such myopia emerges in two phases. First, shareholders are unable to appreciate high-return projects sponsored by R&D managers; therefore, the firm's underevaluation is likely to result in a takeover. Second, after the acquisition, while increased leverage (in addition to managers' replacement) will reduce opportunities for internal R&D funding, debt and equity markets will not provide the necessary financial support for promising, or 'good', R&D projects, which will be cut.

Hall showed that all increases in the debt levels are followed by declines in R&D investments and intensity (Hall, 1990a). First, the result is robust to econometric specifications, and the acquisition effects are insignificant if leverage changes are taken into account. Second, firms that move to a very high debt position decrease their R&D intensity dramatically. Third, leveraged buyouts and private acquisitions financed by debt are more frequent in low-technology, mature sectors; the existence of additional fixed-interest charges to be serviced induces a preference for target firms with steadier cash flow and more redeployable assets.[8] Given the industries of interest, even if R&D projects should be cut, effects on innovation for the overall economy would be negligible. Lastly, in another paper, Hall discussed the relationship between R&D and ordinary investments, on the one hand, and financial restructuring with and without changes in control, on the other, relying upon both her own previous empirical analyses and other works (Hall, 1994). Estimates from an investment equation show that augmented debt is associated with a reduction in R&D investments, whether an acquisition is occurring or not, and the effect is comparable to the cut in ordinary investments.

The motivations advanced by Hall are that the cost of external finance, especially debt, is higher for projects that are more uncertain, less appropriable, subject to more severe information asymmetries, and with fewer redeployable assets; in addition, debt holders prefer collateral, tangible assets as securities (Hall, 1990a, 1994). However, she made the point that both R&D reduction and leverage increase might be endogenously determined by particular contingencies affecting the technological opportunities, rather than by debt impacting on R&D (Hall, 1990a).

The extensive body of Hall's analyses is complemented by few other works. Lichtenberg and Siegel showed that leveraged buyouts are productivity enhancing and involve firms with smaller R&D intensity, further decreasing after the deal (Lichtenberg and Siegel, 1990). Long and Ravenscraft indicated several motivations for leveraged buyouts to be associated with decreasing R&D intensity (Long and Ravenscraft, 1993). First, managers are reluctant to reveal meaningful information concerning their R&D activities. Consequently, debt holders, whose power is especially strong in a leveraged buyout, are likely to be particularly reluctant about new projects. Second, R&D investments create assets that will not easily be sold in the event of financial turmoil. Debt holders are therefore likely to impose higher costs on investments associated with specific, not redeployable assets (Williamson, 1988), such as new knowledge acquired through basic and applied research activities. This is bound to make R&D investments less attractive than the acquiring of new knowledge through technologically-motivated diversification processes, to which the credit market usually attributes a lower risk profile. Third, as is commonly recognized in the corporate finance literature, debts reduce cash flows that are potentially to be allocated to R&D projects. Finally, debt payments associated with leveraged buyouts will reduce tax burdens, making the R&D fiscal incentives less attractive. Ueda modelled the incentives to financial leveraging and merging against the technological cycle (Ueda, 1997); she indirectly supported the view developed by Hall (1990a; 1999b): an increase in financial leverage is especially frequent in stable and low-tech sectors. For mature technologies, debt holders ('banks') have assessing skills that are comparable to those of the firms ('experts'); however, banks (privately) will outperform experts as the financial partners of an inventor/entrepreneur, because banks will not copy new ideas to compete in product markets. In contrast, after a technological breakthrough, an expert will more efficiently assess the idea and provide funds; at the same time, there are incentives to collude in the product markets and the entrepreneur and the expert will merge.

4.   MERGERS AND ACQUISITIONS, R&D PRODUCTIVITY AND INNOVATION PERFORMANCE

The most obvious direct effect of acquisition processes is the increased size of the combined entity, with respect to the original dimension of the acquiring and the target companies. There are two main effects on the innovation process and output: economies of scale and economies of scope in R&D activities. The latter are broadly intended; in addition to cost savings due to the exploitation of common resources by different projects, the resource-based view of the firm predicts a matching between assets and capabilities of the two companies, resulting in a beneficial redeployment of internal resources. We also consider alternative arguments claiming that the possible benefits resulting from R&D economies of scope and from the matching of technological resources are more than outweighed by the inefficiencies related to the diversification process.

4.1 Economies of Scale

When there are economies of scale in the R&D activities, a larger company will have specialist scientists and engineers, and obtain the same innovative output using a smaller amount of input or, alternatively, a greater output with the same input. In addition, given the indivisible nature of most R&D investments, the increase in size could allow the firm to reach the critical mass, thus allowing it to undertake more research projects. Lastly, the scale effect may result in the elimination of parallel R&D efforts; this would imply a reduction of the R&D input in the combined entity. The effect on the R&D output would, once again, be either positive or neutral. The efficiency effect should therefore result in a steady or decreasing input and in a steady or increasing output.

The relationship between firm size and innovation is among the most popular subjects in the economics of innovation literature. Ever since Schumpeter's claim of a positive relationship between size and innovation, a large number of authors have provided controversial results. Prominently, Kamien and Schwartz suggested a non-linear U-shaped relationship between firm size and innovation performance, resulting from the combination of different effects of opposite sign (Kamien and Schwartz, 1982). Among recent empirical studies, Henderson and Cockburn, as a result of a detailed yet wide econometric analysis of individual research programmes carried out by pharmaceutical firms, showed that R&D is more productive, in terms of patents, in larger R&D departments than in smaller comparable activities (Henderson and Cockburn, 1996). However, Henderson has recently pointed out that, in spite of the role played by size in R&D projects, several mergers in the drug industry are unlikely to be driven by research scale economies (Henderson, 2000). In fact, most merging firms already sustain the appropriate R&D critical mass; rather, the combination of pharmaceutical companies is likely to spur scale economies in the marketing and distribution activities and to overcome information asymmetries that are typical of the market for individual R&D projects.

Acquisitions driven by scale considerations are analysed with contrasting results. Hall examined the relationship between size-building acquisitions and R&D, showing no evidence of decline in R&D (Hall, 1990a). Hitt et al. reported that acquisitions are an alternative growth path to internal innovation; in fact, acquisitive growth strategies have a negative effect on firm innovation, even after controlling for the diversification content of the acquisition (Hitt et al., 1991). In addition, organizational studies point out that R&D personnel cuts, even if carried out to enhance the R&D productivity, are detrimental to researchers' motivations. According to a recent study (Bommer and Jalajas, 1999), downsizing and restructuring threats are found to negatively affect R&D personnel's propensity to innovate, both directly and through a set of behavioural variables that influence innovation at individual levels (see Section 6).

Other pieces of evidence derive from the introduction of firm size as a control variable in studies analysing the relationship between innovation and M&As under various perspectives. Size is found to have a mixed effect on innovation after the acquisition: while a firm's large size drives the company to a deeper reliance on strategic control, which in turn favours internal innovation (see Section 5), there is also a direct negative effect of size on internal innovation (Hitt et al., 1996). In a resource-based perspective (see the next subsection), a large-scale survey showed that scale economies play a role in the successful redeployment of R&D resources, provided that the acquirer's resources are recombined into a more innovative target company (Capron et al., 1998). Finally, patent frequency appears to be positively determined by the number of a firm's employees (Ahuja and Katila, 2001).

4.2   Economies of Scope and Resource Redeployment

An increase in size may also be pursued through diversification. Part of the literature provides evidence that companies combining diverse research programmes experience both R&D economies of scope and a successful recombination of their technological resources.

According to the evidence elaborated by Henderson and Cockburn (1996), different R&D programmes in the pharmaceutical industry share basic knowledge accumulated within the company, with no additional cost; in addition, the R&D activity in a specific area strongly benefits from the 'internal spillovers' springing from other, related research programmes.

On the grounds of related but distinct arguments, the resource-based tradition adds new elements to the hypothesis of a positive post-acquisition innovation performance in the merged entity, along two lines of reasoning. First, a firm's assets are merged and put to more productive use in combination with the complementary resources controlled by other firms; in the case of R&D and other assets and capabilities subject to market failures, resources are recombined by buying and selling businesses (on this point, see also Section 5). Capron et al. considered 253 horizontal acquisitions between the late 1980s and the early 1990s, and defined redeployment as the physical transferring of resources from and to target companies and the sharing of resources located with either the acquirer or the target (Capron et al., 1998). They estimated that R&D resources are recombined in both ways, and that the relative technological strength of the acquired company gives momentum to the redeployment process. Second, the combination of the R&D knowledge bases of the acquired and the acquiring firms may be super-additive on its own. Ahuja and Katila carried out a detailed study concerning the innovation output (that is, the number of successful patent applications) of 72 firms (Ahuja and Katila, 2001); the sample companies belonged to the chemicals industry, were situated in different geographic areas and were observed from 1980 to 1991. For our discussion, the crucial variable is the 'acquired knowledge base', as proxied by a time-varying factor combining patents issued to and citations made by the acquired companies; this is complemented by two other indexes, capturing respectively the size difference and the relatedness between the two companies' knowledge bases. Ahuja and Katila's results support a combinatorial perspective on knowledge resources: the larger the acquired knowledge base, the better the post-acquisition innovation performance. However, the 'relative absorptive capacity', as defined by Lane and Lubatkin (1998), plays a mitigating role: if the two knowledge bases are too dissimilar in size, the intra-organizational learning process is more likely to fail.

Finally, if acquisition puts together different innovation projects, the traditional argument of risk sharing holds: the company may spread risks over a portfolio of projects, and therefore access a larger variety of financial means. This provides large firms with an extra advantage over small firms in terms of funds acquisition.

4.3 Diversification

However, in contrast with the hypothesis of R&D economies of scope and resource redeployment, a large body of studies posits and supports the idea of a negative correlation between diversification and R&D; in other words, there would be a partial substitution between diversification and internal R&D strategies.

As outlined by managerial studies of the issue (Hitt et al., 1991; 1996), the need for managing diversification processes through M&As is bound to reduce managers' commitment to R&D activities. A significant amount of managerial time and energy is absorbed by the acquisition process and negotiations, with longer-term decisions postponed; once the deal is completed, the integration process will still divert managers' efforts away from the development of internal innovation, at least in comparison with competitors. In this line of reasoning, one could expect the tension between acquisition and the innovation input, process and output to be especially acute in conjunction with diversifying acquisitions. In this respect, however, the picture emerging from the available studies is a bit more articulated.

A wide array of contributions indicates that diversification implies a decrease in both the R&D input and output (among others: Hoskisson and Hitt, 1988; Baysinger and Hoskisson, 1989). Hitt et al. (1991) provided more complex evidence. R&D intensity is decreased by acquisitions in themselves, that is, after controlling for diversification (proxied by an entropy index), but diversification outperforms acquisitions as a negative predictor of patent intensity. As far as R&D inputs are concerned, Hoskisson and Johnson found that restructuring companies that had reduced the diversified scope of their activities had also increased their R&D intensity, while firms that had increased their diversified scope actually reduced their R&D intensity (Hoskisson and Johnson, 1992). As far as the R&D outputs are concerned, from a different perspective, Ahuja and Katila showed that radical differences between the knowledge bases of merging companies are likely to decrease their R&D output, whereas slighter differences will probably magnify their innovation performance (Ahuja and Katila, 2001).

5.   MERGERS AND ACQUISITIONS, INTEGRATION AND INNOVATION PERFORMANCE

Acquisitions are frequently motivated by the acquirer's willingness to access complementary resources controlled by the target company, for either reaping traditional economies of scope or starting a redeploying process. In this perspective, the post-acquisition relationship between the two firms can be depicted as a case of vertical integration (even in cases of horizontal acquisition), where the acquirer plays the role of a customer owning the upstream supplier.

In particular, whether the acquisition is technologically motivated or not, the target is likely to embody both knowledge and other R&D intangible and material assets, among other resources: a downstream 'customer' integrates an upstream research unit. The market for innovation, and the related arm's-length contracts, have been replaced by hierarchical control. Some of the studies illustrated in the previous section assumed that discrete R&D resources are subject to market failure and, as a consequence, they can be put to more productive use only through integration (for example, Capron et al., 1998). Other studies seem to assume that integration automatically implies a perfect alignment of R&D incentives. In partial opposition to the theory and the evidence discussed throughout Section 4, this section reviews the main motivations why integration can fail to realize the potential synergies between the R&D of the acquired and that of the acquiring firm.

First, the vertical acquisition process is bound to modify the allocation of the property rights on innovation and, consequently, also the target's incentives to innovate. Second, the managerial control on innovation is likely to weaken in the larger organizations resulting from acquisitions, since managers' attention is likely to be diverted from R&D to either the integration process or financial performance.

5.1   Market for Innovation

The first approach builds on the seminal paper of Grossman and Hart on incomplete contracts (1986). As applied to research activities, the notion that research contracts between research units and customers are incomplete is reflected in the fact that, in rapidly evolving technological regimes, it is almost impossible to specify, *ex ante*, the detailed characteristics of the innovation. This makes competitive bidding in the industry very difficult, and motivates the need to allocate property rights on innovation, to either the inventor or the customer.

Aghion and Tirole argued that the research unit will naturally remain independent if its efforts are by far the most critical input to innovation; in this case, the customer will pay a licence fee equal to a share of relevant revenues (Aghion and Tirole, 1998). In other cases, the customer's contribution to innovation is comparable to the input provided by the R&D unit; this may happen, for example, if customization, post-sale services, or continuous incremental innovation are not less valuable than the invention itself. Here, the open question is which vertical arrangement – market for innovation or hierarchical control – will naturally emerge, and whether the outcome will be efficient in terms of innovation performance. In particular, let us consider the cases where, despite a customer's valuable input to innovation, the surplus is larger under separation and the market for innovation is socially preferable; here, there are two possible outcomes. First: the research unit has *ex ante* bargaining power (for example, it is the unique candidate as a knowledge supplier); in this case, it will remain independent and the level of R&D investments will be optimal (or at least second-best). Second: the customer has *ex ante* bargaining power; in principle, it would prefer to allocate its property rights to the research unit and to be compensated by the latter through a cash transfer. However, in many cases, the research unit is cash constrained, and the customer will rather allocate property rights to itself; as a result, the target will underinvest in R&D.

The relevance of Aghion and Tirole's model can be fully appreciated if one considers a sector where small independent high-tech start-ups are racing to develop alternative 'prototypes' of a new technology that can be sold to a large customer. Innovation is crucially determined by the efforts of high-tech start-ups, which are also likely to be cash constrained and to have a relatively small *ex ante* bargaining power. If also the customer's investments affect the innovation output (for example, through product engineering, clinical trials, marketing and so on), they will be acquired, but this will result in R&D underinvestments.

A preliminary analysis by Arora and Merges elaborated on property rights economics, developing a model of R&D 'make-or-buy' that embodies additional incentives for a research unit to stay independent (Arora and Merges, 2000). 'Synergistic' information on new possible applications of the invention spills from the interaction with the customers, but only under separation will the research unit appropriate returns from such new applications of innovation. Both anecdotal evidence and a case study from the chemical and pharmaceutical sectors preliminarily confirmed their analysis.

5.2   Strategic Control

A second stream of literature is linked to the internal control problem. The basic idea is that the transfer of managerial control from the target to the acquirer may affect the internal governance mechanisms of the company, to the detriment of innovation activities. This argument was originally proposed by Walsh and Seward (1990) and Jensen (1993).

A specific aspect of the problem that is particularly acute in the periods immediately preceding and following the acquisition was outlined in several studies (Hitt et al., 1991; 1996). In that circumstance, managers in both the acquiring and the target companies are expected to devote a lot of their time and resources to managing the operation, to the detriment of longer-term activities and especially of R&D investments. For a relatively long time after the acquisition is completed, the integration process is bound to absorb a great deal of the managerial effort, diverting managerial attention from innovation activities (Hitt et al., 1996).

A further and very important issue is related to the control problem in a multi-unit, diversified company. The idea is that, when the organization gets bigger and the control structure more complex, focus tends to shift to financial rather than strategic control, since the latter is far more difficult than the former in complex organizations.

Once again, the issue is tightly linked to the short-termism debate we have dealt with extensively in Chapter 2. The idea that the need to control the division managers' performance implies the use of quantitative performance measures, which bias the managers' incentives towards short-run objectives, was first developed by Chandler (1962). Hayes and Abernathy illustrated how the increased structural distance between those entrusted with exploiting the actual competitive opportunities and those who must judge the quality of their work guarantees reliance on objectively short-term criteria (Hayes and Abernathy, 1980). Hitt et al. stressed that the emphasis on financial control implies that the company's investment decisions are driven by short-run ROI (return on investment) targets rather than by long-run projects, to the detriment of R&D efforts (Hitt et al., 1996).

6.   MERGERS AND ACQUISITIONS, ORGANIZATION AND INNOVATION PERFORMANCE

There are two organizational issues we now wish to survey. First, the efforts aimed at finalizing the deal and at integrating different managerial practices and cultural heritages after the deal completion can disrupt established routines in the target company's R&D activities. Nevertheless, in a longer-term perspective, the differences between organizations may prove to accelerate the learning process. Second, both perspective and completed acquisitions can intervene to limit the individual motivation of the R&D personnel.

The two arguments concern both the R&D input and the output. On the one hand, acquisitions redefine the incentives and motivations of the target company's managers and researchers to search for and to develop new products and technologies. On the other hand, integration of the merged companies intervenes in the innovation process, at either the project or the individual level.

6.1 Acquisition and Integration Process

The period preceding the deal finalization is at the centre of a few managerial studies. However, managerial literature has so far focused especially on the problems (and opportunities) associated with the *ex post* integration of different practices, behaviours and skills in innovation activities.

Before the acquisition completion (according to Hitt et al., 1996), target executives are absorbed by the acquisition negotiations and other routine activities, and enter a state of 'suspended animation'; only residual energy and attention, therefore, are reserved for routine technological activities, while decisions involving long-term and high-risk activities are often postponed. As to the integration process, acquisitions are likely to affect the 'championing' process (Burgelman, 1984). The top management's reduced commitment to innovation translates into lower incentives for R&D and project managers; in this context, the latter will abandon their efforts to identify and pursue promising search patterns and to develop new products and technologies. The post-acquisition performance can be undermined by the lack of communication between the acquired firm and other units of the acquiring firm on technology and joint projects (Chakrabarti, 1990). Cartwright and Cooper investigated, among the possible causes of post-acquisition failures, the incompatibility between the cultures of the organizations involved (Cartwright and Cooper, 1993). Similarity between the two cultures does not, however, guarantee a successful outcome; assimilation will depend on the degree of constraint placed on the individual members of the target firm.

A different hypothesis was developed by the studies belonging to the knowledge-based perspective. While the mere adaptation of historical capabilities is insufficient to successfully merge previously independent companies, the integration endeavours can be managed through the acquiring firm's capability to manage the integration process (Singh and Zollo, 1998). This, in turn, depends upon the tacit and codified knowledge developed through previous acquisitions. A moderate difference between the respective knowledge capabilities and the other technological resources may facilitate integration (Ahuja and Katila, 2001; see also Section 4). Vermeulen and Barkema elaborated the vision that, in spite of a complex confrontation between different cultures and structures, cognitive abilities may benefit from the exposure to different events and ideas (Vermeulen and Barkema, 2001). Once again, conflicts may prove to be constructive, especially if the acquiring companies have acquisition experience in related domains. A survival analysis of the subsidiaries acquired by large Dutch companies empirically supports this idea.

6.2 Individual Motivations

The value of technologically motivated acquisitions is closely related to the number and quality of its researchers. In this context, a worse working climate and depressed individual motivation may follow the event of being acquired, with malign implications for both R&D productivity and quality. In general terms, Cartwright and Cooper documented that, if the acquiring culture is felt to increase employees' participation and autonomy, the acquisition is better accepted by the target organization (Cartwright and Cooper, 1993). However, this is a relatively rare outcome; as a consequence, voluntary separations and layoffs frequently characterize the post-deal evolution of the acquired units.

Turning to implications crucial for the R&D employees, Bommer and Jalajas contested the view that downsizing and restructuring (due to either acquisitions or other causes) can spur the performance of R&D departments (Bommer and Jalajas, 1999). They addressed a survey to a large sample of R&D engineers who survived recent downsizing and who faced the potential threat of a new restructuring process. The 150 respondents provided answers concerning: (i) the degree to which they would be affected by a future downsizing and (ii) a set of personal attitudes that are both conducive to innovation and potentially impacted by a downsizing process. The majority of researchers felt the pressure of a possible downsizing; a decrease in the propensity to innovate can be traced back to the negative impact of downsizing on their willingness to take risks or make suggestions, and on their motivation 'to do the job well'. Ernst and Witt noted that merged companies may lose competitive advantage, due to key innovators (that is, individuals combining high patent frequency and high patent quality) leaving the firm or reducing their performance (Ernst and Witt, 2000). Their study empirically analysed a sample of 43 acquisitions and tracked the careers of target firms' key inventors. There were substantial fluctuations and behavioural changes: the acquired R&D departments had lost 47 per cent of their key inventors; more than half of the remaining researchers had decreased their patenting activity; three out of four key inventors had reduced their patent quality. The reasons for such conduct among key innovators go back to the 'cultural differences' between R&D departments; in addition, researchers often fear that they will not be given the same opportunities to carry on with leading-edge research.

7.   CONCLUSIONS

The aim of this chapter was to review the extensive corpus of literature that has dealt, in the recent years, with the problem of assessing the impact of M&As on the innovative performance of the companies. The width and heterogeneity of that stream of literature makes the task of formulating a coherent framework of hypotheses rather challenging, although our structured review isolates several major findings upon which empirical results seem to converge towards a single interpretation.

First, our discussion of changes in ownership and control has highlighted two possible interpretations, depending on whether one shares the view that the financial market behaves myopically. When the short-termism hypothesis prevails, one should observe a reduction in the R&D input and consequently a decrease in the R&D output as well. On the other hand, if the efficient financial market hypothesis holds, the effects on both the R&D input and output will depend on the *ex ante* nature of the R&D portfolio. If inefficient pet projects are being performed, the efficient control of financial markets is likely to eliminate such activities, resulting in a reduction of the R&D input, but with no effect on the output. On the other hand, no effect on either the input or the output should be observed when the managerial control granted an efficient selection of R&D projects. On this specific matter, the relative ambiguity of empirical results is attributable to the fact that scholars have typically resorted to quantitative measures of the output, while the specific nature of the problem would require more quality-based measures of innovative activity. In fact, in order to achieve a sound assessment of the efficiency effect of the change in ownership and control, one should be able to evaluate whether the part of R&D input that was cut off was actually made up of 'bad' or 'good' research projects, as reflected by the fact that the innovative output quality increased or decreased after the acquisition. Of course, although the empirical problem is in no way simple, some methods of patents weighing through (patent and non-patent) citations seem to represent an interesting line of investigation.

As far as the effect of financial leverage on innovation goes, hypotheses are somehow more homogeneous. The effect on the input is negative, due to the rival nature of acquisitions and R&D projects in terms of financial resources; in fact, a rather abundant literature documents a negative relationship between high debt levels and R&D intensity. In contrast, no specific hypotheses or empirical tests have so far been formulated with reference to the R&D output.

Another large stream of hypotheses discussed in this chapter relates to the R&D productivity issues and in particular to the effects that scale and scope economies play in shaping the incentives to perform R&D before and after an M&A. As far as scale economies are concerned, the literature almost unanimously agrees on an efficiency effect, resulting in a neutral/negative effect on the input side and a positive/neutral effect on the output side. The matter is rather more complex when economies of scope are considered. This is due to the combination of different effects documented in the literature. Many empirical tests evidence a positive relationship between the R&D output and diversifying acquisitions, due to various forms of positive externalities among different lines of research that are well documented in both the knowledge-based and the R&D-productivity literature.

NOTES

1. As to the focal theme of Chapter 2 (that is, the relationship between market structure and innovation), it is clear that, whenever merging companies are rivals, there is a post-merger increase of market concentration with potentially critical effects on the combined entity's R&D activities. However, as Section 2 will clarify, the effects of acquisitions on innovation via market structure are likely to be modest throughout the empirical analysis of Chapter 6; as a consequence, the present survey deserves limited attention to the issue.

2. While acquisitions certainly impact on the R&D input, they also intervene in the R&D process, which in turn determines the innovation output (Hitt et al., 1991). Particular attention will be devoted to the possible effects on patents, because the empirical exercise presented in Chapter 6 is based on patent data. Patents are commonly assumed to estimate the innovation output, even if they may be alternatively interpreted as intermediary input to the innovation process (Griliches, 1990).

3. It should be recalled that, in a broader perspective on M&As and efficiency, even if valuable R&D outputs were found to be cut after a takeover, the net effect of industrial restructuring on social welfare could still be shown to be positive (Berndt, 1990).

4. Of course, this will depend on the notion of relevant market that is applied to the problem. However, as will be discussed in Chapter 6, our sample of acquired companies favoured relatively young firms which had invented and developed new technologies and products; this circumstance seems to allow us to rule out major problems of market concentration.

5. An interesting complement to the market structure hypothesis is the idea that one of the motivations for M&As is the attempt to respond to uncertainty by absorbing part of the environment (Hagedoorn and Duysters, 2002b). This strategy increases the control over the environment and reduces the company's dependency on the market's uncertainty. The idea is that reducing uncertainty would increase incentives towards innovation and the argument boils down to the classical Schumpeter appropriability argument.

6. In Chapter 2 we argued that dividing R&D into its fundamental components (basic and applied research) would contribute to making the empirical testing easier. In fact, in Chapter 6 we demonstrate that Schumpeterian effects prevail as far as basic research is concerned, while Darwinian effects dominate in applied research (see also Calderini and Garrone, 2001).

7. In the symmetric case of a public company acquired by a private company, the information asymmetries between owners and R&D managers should be less significant; however, an increase in financial leverage is very likely to bear the same implications that constitute the second side of the argument, discussed in the next subsection.

8. There are some empirical results in Hall (1999b), pointing out that between 1987 and 1994, private (often leveraged) acquisitions partly ceased to involve low-R&D-intensive sectors.

PART II

Privatization, Liberalization and R&D Activities

4. Privatization's Effects on R&D Investments

Federico Munari and Maurizio Sobrero

1.   INTRODUCTION

In this chapter, we theoretically model the impact of the state as a sole or principal shareholder on the firm's commitment to invest in R&D activities and to protect the results of the innovation process. Drawing on the theoretical arguments introduced in Chapter 1 as to the objectives of the principal, the management incentive system and the amount of information available to principals and agents, we hypothesize that privatization processes negatively affect firm-level R&D investments, while positively affecting appropriability concerns and patent productivity.

To test our hypotheses, we analysed a panel-data set of 35 companies, operating in 11 different industries, fully or partially privatized through public offering in nine European countries during the 1980–97 period. First, we compared pre- and post-privatization R&D efforts and patent quantity and quality. We then explored the possible differences emerging between the privatization announcement and its actual implementation, relatively to the trends in the precedent and in the following periods. We argued that, over this time window, a significant restructuring can affect the allocation of resources to R&D activities and their organization, given the priority to maximize the value of the company to increase the financial returns for the government from the public offer. Finally, we used a fixed-effect regression model to control for alternative explanations (for example, industry effects, scale effects) in assessing R&D and patent behaviour of firms facing privatization.

The results supported our hypotheses, showing a significant reduction of R&D intensity at the firm level, controlling for industry and time effects. Differences emerged with regard to the amount of shares being transferred, to the level of technological opportunities and to the degree of liberalization of the industry. At the same time, our findings documented an increase in patenting by privatized companies. Moreover, using citations to measure patent quality, we found that the rise in patenting activity following privatization is not accompanied by a decline in the quality of the awards, which remains constant or even, in some cases, increases. These combined results suggest an improvement in terms of R&D productivity of privatized firms. We conclude by discussing the implications of these results for future research and for public policy decisions to proactively address possible underinvestment risks in R&D accompanying privatization processes.

2.   THEORETICAL BACKGROUND

The differences between state-owned and private firms in terms of objectives, efforts and outcomes of the innovation process have not been assessed in the literature in a direct and systematic way. However, as we saw in Chapter 1, several studies analysed the relationship between governance and ownership systems and different aspects of the innovation process. These results are particularly interesting in the context of privatization, since government divestment impacts consistently on the principal–agent relationship. More precisely, the change in the allocation of property rights from the public to the private sector impacts upon the objectives of the principal and, as a consequence, upon the agents' incentives structure (De Alessi, 1987; Laffont and Tirole, 1993; Vickers and Yarrow, 1988). These changes may present significant implications for both innovation processes and their outcomes.

State-owned enterprises present important peculiarities as to the objectives of the principal, the management incentive system, the amount of information available to principals and agents, and their risk profile. Privatization brings a shift in the objectives of principals and hence a different structure of incentives for the management (Vickers and Yarrow, 1988).

First of all, it is important to consider whether and how the objectives of the state as a firm owner diverge from those of private shareholders relatively to R&D investments. State-owned enterprises (SOEs) are set up – or nationalized – to achieve a wider set of objectives, targeted to the maximization of social welfare through the control of market asymmetries, which would generate inequality in the distribution of (or in the access to) not only the revenues coming from the activities controlled, but also their physical or non-physical output (Vickers and Yarrow, 1988; Ramamurti, 2000).

Therefore, while private shareholders are mainly interested in private returns to innovative activities, an SOE's mission on the R&D side is not only to pursue business-specific objectives, but also to support the advancement of knowledge and the creation of public goods (Munari, 2002; Munari et al., 2002). As a consequence, it is likely that an SOE's R&D laboratories tend to allocate substantial funds to long-term research projects and to make specific commitments to scientific and downstream activities in order to diffuse their results to the national R&D system in general.

Overall, the presence of an institutional investor such as the government in companies engaged in R&D activity can generate profound differences not only at the macrolevel of investments, but also at the microlevel of structures, processes and employee attitudes (Cuervo and Villalonga, 2000; Zahra et al., 2000). Given the peculiarities of this type of principal, expectations or manifestations of changes of its role and presence in the company would determine profound adjustments or reformulation of the agents' mandate and, as a consequence, of the organization goals and processes.

After divestiture by the state, private shareholders seek to maximize their expected financial returns from the company. In general, the firm no longer has any implicit or explicit obligation to act in the interest of public welfare or of the overall industry, carrying out research programmes going far beyond its own immediate business needs.[1] For this reason, managers within a privatized company, under a tighter control of the capital market, may have more incentives to reduce investments in long-term, high-risk projects and to focus on short-term results. This should encourage the management to reconsider the scope of the R&D projects undertaken, by focusing on those most closely linked to the needs of the core business.

This concept is clearly summarized by a former director of procurement and technology of British Telecom (BT), privatized in 1984 by the Thatcher government: 'For Research and Technology the first priority must be the BT Operating Divisions and the Corporate Headquarters. Recognizing BT's public sector background it has been emphasized that this first priority does not include «British Industry», the «UK Government», or even the «National Good» except where BT's interests coincide' (Rudge, 1990). Qualitative studies on privatization processes offer evidence consistent with this claim, for instance in the case of the telecommunications and energy sectors in the United Kingdom or in the steel industry in Italy and in France, as we show in Chapter 7.

According to public choice theory (Buchanan, 1972; Niskanen, 1971), the reduction of resources devoted to R&D can also be interpreted not so much as a shift from national interest objectives, but rather as a consequence of the elimination of the wastes or duplication of resources characterizing the company under state ownership. Under this perspective, in the absence of an effective control system, SOEs' managers are granted more freedom in pursuing their particular interests, for example by inflating budgets or defending their personal position. Privatization should produce a better alignment of managerial incentives with the firm's financial performance, ultimately promoting a more efficient use of resources. Indeed, most of the studies on the economic consequences of privatization generally showed consistent efficiency gains and improvements in productivity after divestiture by the state

(Galal et al., 1994; La Porta and Lopez de Silanes, 1999; Megginson et al., 1994; D'Souza and Megginson, 1999).

Obviously, the process of privatizing a company does not occur overnight, since the government has to face many important and interrelated decisions, such as which method to choose (for example, IPO [initial public offering] or direct sale); how to transfer control; how to price the offer and how to allocate the shares; if and how to anticipate state divestments with new market regulatory frameworks (Siniscalco et al., 1999; Vickers and Yarrow, 1988). In most cases, the announcement of privatization made by the government considerably precedes the actual divestiture. For instance, in the case of the British privatization programme, the period between the date of announcement and the date of sale on average amounted to two and a half years (Cragg and Dyck, 1999).

Thus, it is likely that the hypothesized reduction of R&D resources has already started during the general restructuring of the company beginning long before state divestment. In this sense we view privatization as a process, and we expect that its effects on the firm's commitment to innovate start before the date of the selling. This leads us to the following hypothesis:

Hypothesis 1
Ceteris paribus, there is a negative relationship between
a firm's privatization and its R&D investment levels.

The impact of privatization on firms' performance is likely to be highly dependent on how SOEs are privatized, in particular with regard to the government's residual ownership after privatization and the kind of private capital they attract (Ramamurti, 2000). A government's decision to retain a majority or a minority stake – or no stake at all – has a direct influence on the distribution of control over the company after the public offering, as well as on the lasting presence of the same principal. Restructuring following privatization is more likely to occur when private shareholders get control rights, since the objectives of privatized firms become independent from politicians (Boycko et al., 1996). Thus, selling voting control to outside private investors leads more directly to efficiency improvements after privatization. D'Souza and Megginson (1999) compared the performance changes following state divestments of 85 companies from 28 countries, privatized through public offer during the period from 1990 to 1996, distinguishing between cases where the state voting control had been sold (companies privatized for more than or equal to 50 per cent) or retained (companies privatized for less than 50 per cent). Their findings showed that the post-privatization increase in real sales and in sales efficiency (sales to total employment) is significantly higher for the first group, whereas post-privatization changes in the return on sales, dividend payout, capital expenditures, leverage and total employment do not differ significantly between the two groups. We would therefore expect the following,

Hypothesis 2
Ceteris paribus, the lower the amount of shares retained by the government after privatization, the stronger the pressure on R&D investments.

Privatization may also affect R&D outcomes. The shift from public to private ownership influences significantly firms' propensity to patent, since it induces a series of mutually reinforcing changes leading to an increase in patent production. First, it is likely that, under state control, R&D facilities pay less attention to control mechanisms against information leakage and know-how spillover, as a consequence of their status as national laboratories and their explicit or implicit mission to maximize the social returns to R&D activities. In contrast, after privatization the company no longer has an obligation to act in the interest of public welfare and can focus on the maximization of private returns. Therefore, the appropriability concerns become critical. Second, the increase in patenting may also reflect a major shift in the orientation and balance of the research portfolio towards more applied work and development activities, at the expense of basic research, given the new priority to focus on those research projects most likely to offer a more direct and faster commercial application (Roberts, 1995; 2001).

Finally, we can argue that, after privatization, firms will manage R&D activities in a more efficient way, so that any currency unit invested in R&D will have a higher impact in terms of inventions realized. In this sense, any increase in the number of patents issued should be ascribed to the improved productivity of research efforts, rather than to a shift in firms' propensity to patent. This explanation is consistent with the findings of the empirical literature on privatization, suggesting that the switch from public to private ownership is associated with improvements in operating performance (Dewenter and Malatesta, 2001; D'Souza and Megginson, 1999; La Porta and Lopez de Silanes, 1999; Megginson et al., 1994). Ultimately, these three different but interrelated explanations support the expectation of a rise in patent production following privatization.

Hypothesis 3
Ceteris paribus, there exists a positive relationship between a firm's privatization and its patenting activity.

However, considering the simple number of patents as an output indicator of inventive activity presents widely-known limitations, because: '[N]ot all inventions are patentable, not all inventions are patented, and the inventions that are patented differ greatly in quality' (Griliches, 1990, p. 1669). Since patents vary significantly in their technological and economic value (Griliches, 1990; Trajtenberg, 1990), it seems necessary to capture the impact of privatization on the average quality of the patented inventions, not only on their overall quantity. Indeed, it is possible that the expected rise in patent production within privatized companies is due to a lower threshold adopted in the decision to patent.

Henderson et al. (1998) suggested that a similar pattern can be traced for US university patenting after the changes in federal law in the early 1980s. Although the university patenting activity had risen dramatically over that period, it seems that there was no significant improvement in patent quality, as measured by the number of citations received. On the contrary, Jaffe and Lerner (1999) documented that, after similar reforms were carried out at the beginning of the 1980s, the quality of the patents assigned to national laboratories of the Department of Energy remained constant or even increased as patenting was rising.

Following those different and controversial theoretical expectations, we advance the following alternative hypotheses:

Hypothesis 4a
Ceteris paribus, there exists a negative relationship
between a firm's privatization and its average patent quality.

Hypothesis 4b
Ceteris paribus, there exists a positive relationship
between a firm's privatization and its average patent quality.

3. RESEARCH DESIGN

3.1 Sample and Data

We started our data collection with the sample taken from two articles by Megginson et al. (1994) and by D'Souza and Megginson (1999), including 174 companies, operating in 35 different industries that had been fully or partially privatized worldwide through public share offering in 32 countries between 1980 and 1997. Following Megginson et al. (1994), our definition of privatization includes any measure transferring part or all of the ownership (and/or control) of an SOE to the private sector. Moreover, we decided to consider only the companies that were privatized through public sale, in order to control for information asymmetries, which might be generated by private solicitation processes and which could not, otherwise, be controlled effectively.

We further integrated our sample with information on privatization processes derived from: (1) the complete list of companies privatized worldwide in the

1980s compiled by the World Bank (Candoy-Seske and Palmer, 1988); (2) the description of the privatization programmes adopted by the countries of the European Union provided by Parker (1998); (3) additional information taken from business journals and publications reported in the archive Lexis-Nexis. The final sample we were able to draw on after the initial phase included 182 firms from 32 countries.

We then decided, for several reasons, to limit our analysis to the firms that were privatized in Western European countries. First, the vast majority of the privatization programmes occurring worldwide in the 1977–97 period took place in Western Europe. Using a database compiled by *Privatization International* including 1 867 privatizations in 113 countries between 1977 and 1997, Siniscalco et al. (1999) concluded that privatizations in Western European countries account for about 30 per cent of all operations and about 50 per cent of global privatization revenues.

Second, gathering information on the key variables for non-Western-European firms is extremely difficult, especially with regard to the data on research and development expenditures. Moreover, by considering firms from Western Europe, we were able to collect data at both the country and the industry levels, using the OECD official statistics, and to take into account the potential effects of the contextual variables affecting firms' incentives to invest in R&D over time, as we shall describe below.

We then identified all the R&D-performing firms in Western European countries from the initial sample, and focused only on those reporting R&D expenditures in their financial figures at least once in the period –3 to –1 and in the period +1 to +3, where the year of privatization is defined as year 0. After cleaning the initial sample according to the above-mentioned criteria, we were left with a final sample of 35 privatized companies operating in nine Western European countries and 11 different industries.[2]

The financial figures on these firms were drawn from Datastream, Worldscope and several company annual reports, then converted to constant (1990) US dollars to ensure standardization within the sample. Industry- and country-level R&D data were collected from the Anberd database published by the OECD, reporting information on the R&D activities carried out in the business enterprise sector on a consistent basis across the main OECD countries since 1973, regardless of the origin of funding, and including the R&D performed by the SOE. The data are reported at country level, using an industrial disaggregation based on the second and third revisions of the International Standard Industrial Classification (ISIC, Rev. 2 and ISIC, Rev. 3), covering 58 sectors. We then matched the R&D data with information on the gross output (production) at the industry and country levels from the OECD Stan data set (which is compatible with Anberd) to calculate the ratio of business enterprise R&D to output for every industry and every country in our sample.

Turning to the patent data analysis, following other studies based on international samples (Ahuja and Katila, 2001; Stuart and Podolny, 1996) we decided to employ US patent data in order to maintain comparability. The procedure followed to collect patent data is straightforward. We started by considering the initial sample taken from Megginson et al. (1994) and D'Souza and Megginson (1999) including 174 companies privatized worldwide in 32 countries between 1980 and 1997, and retained only the European companies. For each of them, we referred to Chi Research to obtain the annual data on patents assigned at the United States Patent and Trademark Office (USPTO) during the period –5 to –1 and the period +1 to +5, where the year of privatization is defined as year 0. However, Chi Research keeps tracks only for the companies presenting a patenting activity above a minimum threshold of about ten patents per year. We therefore complemented the data provided by Chi Research, regarding 21 companies, by searching directly on the USPTO web site for patents assigned to the remaining companies of the initial sample.

At the end of this process, we were left with a set of 33 companies that were assigned at least one patent at the USPTO over the time window from five years before to five years after the privatization year. The 33 companies operated in 12 industries and nine Western European countries. In 27 cases out of 33, the companies of the second sample coincided with those considered in the analysis on R&D investments. For each company represented in this sample, we obtained information on the total number of patents assigned at the USPTO in any given year, as well as on the average number of citations per patent received by following patents, over the time window from year –5 up to year +5, where we define the privatization year as 0.

In order to control for more general trends across time and industries in the propensity to patent and to cite, we collected the same kind of patent indicators (average number of patents granted per company and average citations per patent) at the industry level as well. A major difficulty in collecting patent data at the industry level arises from the fact that they are classified by the Patent Office into various technological classes, and the development of a concordance between the patent class and industry classification is inherently ambiguous (Griliches, 1990). We adopted the concordance developed by Chi Research, which categorizes all patents into 26 industry groups, roughly corresponding to the two-digit Standard Industrial Classification (SIC) coding scheme. Under this classification, our sample companies were assigned to eight industries (aerospace, automotive, chemicals, energy, machinery, metals, pharmaceuticals, and telecommunications).

3.2   Measures

3.2.1   Critical events
Several studies in different fields showed the relationship between organizational adaptation to critical events and the actual occurrence of critical events

(for example, Ghemawat, 1991; Keck and Tushman, 1993; Hitt et al., 1996), pointing to the importance of conceptually and empirically separating the critical event itself from the moment the organization chose to prepare for the event. In our case, this means considering the time window between the announcement and the public offering, which we have previously called the 'preparation time', during which the pressure towards restructuring and reorganization efforts may be strongest. It must be noted, in fact, that changes in corporate governance are very often anticipated by changes in strategy and organization, which can start well before the actual selling of the company, and are promoted by governments in order to maximize the value of the company and, consequently, the financial returns from the divestiture (Cuervo and Villalonga, 2000).

In our sample we had complete information on both events in 21 cases out of 35. In these cases the period between the announcement and the public offering is on average equal to two years. Such value was confirmed by anecdotal evidence collected from press releases on some of the countries observed in our sample. We therefore decided to consider the announcement date as critical, and to use a two-year window before the public offer as an indirect way of identifying the event for all our observations. To further validate our analysis, we also coded our data using a second time window of one year only, and a third one of three years.

3.2.2 R&D and patent indicators

We used four different dependent variables to measure firms' commitment in R&D activities. First, we used the log transformation of R&D expenditures in any single fiscal year, converted to constant (1990) US dollars, to control for the skewness in the distribution of the variable. Second, we computed the R&D intensity at the firm level, defined as the total R&D expenditure divided by the total sales in any given year (expressed as a percentage). Third, we computed 'industry-adjusted' R&D intensity to control for industry influences, by subtracting the average industry R&D intensity from the R&D intensity of each firm in the sample. The target industries were the dominant industries of every firm as reported in Worldscope and defined using the four-digit SIC system. As described above, we defined the industry R&D intensity as the business enterprise R&D/output percentage ratio in each industry and each country. Since the coverage of service sectors is very limited in the statistics provided by the OECD, we were able to completely compute this indicator over the analysed period only for ten manufacturing industries, corresponding to 24 companies in our sample. For the remaining ones, we decided to turn to the average value of R&D intensity for the whole manufacturing sector at country level. Finally, we calculated our fourth indicator as the ratio of firms' 'industry-adjusted' R&D intensity to the average industry R&D intensity, in order to compare the marginal change of the individual firm with respect to the industry average.

To measure firms' patenting activity, we used three indicators. First, the number of patents assigned at the USPTO in each year of observation. Second, we constructed 'industry-adjusted' patent count for each company in any given year, calculated as the difference between the actual number of patents received by the company and the average number of patents assigned, per company, within the industry in the same year. Third, we used a second normalized indicator calculated as the ratio of 'industry-adjusted' patent count (the difference described above) to the average number of patents granted to companies within the industry, to control for differences across industries and time in the propensity to patent.

Following previous studies (Henderson et al., 1998; Jaffe and Lerner, 1999; Trajtenberg, 1990), we considered the number of citations per patent received by following patents as a measure of patent quality. The underlying assumption is that a large number of citations received by a patent indicates that it led to many subsequent technological improvements. The literature has confirmed that the intensity of citations received by a company's patents is strongly associated with its patents' technological and economic value (Trajtenberg, 1990) and with the company's market value (Hall, 1999a).

To measure the quality of the patents assigned to each company in our sample, we therefore calculated two normalized citation-intensity indicators, to control for variations in the propensity to cite across time and industries, and for the truncation in time of citations, given that – *ceteris paribus* – older patents are likely to receive more citations. The first indicator is computed as the difference between the average number of citations received by each patent of a certain firm and the industry citation intensity. The latter is defined as the average number of citations per patent received by firms operating in the same industry in any given year. The second indicator is the ratio of the normalized citation intensity (as described above) and the industry citation intensity.

3.2.3 Independent variables

Our first independent variable is a dummy variable establishing, for each company, a value of 0 for the pre-privatization estimation period and of 1 for the post-privatization period, including the year of the public offering. However, this simple variable does not permit an assessment of the extent and credibility of the government divestiture, since in many cases governments privatize SOEs without selling the full amount of shares in their possession. We therefore decided to control for these asymmetries and to compute for each company the total amount of shares owned by the private sector in any given year.

3.2.4 Control variables

To include in our analysis the results of previous studies on the relationship between R&D expenditure and corporate governance (Baysinger et al., 1991; Hall, 1990a; Hansen and Hill, 1991; Zahra, 1996), we used four controls. First, to control for scale effects in R&D investments, we considered the firm's size in any given year as measured by the log transformation of total sales. Second, following the evidence provided by Hall (1990a), showing a negative association between R&D investments and a firm's debt level, for each firm in each year of observation we calculated leverage as total debts divided by total assets. In addition to firm-level control variables, we also tried to assess the potential effects of industry-level variables that could influence managers' decisions to invest in R&D. Zahra (1996) showed that the level of technological opportunities in the industry has a moderating effect on the association of governance and ownership with corporate entrepreneurship. Similarly, Chan, et al. (1990) showed that the market response to R&D investment was positive in the case of firms operating in high-tech industries, but not for firms operating in low-tech industries. We therefore partitioned our sample into two categories and used a dummy variable (*low-tech*) to separate firms operating in low-technology industries (1) from firms operating in high-technology sectors (0). The categorization into high-technology or low-technology groups is based on the classification provided by the OECD.

Although privatization (the transfer of ownership) and liberalization (the opening up of markets to competition) are two distinct concepts, they are very often intertwined and simultaneous processes, especially in the case of public utilities. Vickers and Yarrow (1988) clearly stated that, in those cases, new ownership arrangements are contingent on the competitive structure of the industry where the firm is operating and on the regulatory constraints it faces. To this purpose, similarly to other studies on the effects of privatization (Cragg and Dyck, 1999; D'Souza and Megginson, 1999; Megginson et al., 1994), we used a dummy variable (*Monop*) to separate companies operating in noncompetitive industries (1), for instance those public utilities that used to act in a monopoly regime under state ownership, by those operating in more competitive industries (0). Following D'Souza and Megginson (1999), we defined 'competitive firms' as companies operating in industries subject to international product-market competition, whereas 'noncompetitive firms' are relatively free of product market competition. Consequently, we included public utilities in the latter group, such as telecommunications carriers or energy utilities, and we classified all the other firms in the 'competitive' group.

4. THE EMPIRICAL ANALYSIS

4.1 Descriptive Statistics

While almost all sectors were affected by privatization processes worldwide, the majority of revenues came, respectively, from public utilities and manufacturing (Siniscalco et al., 1999). Our sample reflects this distribution with 12 public utilities, such as energy or telecommunications service providers, and 23 manufacturing companies, from both high-technology industries (such as pharmaceuticals, aerospace or telecommunication equipment) and low-technology industries, such as steel or oil distribution.

Table 4.1 displays descriptive statistics. Firms' average annual sales are $12 088 million, with a maximum of $70 969 million and a minimum of $424 million. They spend between $0.2 million and $2 603 million on R&D, with an average of $105 million.

On average, the R&D intensity of our sample companies is 2.51. Firms operating in low-tech industries show an average R&D intensity ratio of 1.27 per cent, the value increasing to 4.9 per cent for firms operating in high-tech industries. For firms operating in highly regulated industries, such as telecommunications or energy utilities, the ratio of R&D intensity is 1.07 per cent and it becomes 3.59 per cent in the case of competitive industries. In 79 per cent of the observations for which data on industry R&D intensity are available, the average firm in the sample is 60 per cent less R&D intensive than the average firm in the industry.

Table 4.1   Summary statistics for all variables

Variable	Mean	Standard deviation	Min	Max
R&D expenses (Log)	18.47	2.59	5.17	21.68
R&D intensity (R&D/Sales*100)	2.51	2.46	0.01	16.11
Industry-adjusted R&D intensity[a]	−0.28	2.15	−11.22	3.93
Industry-adjusted R&D intensity /Industry R&D intensity	0.69	1.71	−0.96	6.63
Patent count (number)	40.90	50.52	0	274
Industry-adjusted patent count[b]	−23.67	59.53	−171.23	214.92
Industry-adjusted patent count /Industry patent count	−0.27	0.95	−1	6.33
Industry-adjusted citation intensity[c]	−1.17	3.07	−10.64	12.41
Industry-adjusted citation intensity /Industry citation intensity	−0.17	0.76	−1	7.07
Dumpriv	0.62	0.48	0	1
Privshare (%)	54.66	38.16	0	100
Sales (Log)	9.09	1.15	6.05	11.17
Leverage	24.74	15.23	0	71.88

Notes:
a) The industry-adjusted R&D intensity is the difference between firm R&D intensity (%) and industry R&D intensity (%).
b) The industry-adjusted patent count is the difference between the firm patent count and the industry average patent count.
c) The industry-adjusted citation intensity is the difference between firm average citations per patent and industry average citations per patent.

Turning to patent data, the mean patent count is 40, although it presents a very high variability (the standard deviation is equal to 50). Our sample companies generate a lower number of patents per year than the average firm in the industry, as suggested by the negative values of the normalized patent count indicator (−24 in absolute terms and −27 per cent in relative terms). With regard to this, we should bear in mind that Chi Research keeps tracks only for companies that presented a patent activity above a threshold of about ten patents per year, so that companies included in the industry samples are generally very active in patenting. The normalized citation-intensity indicator is −1.17, suggesting that the patents from our samples are less frequently cited by subsequent patents than those included in the industry benchmark.

4.2 Pre- and Post-privatization Cumulated Differences

To measure company-level changes in R&D investments after privatization announcements, as explained in Subsection 3.2.1, we assumed that the announcement preceded the public sale by two years. To control for possible biases in the exact definition of our critical date, we conducted a sensitivity analysis, considering that privatization announcements may precede the public offering respectively by one year, by two years and by three years. However, the results did not vary significantly in the three cases.

We divided our firm-level observations into two subgroups, representing data referring to the pre-privatization and to the post-privatization period. We then treated our observations as two independent samples with unequal variance and used a corrected *t*-test to statistically compare the mean value of the four different measures of R&D investments. Table 4.2 reports the means, the *t*-tests and the corresponding *p*-values. We used one-tailed tests because we were *ex ante* expecting a directionality of the effect. More restrictive two-tailed tests, however, do not change significantly the magnitude of our results.

Table 4.2   Changes in R&D investments before and after privatization announcement, assuming it occurs within two years of public offer

Variable	Pre	Post	*t*-test	*p*-value (one tail)
R&D expenses (Log)	17.55	18.27	−1.77	< 0.05
R&D intensity (R&D/Sales*100)	2.93	2.37	1.91	< 0.05
Industry-adjusted R&D intensity[a]	0.10	−0.41	1.85	< 0.05
Industry-adjusted R&D intensity /Industry R&D intensity	1.2	0.51	3.09	< 0.01

Note: a) The industry-adjusted R&D intensity is the difference between firm R&D intensity (%) and industry R&D intensity (%).

In all cases, contrary to our expectations, we observed an increase in the overall amount of R&D investments. In the first case we recorded a shift from an average annual value of the log transformation of R&D expenditures of 17.30 before privatization, to 18.50 after privatization. In the second and third cases, the pre- and post-privatization values for the log transformation of R&D expenditures were, respectively, 17.55 and 16.94, and 18.27 and 18.35.

The analysis of the relative percentage of R&D spending over the total firm sales, on the contrary, offered opposite results. In all three cases, in fact, the ratio decreases and the differences are statistically significant. If we look at this result in conjunction with the previous one, a possible explanation lies in the changes experienced by the observed firms not only in the numerator (the absolute amount of R&D spending in any given year), but also in the denominator (the firm's sales). As the first clearly increases significantly over time, the lower value of the ratio signals a more than proportional increase in the denominator as well.

These observations are confirmed when we take a closer look at the firm-level R&D intensity with respect to the overall industry average. One can observe that the R&D intensity values are slightly higher than the industry average before privatization, and then become lower. These differences are all strongly statistically significant and especially interesting, as they control for inter-industry differences, which might have gone unnoticed in previous analyses.

One objection to these results could be that the firms in our sample were generally underinvesting in R&D, regardless of their ownership structure. To control for this possibility, we used our fourth and last variable, the ratio of the difference in R&D intensity to the industry average R&D intensity. The data reported in Table 4.2 confirmed an overall tendency of the firms observed to reduce the commitment to R&D activities with respect to the industry average following the announcement of privatization.

We replicated this analysis using patent data. In this case, it is important to bear in mind that we employed the number of patents *granted* as a measure of innovation output. Given that there is a delay of about two years between applying for and being granted a patent, it is likely that changes in the R&D overall effort and shifts in the focus from basic to applied research, which may begin during the preparation time, will be reflected in a different number of patents granted with a consistent time-lag. In the previous analysis we singled out the privatization announcement as the critical event and assumed that it took place, on average, two years before the divestment. To account for possible delays in granting a patent, we then considered the year of privatization as the turning point, in order to divide all our annual patent observations into two subgroups.

We calculated the mean of each patent variable over the pre- and post-privatization period (pre-privatization: −5 to −1 and post-privatization 0 to +5) and then used a *t*-test to examine whether significant differences existed between the two subsample groups (see Table 4.3). The number of patents granted by the USPTO goes from an average 35.8 value during the pre-privatization period to 45 patents granted in the post-privatization period. However, if we compare this trend to the average patent production in the industry, the increase tends to shrink until it becomes statistically insignificant: following privatization, the sample firms reduced the gap in patent production from the industry average, since the negative difference decreased from 25 patents to 22 patents (from 28 per cent to 26 per cent in terms of marginal change with respect to the industry average patent frequency).

To test whether the surge in the propensity to patent may lead to a decline in patent quality after privatization, we then examined the changes in the mean values of citations per patent. Results in Table 4.3 show that the sample firms' patents were, on average, less frequently cited by subsequent patents than industry ones, but this difference tends to decline following privatization.

Prior to divestment, our sample firms' patents had 1.6 citations less than industry ones, whereas, by the year of privatization, the difference in normalized citations intensity reduced to –0.8 citations per patent (from –21 per cent to –13 per cent in terms of marginal change with respect to industry average citation intensity per patent).

Table 4.3   *Changes in patent quantity and quality before and after the privatization year*

Variable	Pre	Post	*t*-test	*p*-value (one tail)
Patent count (number)	35.83	45.01	–0.17	< 0.5
Industry-adjusted patent count[a]	–25.11	–22.47	–0.41	ns
Industry-adjusted patent count / Industry patent count	–0.28	–0.26	–0.16	ns
Industry-adjusted citation intensity[b]	–1.63	–0.80	–2.50	< 0.01
Normalized citation intensity /Industry citation intensity	–0.21	–0.13	–1.00	ns

Notes:
a) Industry-adjusted patent count is the difference between the firm patent count and the industry average patent count.
b) Industry-adjusted citation intensity is the difference between firm average citations per patent and industry average citations per patent.

4.3   The Privatization Period Effect

Similarly to research on the effects of public announcements on companies' share value (Chan et al., 1990), in the previous analysis we singled out a specific instant of time as the marker between two distinct moments of organizational life. As in the case of publicly-traded stocks, however, the observation of our variables of interest too near or too far away from the critical date might carry some unobserved variance, which could not be properly accounted for in the model. Moreover, in our case, we are interested in a critical period, more than in a single critical event. This period is the time during which state assets are being prepared to be sold on the market. If we limit our analysis to the comparison of pre- and post-privatization data, we risk underscoring the role played by the transition period, which is also the area where the impact of the government measures accompanying privatization could be the greatest. To account for these elements, therefore, we decided to distinguish three different periods: the period preceding the privatization announcement, the period from the announcement to the public offering, and the period after the public offering.

We used Anova to compare between group differences in the average values of our four indicators of R&D investments in the three periods for the whole sample. The F-test derived from Anova statistically supports (or not) the presence of a difference in the means observed. It does not, however, provide any information on the directionality of the effect observed. To test for a decreasing level of R&D investments in the three periods observed, we therefore decided to calculate a linear contrast test, with coefficients set equal to 1 for the first period, equal to 0 for the second period, and equal to –1 for the third period. As the length of the three periods and the number of observations in each period differ, we computed the test assuming unequal variance in the three distributions.

Table 4.4 reports the results of this analysis, which offer additional support to the hypothesized negative relationship between privatization processes and the amount and quality of R&D investments. In addition to that, they also highlight the specific role played in this process by the period dedicated to the preparation of the SOE to the market investors. The value of the log transformation of R&D expenditures before the privatization announcement is, on average, equal to 17.18, and it increases significantly during the time between the announcement and the public offering. However, if we look at the rough and industry-adjusted R&D intensity indicators, we notice a decreasing tendency, which starts during the preparation period and continues after the public offering, signalling the continuation of a significant restructuring effort, initiated by the state and carried forward by private investors.

We repeated the same analysis for patent variables. As before, we assumed that changes in the organization of R&D activities, which are likely to begin after the privatization announcement, will lead to changes in the number of patents granted with a lag of around two years, in order to consider the delay between the request for and the grant of a patent. Therefore, we now distinguished three different periods: the period before the public offering, the period from the public offer to two years later, and the period from the third year on.

The results of the Anova analysis reported in Table 4.5 highlight that changes in patenting behaviour may have begun before privatization, since there are significant differences across the three periods in terms of the number of patents assigned at the USPTO. The average number of patents granted per year before privatization is 35.80, and it increases significantly during the two following periods. However, these differences tend to disappear once the trends in patenting activity within the industry are considered, given that the industry-adjusted patent count remains stable. Contrary to our expectations, the citations received per patent seem to increase significantly over the three periods as compared to industry trends in citation intensity.

Table 4.4   *R&D commitment: group differences in the three periods for the whole sample*

Variable	Pre[a]	During[b]	Post[c]	F-test	Contrast t-test[d]
Ln R&D expenses	17.18	17.67	18.63	6.87	−1.48 ***
R&D intensity (R&D/Sales*100)	2.93	2.40	2.35	1.91	0.57
Industry-adjusted R&D intensity[e]	0.17	−0.26	−0.50	2.84	0.69 *
Industry-adjusted R&D intensity /Industry R&D intensity	1.24	0.63	0.44	6.28	0.80 ***

Notes:
a) Until two years before the public offering.
b) From two years before to the public offering.
c) After the public offering.
d) Linear contrast coefficients 1, 0, −1.
e) Industry-adjusted R&D intensity is the difference between firm R&D intensity (%) and industry R&D intensity (%).
* $p < 0.05$, *** $p < 0.001$.

Table 4.5   *Patent quantity and quality: group differences in the three periods for the whole sample*

Variable	Pre[a]	During[b]	Post[c]	F-test	Contrast t-test[d]
Patent count (number)	35.80	41.00	47.12	1.74	5.57***
Industry-adjusted patent count	−27.06	−26.56	−18.02	0.89	1.26
Industry-adjusted patent count /Industry patent count	−0.27	−0.27	−0.26	0.99	0.01
Industry-adjusted citation intensity	−0.19	−0.22	−0.10	0.47	0.06
Industry-adjusted citation intensity /Industry citation intensity	−1.48	−0.93	−0.92	1.42	−6.06***

Notes:
a) Before the public offering.
b) From the public offering until two years after.
c) From the third year after the public offering.
d) Linear contrast coefficients 1, 0, −1.
*** $p < 0.001$.

4.4   Regression Models

Changes in the ownership structure could not be the only reason for changes in the attitude towards R&D investments, as is suggested throughout the book. In the previous subsections we controlled for possible inter-industry differences by adopting 'industry-adjusted' R&D indicators and found consistency in our results. To consider the influence of additional variables that may impact on R&D investment decisions according to previous research, we estimated the following regression model:

$$R\&D_{it} = a + \beta_1 Log (Size_{it}) + \beta_2 Priv_{it} + \beta_3 Privshare_{it} + \beta_4 Leverage_{it} + \varepsilon_{it}$$
(4.1)

where i denotes firms and t years. Firms' size is measured by the log transformation of total annual sales. *Priv* is a dummy variable that takes the value 1 in the estimation period following the public offering, including the year of the divestiture, and the value 0 in the pre-privatization period. *Privshare* is the proportion of firm shares not owned by the government in any given year. *Leverage* is defined as the ratio of total debts to total assets in any given year. For each firm i, we used all the available observations. We performed a sensitivity analysis by considering the observations for a shorter time window around privatization, and included observations up to three years before the privatization and for three years after the years in which the privatizations were completed. However, such changes in the time window did not generate any significant change in the estimates obtained.

We adopted a fixed-effect (within group) estimator to take into account the effects of unobserved heterogeneity, or the possibility that unobservable individual firm-specific effects lead to permanent differences in the amount of R&D investments across firms. The fixed-effect approach takes the unobserved individual effect to be a group-specific constant term in the regression model (Greene, 1996). This technique essentially transforms the data into deviations from individual means and it drops the time-invariant terms out of the final estimating equation.

Table 4.6 reports the results for the four models estimated, each using a different measure for the dependent variable. In this model, the dummy variable that measures the post-privatization period has a significant positive relationship with the dependent variables in all the models. In contrast, *Privshare*, which captures the percentage of shares owned by private shareholders, has a negative relationship that is highly significant in the models with 'simple' and 'industry-adjusted' R&D intensity as dependent variables. This suggests that the higher is the transfer of control, the higher becomes the change in the investment horizons of the companies and the discontinuity with former practices. Company size has a statistically positive effect only on the log transformation of annual R&D investments, offering mixed results with respect to the presence of scale effects. Finally, the evidence on firms' leverage values offers some mixed support to the results provided by Hall (1990a).

Table 4.6   Estimates of the R&D investment model: models with fixed effects (standard errors in parentheses)

	Model 1	Model 2	Model 3	Model 4
Dependent variable	Log R&D	R&D intensity (R&D/Sales)	Firm R&D intensity vs. industry average R&D intensity	Difference of firm R&D intensity over industry average R&D intensity
Intercept	12.270***	4.332**	−3.985*	1.688*
	(0.587)	(1.461)	(1.670)	(0.826)
Log Sales	0.657***	−0.179	0.432*	−0.121
	(0.066)	(0.164)	(0.190)	(0.094)
Priv	0.418***	1.238***	0.662**	0.307*
	(0.086)	(0.217)	(0.237)	(0.117)
Privshare	−0.002	−0.023***	−0.012**	−0.002
	(0.001)	(0.003)	(0.004)	(0.002)
Leverage	0.013***	−0.008	0.001	0.01
	(0.003)	(0.007)	(0.008)	(0.01)
R^2	0.43***	0.12***	0.06**	0.03**
No. of firms	35	35	33	33

Note: * $p < 0.05$, ** $p < 0.01$, *** $p < 0.001$.

In order to investigate empirically how the interaction of privatization with industry-level variables affects R&D investment, we then estimated a regression model including direct and interaction terms referring to the level of technological opportunities and the intensity of competition within the industry. Under this specification, our estimation equation takes the following form:

$$R\&D_{it} = \alpha + \beta_1 \, Log(Size_{it}) + \beta_2 \, Priv_{it} + \beta_3 \, Privshare_{it} + \beta_4 \, Leverage_{it}$$
$$+ \beta_5 \, Low\text{-}tech_{it} + \beta_6 \, Monop_{it} + \beta_7 \, (Low\text{-}tech_{it} * \, Priv_{it})$$
$$+ \beta_8 \, (Monop_{it} * \, Priv_{it}) + \varepsilon_{it} \qquad (4.2)$$

where the coefficients β_5, β_6 and β_7, β_8, respectively, pick up the direct and interaction effects of the level of technological opportunity and of the intensity of competition. As described above, *Low-tech* is a dummy equal to 1 for low-tech firms and to 0 for high-tech firms, whereas *Monop* is a dummy equal to 1 when firm *i* operates in regulated/noncompetitive industries, but equal to 0 when it operates in competitive industries. However, it should be stressed that it will not be possible to separately identify the linear effect of these two variables in the 'within-group' regression model, since this estimator does not permit estimates of any time-invariant explanatory variables to be obtained (Bloom and Van Reenen, 2000), as the within-group transformation removes not only the unobserved individual effects, but also the effects of any time-invariant observed variable.

The results in Table 4.7 show that the technological opportunity–privatization interaction term is negative in the last two models, but insignificant at the conventional level, suggesting only a limited decrease of R&D efforts after privatization, as compared to the industry average in the case of low-tech industries. This only partially confirms the results obtained by Chan et al. (1990). In contrast, for all of the four models, privatization leads to a negative impact on R&D investments for noncompetitive firms, as in the case of public utilities, as suggested by the negative and significant coefficients of the regulation–privatization interaction term. We interpret this observation in the light of the simultaneous process of market liberalization that very often accompanies the divestiture by the state in the case of public utilities. Our results suggest that in these industries the pressure of competition on the product/service market further encourages the reduction in R&D commitment, as will be seen in detail in Chapter 7.

Table 4.7   Estimates of the R&D investment model: models with fixed effects and interaction (standard errors in parentheses)

	Model 1	Model 2	Model 3	Model 4
Dependent variable	Log R&D	R&D intensity (R&D/Sales)	Industry-adjusted R&D intensity	Industry-adjusted R&D intensity /Industry R&D intensity
Intercept	12.390*** (0.595)	4.202** (1.497)	–3.596 (1.694)	1.885 (0.835)
Log Sales	0.648*** (0.067)	–0.163 (0.168)	0.402* (0.192)	–0.135 (0.095)
Priv	0.093 (0.145)	1.17*** (0.250)	0.814** (0.275)	0.379* (0.136)
Privshare	–0.002 (0.001)	–0.023*** (0.003)	–0.011** (0.004)	0.002 (0.002)
Leverage	0.012*** (0.002)	0.009 (0.007)	0.002 (0.008)	0.000 (0.004)
Inttech	0.057 (0.104)	0.192 (0.264)	–0.156 (0.293)	–0.04 (0.14)
Intregul	–0.353** (0.130)	–0.142 (0.339)	–0.668 (0.401)	0.421 (0.198)
R^2	0.44***	1.13***	0.07**	0.05*
No. of firms	35	35	33	33

Note: $* \; p < 0.05$, $** \; p < 0.01$, $*** \; p < 0.001$.

Turning to patent analysis, the number of patents assigned to a company in a given year (the first dependent variable of our analysis) is a typical example of count data, since they have a non-negative discrete nature and generally present small values and have an excess of zeros. In this context, a Poisson regression approach is appropriate. Consequently, we decided to adopt the following Poisson regression model:

$$Patent_{it} = \exp[\beta_1 \text{ Log } (Size_{it}) + \beta_2 Priv_{it} + \beta_3 Privshare_{it} + \beta_4 Leverage_{it}$$
$$+ \beta_5 \text{ } Indpat_{it} + \varepsilon_{it}] \qquad (4.3)$$

where $Patent_{it}$ is the number of patents assigned to company i in year t, and the explanatory variables are the same as adopted in the R&D investment model, except for $Indpat_{it}$, measuring the average number of patents assigned per company in the industry. However, this simple model does not account for the presence of unobserved heterogeneity. The standard approach to consider the problem of unobserved heterogeneity in panel data with a count model is the Poisson conditional maximum likelihood estimator proposed by Hausman et al. (1984), separating persistent individual effects by conditioning on the total sum of outcomes over the observed years.

We have therefore adopted this estimator in our regression model. Table 4.8 reports results from the Poisson conditional specification in column 1. The variable $Priv$, which captures the post-privatization period, has the expected positive sign, but it is statistically insignificant. In contrast, $Privshare$, measuring the percentage of stake held by private shareholders is positive and significant, suggesting that the more credible is state divestment and the transfer of control to the private sector, the higher is the increase in patent productivity. Among the control variables, firm size and especially the level of patenting activity in the industry ($Indpat$) are significant.

A major shortcoming of the Poisson conditional is the underlying assumption of equality between the variance and the mean. To assess the problem posed by overdispersion in the data, we then adopted a fixed-effect version of the negative binomial model proposed by Hausman et al. (1984). The estimates from the negative binomial specification are reported in column 2 of Table 4.8. The estimate of the coefficient of the post-privatization period is still positive and greater (0.23) than the estimate in the Poisson model (0.01), and it is now statistically significant, a result that confirms the increase in the patenting activity after privatization. In contrast, the coefficient of $Privshare$ is now negative, although not significantly. Moreover, the control variables we introduced in the model are all statistically significant.

Table 4.8   Estimates of the patent models (standard errors in parentheses)

	Model 1 Poisson model with fixed effects	Model 2 Negative binomial model with fixed effects	Model 3 Within-group estimator
Dependent variable	Number of patents	Number of patents	Industry-adjusted citation intensity
Intercept			7.68 (4.22)
Log sales	0.036 (0.040)	0.147 *** (0.024)	−1.08 * (0.48)
Priv	0.010 (0.029)	0.227 * (0.094)	−0.04 (0.01)
Privshare	0.001 * (0.000)	−0.001 (0.001)	0.32 (0.45)
Leverage	−0.001 (0.001)	−0.014 ** (0.004)	0.01 * (0.01)
Indpat	0.008 *** (0.001)	0.008 ** (0.002)	0.03 * (0.01)
Log likelihood	−1136.13	−835.59	
R^2			0.54 *
No. of firms	28	28	28

Note: * $p < 0.05$, ** $p < 0.01$, *** $p < 0.001$.

We then turned to the citation intensity regression, to test our hypothesis that the increase in patenting after privatization, emerging also in the regression analysis, may negatively affect the average patent quality. The dependent variable, the difference between sample company citation intensity per patent and mean industry citation intensity, is now a continuous variable. Accordingly, we adopted a fixed-effect (within-group) specification to account for permanent differences in behaviour across individual firms. Column 3 of Table 4.8 provides the regression estimates for the citation intensity regression, where the explanatory variables are the same of the patent count model. The coefficient of *Priv* now has a negative sign, as we would have expected, whereas the share of private ownership has a positive sign. However, neither of the variables capturing the transfer of ownership is statistically significant. Thus, it is not possible to draw any strong conclusion from the citation intensity regression about the association between privatization and an increase in the value of patented inventions. Among the control variables, firm size, leverage and the level of patent production in the industry are all significantly associated with citation intensity. The last relationship suggests that the patents assigned to companies operating in industries with high patenting activity are more likely to be cited by subsequent patents, as it is logical to expect.

5.   CONCLUSIONS

Over the last two decades, privatization programmes have profoundly transformed the economies of a variety of countries, consistently reducing the role of the state as a major owner of productive assets. However, the literature on privatization has focused mainly on assessing its consequences on static efficiency, while tending to ignore dynamic efficiency gains, involving investments, R&D and innovation.

In this chapter we investigated the consequences of the privatization processes on the incentives to invest in R&D and innovation output. Our findings support the hypothesis of a negative association between privatization processes and R&D investments. We documented a significant decrease in the mean levels of R&D intensity after privatization, even relatively to industry trends, and highlighted the impact of prior restructuring undertaken by the government to maximize firm value and thus obtain a higher price from the sale. Moreover, the amount of shares being sold to private shareholders, the level of technological opportunities and the degree of market competition of the industry, all seemed to affect significantly the R&D commitment within privatized companies.

Since R&D is just one measure of innovative input, we also assessed the impact of privatization on patenting activity. We documented a rise in the average number of assigned patents after the state divestment, which is largely in line with the trends in patenting occurring contextually within the industry. At the same time, patent quality, measured by the citations received by subsequent patents, did not seem to decrease significantly. This last result suggests that the switch in ownership induces privatized companies to produce more patents, by reorienting their research activities towards areas with more direct commercial applicability. This is consistent with the findings of Jaffe and Lerner (1999) on the impact of legislative reforms of the early 1980s on patenting and technology transfer activities at US national laboratories.

Taken together, these findings suggest that privatization may lead to an overall improvement in R&D productivity, and the innovative outcomes deriving from restructuring processes may be considered positive from the perspective of private investors. These results are consistent with the literature on the impact of privatization, which on average documented significant improvements in financial and operating efficiency of privatized firms (D'Souza and Megginson, 1999; Galal et al., 1994; La Porta and Lopez de Silanes, 1999; Megginson et al., 1994).

Our study presents several implications from a public policy perspective. First, we found that privately-owned companies are unlikely to make the same long-term commitment as did state-owned enterprises, and that the barriers to private risk taking vary across industrial sectors. We argue that this reduction is to be considered positive in terms of private interest, since it is driven by a better use and higher productivity of R&D resources. However, a critical situation arises when the abandoned R&D activities, of limited interest for the company at least in the short term, but important in a more general sense for the industry or for society as a whole, are not undertaken by other subjects, since in this case their abandonment can have a negative impact on social welfare. A typical situation of market failure emerges and the intervention of the state should be requested in forms that differ from ownership and control.

This should be opportune and in the interest of general welfare, but it is not always likely to happen. For instance, in the UK electricity sector, the huge cuts in R&D expenditures made by the successors of the formerly state-owned Central Electricity Generating Board were not accompanied by a corresponding increase in government spending on energy research. As a consequence, research in important areas, such as environment protection, was negatively affected (Kenward, 1993). Further research is needed to assess the impact of privatization on the social returns to innovative activities.

Finally, it is important to acknowledge this chapter's limitations, which indicate fruitful avenues for future research. A first weakness derives from the limited number of companies constituting our sample, which is strictly related to the limited number of privatization programmes of significant size occurring worldwide over the last twenty years. The possibility of considering larger samples in future research, for example by including firms privatized in developing economies, will largely depend on the objective difficulties of collecting reliable financial and innovation data on international companies. Second, a major difficulty in the assessment of firm-level changes in performance after privatization regards the multiplicity of variables that typically intervene at different levels (firm, industry and country) to generate substantial noise around the ownership effect (Cuervo and Villalonga, 2000; Ramamurti, 2000). This was our main concern and we tried to control for different factors both at the firm level, for instance by separating the individual permanent effects in the regression models, and at industry level, by adopting industry-adjusted indicators and by differentiating between competitive and noncompetitive firms or between high-technology and low-technology firms. However, future studies may employ more sophisticated control variables (for instance to measure the level of competition within the industries) or research approaches (such as matched-pair research designs) in order to account for these critical issues. Another limitation of this study derives from the use of patents as a measure of innovative output. We addressed the problems of high variance in the value of patents by considering citation-based measures to proxy patent quality. Future research might tackle this issue more directly by analysing the impact of privatizations on the underlying economic value of innovations.

Despite these limitations, we believe that this study provides the first empirical evidence of the impact of privatization on innovation activities and contributes to deepening our understanding of the long-term consequences of the decision to privatize public sector activities, a rich area for future research.

NOTES

1. In the case of public utilities, typically characterized by the concurrent undertaking of privatization and liberalization processes, the national regulatory authorities aim at regulating the market through welfare-maximizing schemes. In most cases, however, a static definition of welfare is adopted, so that R&D obligations are not imposed on either the former monopolist or the new entrants.
2. A list of the sample firms is available from the authors.

5. Liberalization and the Balance of R&D Activities: An Empirical Analysis

Mario Calderini and Paola Garrone

1. INTRODUCTION

The relationship between market structure and R&D is still a matter of theoretical debate. Chapter 2 of this volume has surveyed a number of contributions to the issue from endogenous growth theory and financial economics, and has made a case for discriminating between basic (or 'long-term') and applied (or 'short-term') research.[1] While applied research is the domain of the so-called 'Darwinian' market effects, basic research is more consistent with a Schumpeterian framework: it reacts only weakly to competition stimula and, in managerial firms, suffers from short-termist decision making. As a consequence, we proposed the hypothesis that basic and applied research are likely to respond to the competition acceleration in opposite ways: while the former decreases, the latter increases.

In the application presented in Chapter 5, we stylize the liberalization process as a transition from a monopolistic regime to a competitive one. Therefore, we claim that the liberalization event can be identified as one that induces a higher degree of product market competition.

With respect to the notion of competition used in Chapter 2, a few important remarks are in order. In the empirical exercise that is presented here, we reduce our notion of competition to a much more restricted and limited concept than the one used to review the literature in Chapter 2. Namely, we refer specifically to product market competition, that is, competition in the final market of telecommunication services. This definition has at least two relevant implications. First, it excludes the notion of technological competition. The change that the companies are assumed to face in this context is purely related to the number of competitors that operate in the same relevant market. Therefore, when we refer to the effects of competition on R&D incentives, we mean exclusively the effects of product and service competition and not those related to technological competition. Second, our notion of competition excludes other dimensions of competition that might be equally relevant in determining the change in the incentive to innovate. It should be noted that the liberalization date implies a change in the competitive scenario in several dimensions, in particular the capital market and the labour market. Although it is beyond the scope of this review to discuss these specific dimensions of the problem, it can be useful to bear in mind that the empirical models that are presented throughout this chapter cannot distinguish among these different sources of discontinuities in the competitive regime.

Many policy makers have recently expressed concern about the fate of industrial basic research in a world of increasing competitive pressure. This vision was clearly expressed in a planning report of the US National Institute of Standards and Technology (see Tassey, 1999). According to this analysis, the scope of R&D market failures seems to have broadened in several key respects, resulting in significant underinvestment relative to the optimum level and composition of R&D needed for economic growth. The report stresses that the composition of US private sector R&D is shifting towards shorter-term objectives, at the expense of next-generation research. US industry is attempting to become more efficient in the conduct of applied research, the effort manifesting itself in the 1990s in the form of shorter R&D cycle times, cutting the average time by 45 per cent (18 months to 10 months in a five-year period).

Whether such strategy shifts suppress private sector incentives to invest in next-generation research seems to be chiefly an empirical question. In some sectors, shorter R&D cycles are accomplished by adopting new technology management practices and systems without prejudice to long-term innovation rates. However, Tassey found that, in most US high-tech sectors, shorter R&D cycle times were accompanied by a drift from more radical and risky innovation efforts, which are crucial to prepare the transition to new technologies (Tassey, 1999). Telecommunications (tlcs) are an ideal field to empirically address the issue. On the one hand, the industry labs have traditionally carried out long-term research, whose output is widely assumed to have sustained productivity growth in both information and communication technology (hereafter, ICT) sectors and other downstream industries. On the other hand, over the last two decades, in most industrialized countries, liberalization has implied a sharp discontinuity in the market structure of tlc services. The main empirical question motivating the present analysis is whether the institutional change has redirected the industry R&D activities towards applied research at the expense of basic research.

This chapter empirically analyses whether the incumbent tlc firms changed the composition of R&D activities in coincidence (or in anticipation) of the liberalization date. The data set includes innovation measures for 17 European former monopolists. It is to be noted that our empirical proxies were likely to over-represent the US (see Section 3). Accordingly, despite the somewhat richer evidence on that country, we were forced to exclude the US firms from our sample. Basic research activities are observed from 1988 to 1999, while applied research activities are observed from 1980 to 1999. The hypothesis that the R&D resources were shifted by the institutional change towards more applied tasks is preliminarily discussed through the analysis of cross-tabular and graphical evidence; subsequently, it is specified and submitted to testing through Poisson and latent variable models.

The remainder of the chapter is structured as follows: the next section reports on recent trends in industrial basic research in both the whole industry and tlcs; Section 3 presents data and a preliminary analysis of the sample; Section 4 specifies the econometric model; Section 5 illustrates the results obtained; Section 6 concludes.

2.   RECENT TRENDS IN BASIC RESEARCH

In the mid-1990s, a large number of comments pointed at a sharp redirection in industrial R&D. Anecdotal evidence is especially rich for the US economy and for the ICT industries.

In the early 1990s, Bell Labs were reported to have stopped most long-term research in physics to focus on the immediate needs of the customers, and the same was true for IMB, AT&T, Exxon and Dupont (Business Week, 1994; Odlyzko, 1995). Most US firms manifested their ambition to get their blue-sky research down to earth (Business Week, 1995), leading the former Bellcore's president to express his concern in these terms (Business Week, 1994): 'It is now legitimate to ask who will do long-term, more basic research in the future'. Worries about this trend were legitimated by the comparison with Japanese industry; in 1994 the Council on Competitiveness estimated that Japanese industry spent nearly 50 per cent on long-term projects, versus less than 22 per cent for the US industry. In this respect, it should be recalled that many analyses of the potential risks of a drift from longer-term R&D projects take root in the long-debated differences between Japanese and US/UK management attitudes towards time horizons.

Almost every commentator seemed to attribute the insurgence of this trend to increasing competition on global markets. This was utterly true in R&D-intensive sectors, such as tlcs. The US tlc industry, though, seemed to perceive the threats intrinsic in a massive downsizing of long-term R&D, and many signs of awareness of and determination to offset the phenomenon can be traced in the words of several commentators and managers. In particular, the problem of coordinating basic and applied research efforts emerged as a top priority in research managers' agenda. Lucent's Bell labs in 1998 could spare a $3.7 billion budget for R&D, thanks to the decision to allocate a fixed 11 per cent of the revenues to research. Lucent also established an internal venture capital operation to fund researchers' ideas that would not fit into existing business (Business Week, 1999). The New Ventures Group at Lucent, just like the Xerox Technology Venture at Xerox, are there to ensure that any scientist coming up with a good idea has a legitimate chance of getting it financed (Valery, 1999). The Industrial Research Institute has been surveying its membership annually since 1993 to identify the biggest problems for technology leaders (IRI, 1993–1999). The item 'Balancing long-term/short-term R&D objectives/focus' was identified as the second most important problem every year of the survey except 1996 (when it ranked first) and 1993 (third).

Our claim that basic research is increasingly viewed as just one more expense item that competes against applied research, sales, marketing and general management expenses is better understood when it is recalled that, in the US, in the last decade, business was conducted in the context of increasing R&D expenditures (Roberts, 2001). Payson and Jankowski reported that the US economy and, in particular, US industry, experienced unprecedented growth rates in R&D over the 1990s (Payson and Jankowski, 2000). However, the positive trend is chiefly led by downstream R&D activities: development grows at a 6.1 per cent annual rate (expenses, real values, 1994–2000), while the growth rate of applied and basic research is equal to, respectively, 5.8 per cent and 5.7 per cent.

Let us now focus on the worldwide tlc sector. All over the world, during the 1990s, tlc carriers experienced serious problems in accommodating long- and short-term research objectives.

A comprehensive review is provided by Fransman (1994a; 1994b). British Telecom (BT) and Nippon Telegraph and Telephone (NTT) allocated, in 1994, about 10 per cent of their R&D budget to projects with a commercial time horizon of 10–20 years. There seemed to be little, if any, basic research undertaken in the BT laboratories, at least in so far as that refers to research undertaken without any practical or commercial objective in mind. Even in the case of long-term research, BT put in practice a tight 'customer–supplier' principle, establishing a structure in order to define a portfolio of research projects. The portfolio is managed to comply with the broad strategic directives agreed by the Technology Research Board; in addition, the project scope is strictly monitored by an advisory committee of experts selected from business units across the group.

The same can be said about NTT; the Basic Research Laboratory consumes about 6 per cent of NTT total R&D budget and it has been protected as a priority area from budget cuts. Nevertheless, the Basic Research Laboratory is characterized as undertaking long-term-oriented basic research. It is here interesting to notice that the different attitude of BT and NTT towards basic research is probably the result of different obligations to do research in the nation's interest, which are very strong for NTT, but weaker for BT.

A greater attention to applied, commercial R&D activities *per se* should raise no concerns for the long-term perspectives of technological progress, and could even signal a superior efficiency of the innovation process. However, a common perception among industry experts is that the redirection towards applied research occurs at the expense of basic research efforts, in both relative and absolute terms. Unfortunately, corporate documents do not provide comprehensive evidence on long-term research investments, because the 'basic' portion of R&D expenses (or employees) is not reported. As a consequence, the long-term component of R&D efforts can be observed only indirectly, and in the next sections we shall resort to R&D output indicators.

3.   DATA AND QUALITATIVE EVIDENCE

In the last section, we limited ourselves to illustrating signals of a recent increase in the applied research investments by industry. Such a trend is likely to imply, in a context of either stable or decreasing R&D expenses, as for some European tlc incumbents (see Table 5.1 below), a cut of R&D resources devoted to basic activities. In turn, a reduction of basic research resources is likely to translate into a reduction of basic research output (only if R&D productivity is assumed not to increase).

We tracked the R&D output portfolio of 17 firms from the 15 countries of the European Union, plus Switzerland and Norway, in a 15-year time window embracing the liberalization dates of different national markets. The companies are the tlc incumbents (former monopolists); as liberalization date, we considered the year when voice services over the public network are liberalized.

We considered patents as a proxy of applied research output and publications as a proxy of basic research output. However, if we assume a constant R&D productivity, trends in patents and publications also depict trends in R&D efforts. We empirically characterized the R&D activities of a given firm in a given year through two fundamental variables: the number of papers published in peer-reviewed journals and the number of patents obtained by the largest world patent office, that is, the US Patent and Trademark Office. We have patent data from 1980 to 1999 and publication data from 1988 to 1999.

3.1 Measuring Basic Research

In the following paragraphs, we discuss major potential problems with bibliometric indicators as proxies of basic research activities, especially those undertaken in the tlc industry labs. The debate on the parallel issue, namely the validity of patent indicators as proxies of applied research, is to some extent more consolidated, and economic literature has extensively used patents as indicators of applied and development activities. The reason for this is that patents are the outcome of science and technology activities of a proprietary nature, and are likely to generate business applications. This argument is to be found in many contributions from different authors, but prominently in Griliches (1990) and Archibugi and Pianta (1992).

First, bibliometric measures that are not integrated by citation indexes, as publication counts, indicate the output quantity, not its quality; in addition, undesirable publishing practices (artificially inflated numbers of co-authors, artificially shorter papers) are increasing in various fields, but in particular in medicine and the related fields. However, many authors emphasized that in large statistical samples, publication and citation anomalies have little effect, since they are like random noise in the presence of strong repetitive signals (for example, Cawkell, 1977).

Second, publication practices may vary across scientific and technological fields. However, this problem is particularly acute when publications are used in cross-sectional studies, and this is not our case.

Third, the appearance of a publication in a scientific journal lags the research effort by, on average, 18 to 24 months. We tried to cope empirically with this drawback: the models of Section 4 test the anticipated effects of liberalization; alternatively, the inclusion of lead liberalization dates controls for lags in the publication dates.

Fourth, and most important, publication productivity may be highly dependent on the structure of incentives defined in different institutional systems. In particular, when publication counts are used to evaluate industrial basic research, it should be taken into account that the management of basic research by private corporations is typically inspired by secrecy and appropriation policies rather than by the circulation of knowledge. This problem is of the utmost importance when dealing with the ICT sectors, where research is intended mainly to generate new products and processes, and not to produce publishable results.

The criticism should not be dismissed heedlessly. However, many authors discussed thoroughly the general reasons why companies tend to publish and circulate their basic research results (prominently, Pavitt, 1991, and Hicks, 1995). The idea is that large firms have to invest in long-term, fundamental research for creating in-house capabilities for recognizing, assimilating and exploiting the knowledge created elsewhere. Accordingly, they need to establish their links to the public research sector. Publications are what David called 'the entry fee' to the scientific community; moreover, scientific publications may help the firm to establish and consolidate its reputation in science-intensive industrial sectors. In addition, researchers at private companies release their competencies and knowledge in order to present themselves to the scientific community and get accepted; Stern showed that scientists accept a wage discount if they are allowed to publish in scholarly journals (Stern, 1999a). Research papers by industrial researchers can therefore be regarded as deliberate signals of the existence of tacit knowledge and skills. Tijssen and Van Wijk argued that the need for consolidating such capabilities and maintaining a close link to the scientific community exerts an important influence on researchers at large corporations, motivating them to adapt their publication strategies in favour of more publications in the scientific and technical literature (Tijssen and Van Wijk, 1999). As to telecommunications and other ICT sectors, many companies do produce many scientific publications, as do large private laboratories (Godin, 1996; Hicks et al., 1996).

Lastly, as Tijssen and Van Wijk (1999) rightly pointed out, large companies tend to publish only a small fraction of their research output; scientific articles usually go through a selective internal process, by means of which they are often amended or kept secret. In this sense, bibliometric indicators based on articles in international journals will tend to be biased towards basic research and to underestimate applied and development results; accordingly, publications may, in many respects, be a consistent proxy of tacit and embedded knowledge. We appreciate this element of bibliometric indicators; since our primary objective is specifically to evaluate the evolution of basic research output, we shall use articles in selected scientific journals as a proxy of basic research and complementarily shall analyse the evolution of applied research output through patent indicators.

3.2   The Data Set

We referred to the US Institute of Electrical and Electronics Engineers and the UK Institution of Electrical Engineers (hereafter, IEEE/IEE) database for publications. The IEEE/IEE database includes the most quoted scholarly journals related to communication and information technologies. The IEEE is the most important scientific organization in the field and publishes about one hundred scientific and non-scientific journals. Furthermore, the IEEE organizes the most important conferences in this field and coordinates the standardization activities. The IEEE publishes about 30 per cent of the total number of scientific papers in the field and the journals published by the IEEE rank among the very first positions in terms of impact factor. Given the positioning of IEEE, we are not able to estimate a possible shift of publications towards lower-quality journals; in other words, we are likely to observe higher-quality output from basic research.

Within the database one can easily distinguish three types of papers: journal papers, conference proceedings and technical documents related to the definition of standards. Given the purpose of our analysis, we selected a subset of journals that publish only scientific papers: Transactions or Letters. In fact, these series are exclusively dedicated to the publication of scientific papers on ICT topics and the papers go through a very selective peer-reviewing process.

We used the US Patent and Trademark Office (hereafter, USPTO) database in order to build our patent data set. The main reason for choosing the USPTO database instead of the European Patent Office (EPO) is that the USPTO represents an unbiased source of information with respect to European companies. Furthermore, its accessibility, depth and width allow the accurate kind of queries that will be used throughout this work. Our data sources prevented us from including US firms in our sample. In fact the incentive of US firms to patenting and, to a lesser degree, to publish in the US is much higher than that of European firms, and this would have introduced a strong bias in our population.

The patent search was performed in a 20-year time window, from 1980 to 1999. The reference date is the 'issue date' on the front page of the patent, although the use of this latter may introduce some delay between the moment in which the innovation is generated and the moment the patent becomes available in the database; Griliches estimated that between the two dates there is a delay that is on average eighteen months (Griliches, 1990). Moreover, in order to control for the overall trend in patenting activity (see the definition of *Wpat* in Table 5.3), a patent search was performed on telecommunications-related classes, irrespective of the assignee. As far as classification of patents by industry is concerned, we used the USPTO concordance manual (USPTO, 1998). This opened a serious methodological problem, since there was no way to define univocally the patent classes that are related to telecommunications. The USPTO provides a comprehensive classification of technological classes (Current US Class) on the basis of which USPTO examiners assign each patent to a specific technological class. Such classification is multiple, meaning that the same patent may be assigned to different classes, depending on its applications. In order to identify all the classes that must be considered relevant to telecommunications, we relied on the USPTO manual (USPTO, 1998). The manual allows identification of the correspondence between SIC codes and patent classes; in particular, a subset of classes is characterized by including all the subclasses related to telecommunications. Such a restricted set is: R = {117, 178, 216, 257, 314, 315, 326, 327, 329, 330, 331, 332, 333, 334, 336, 338, 341, 342, 343, 349, 358, 365, 367, 370, 375, 379, 380, 381, 386, 438, 455, 505}.

3.3   Preliminary Evidence

In Section 2 we gave some hints that, especially in ICT, the increase in applied research investments observed throughout the last decade is likely to have occurred at the expense of basic research activities. In this section, we present and discuss qualitative evidence of the ongoing unbalance between basic and applied research in European tlcs.

First of all, many sector experts point out the fact that, in Europe, major tlc firms have relatively stable (or decreasing) R&D expenses: larger resources were progressively absorbed by more downstream functions, as service development and engineering, marketing, advertising, or customer relationship management. Given a stable, or declining, R&D budget, any drift towards applied, short-term objectives is likely to imply a cut of basic, long-term research projects.

Data from public sources allow us to present in Table 5.1 the time series of R&D expenses (when available) and intensity (the ratio between R&D expenditures and sales) for the most important European tlc carriers: British Telecom (BT) (UK), France Télécom (FT) (France), Deutsche Telekom (DT) (Germany), Telecom Italia (Italy), Telefónica (Spain) and Telia (Sweden). As far as expenses are concerned, minor changes can be observed in the corporate R&D efforts for most carriers, with the exception of BT, which has increased its R&D expenses starting from 1993, and FT, which has sharply decreased its engagement in the research activities.

The second half of Table 5.1 shows that the R&D intensity ratio does not have any appreciable trends, again with the exception of BT after 1994 and FT after 1999. The relative stability of R&D intensity over time is an indirect confirmation of the widespread perception that tlc firms use a rule of thumb in determining the R&D budget.

The data reported in Table 5.1 document that R&D expenses are, with the exception of BT, stable or decreasing over time; given such an R&D budget, basic and applied research are natural competitors. This trade-off, when coupled with anecdotal evidence on the recent drift towards applied R&D (Section 2), speaks indirectly in favour of our hypothesis: the European tlc incumbents' shift from basic research coincides with the liberalization dates. More explicit evidence arises from the analysis of bibliometric indicators for the two European incumbents that, with their affiliated research labs, have been most active in publishing papers: BT and FT. In order to interpret the evidence, it is to be recalled that the UK Duopoly Review can be traced back to 1991, while the liberalization of the French tlc market started in 1998.

We give an account of the evolution experienced by tlc incumbents by means of the 'scientific strength' indicator, a measure of the firm's bibliometric performance that takes into account the fact that the world's science base varies over time. This latter aspect is accounted for by dividing *Pub*, the number of a firm's yearly papers in the IEEE/IEE set of scholarly reviews (Transactions or Letters), by the total papers in the same reviews. Formally, the scientific strength indicator *SS* is defined as follows:

$$SS = Pub \ / \Sigma_i \ Pub \qquad (5.1)$$

with $i \in \{1, 2, ..., M\}$, where M is the number of all the firms or research institutions that have published articles in the specified set of reviews.

Table 5.1   *R&D expenses (UK£000) and intensity (%), European tlc incumbents*

	BT	DT	FT	Telecom Italia[a]	Telefònica	Telia
			Expenses			
1991	243 000	na[b]	na	na	na	na
1992	240 000	na	na	na	na	na
1993	233 000	na	na	na	na	na
1994	233 000	na	na	254 647	na	na
1995	265 000	na	na	267 925	na	na
1996	271 000	na	na	296 381	na	na
1997	282 000	na	na	226 746	95 105	118 872
1998	291 000	405 611	541 092	na	78 486	117 961
1999	307 000	469 128	576 286	328 056	na	126 724
2000	345 000	435 323	368 910	na	na	124 121
2001	364 000	439 947	282 195	na	66 557	110 963
			Intensity			
1991	1.00	na	na	na	na	na
1992	1.00	na	na	na	na	na
1993	1.00	na	na	na	na	na
1994	1.76	na	na	2.37	na	na
1995	1.90	na	na	2.30	na	na
1996	2.00	na	na	2.20	na	na
1997	2.00	na	na	1.60	1.10	3.20
1998	1.90	1.80	3.40	na	0.80	3.30
1999	2.00	1.90	3.40	2.10	na	3.30
2000	1.80	2.00	2.20	na	na	3.30
2001	1.80	1.70	1.30	na	0.40	2.90

Notes:
a) Telecom Italia (formerly Sip) includes other smaller tlc carriers and manufacturers of the Stet group.
b) Not available.

Source: UK R&D Scoreboard (Department of Trade and Industry).

In order to represent in a synthetic way the evolution of the publication activity for the two companies, in Figure 5.1 we plotted the bibliometric indicator, defining an index that is set to 1 in 1988. Both the *SS* indexes tend to decrease in the second half of the decade. The decrease for BT is anticipated, and we might interpret this as preliminary evidence of the fact that the phenomenon is somehow related to the change in the domestic market structure; FT seems to start steadily decreasing with a one-year anticipation of the liberalization date.

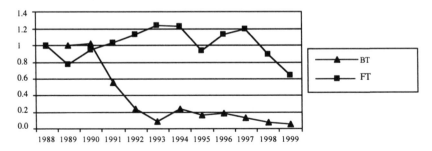

Figure 5.1   Scientific strength: BT and FT

As will be clear in Section 5, the econometric evidence confirms this preliminary picture; all the European incumbents with a large historical stock of published papers will be shown to have decreased their publication activity in proximity of the liberalization event. In that section, we shall discuss in some detail the scope of our results, and point out that the process is not necessarily inefficient, nor does it exclude an outsourcing of basic research to universities or upstream sectors. Here, we shall give a preliminary hint that the companies that have traditionally provided the European industry with a significant amount of knowledge in the tlc technological fields are apparently cutting corporate long-term research projects.

4.   THE MODEL

The econometric model presented in this section tests the hypothesis that liberalization in the tlc sector has caused a relevant mutation in the companies' R&D portfolio. Specifically, we claim that the allocation of resources has drifted away from basic research in favour of applied activities.

The model will pivot around the following hypothesis: the composition of the European tlc incumbents' R&D activities was significantly modified by the liberalization of the tlc market. Specifically, we claim that the relative share of basic research activities decreased after (or in anticipation of) the institutional discontinuity, having taken into account changes in firms' size and in the world's basic research activity in the same fields.

We resort to two different empirical strategies, in order to assess the robustness of our results and to encompass the inherently complex nature of firms' R&D processes: first, a count data model; second, a latent variable, or Tobit, model. The former has to be regarded as the standard methodology for modelling innovation output; the latter is more appropriate for taking into account the fact that publications or patents are just the contingent output of a firm's underlying innovation activity.

4.1 The Model for Basic Research

We shall estimate the relationship between the number of scientific publications (*Pub*) as a proxy of basic research, on the one hand, and a vector of independent variables describing both firms' characteristics and liberalization, on the other.

The variables are listed in Table 5.2. *Wpub*, the overall number of scholarly publications obtained by all firms and organizations in the IEEE/IEE scholarly journals (see Section 3), allows us to insulate the effects of any autonomous trend in the world scientific basis on the firm's R&D output. *Size*, the number of the Post Telecommunication Office (PTO) employees, allows us to control for the dimensional factor. *Basepub* captures one of the main sources of unobserved heterogeneity between organizations in basic research, namely their 'basic knowledge stock', measured as the average number of publications in the two pre-sample years.

Table 5.2   Variables in basic research models

Variable	Definition	Source
Pub	Number of scholarly publications in tlc technologies	IEEE/IEE
Wpub	Number of world scholarly publications in tlc technologies	IEEE/IEE
Size	Number of employees	OECD, 1990, 1993, 1995, 1997, 1999, Communications Outlook (Organization for Economic Cooperation and Development, Paris)
Basepub	Average yearly number of firm's scholarly publications in information and communication technologies before 1990	IEEE/IEE
Nullpub	Binary variable: *Nullpub* = 1 if *Basepub* = 0	IEEE/IEE
Omkt*	Binary variable: *Omkt* = 1 from the year of liberalization of the firm's home country market to 1999	ESIS, ISPO project European Commission

Note: * Similarly, *Omkt1* = 1 from one year before liberalization, and *Omkt2* = 1 from two years before liberalization.

According to Blundell et al. (1995), the firms' historical knowledge stock allows problems related to the estimation of individual fixed effects to be circumvented. A complementary variable, *Nullpub*, allows us to take into account the fact that the difference between a firm without publications and one with few publications is larger than the difference between one with few and one with many. *Nullpub* is a binary variable, which takes value 1 for firms that do not have any publications in the 1988–89 period. The institutional shock is modelled through the variables *Omkt*, *Omkt1*, *Omkt2* which will enter the model separately. The three variables are dummies that take a non-null value respectively on the year the market is liberalized, on the year before and on two years before.

To begin with, a *count data* model was specified. Available data for publications are peculiar in the sense that they are small integer numbers with a large component of null values. Therefore we need to treat them as count variables. In such cases, standard empirical literature suggests that the likelihood that firm *i* in year *t* has n_{it} scientific publications follows a basic Poisson distribution. Therefore we assume, for $i \in I$, the set of 17 former monopolists, $t = 1990, ..., 1999$:

$$\text{Prob}(Pub_{it} = n_{it}) = \frac{e^{-\lambda_{it}} \lambda_{it}^{n_{it}}}{n_{it}!} \tag{5.2}$$

where λ_{it} is the expected value of Pub_{it}; as will be shown by (5.5), λ_{it} is a function of the vector of explanatory variables. This approach was criticized by some econometric studies, since it imposes a strong hypothesis on the relationship between mean and variance, namely that the mean value and the variance of the distribution are identical. Of course, this might well not be the case for innovation data, which are typically rather dispersed. For our estimates, we took this into account by assuming a basic Poisson distribution and modelling the firms' heterogeneity through *Basepub_i* and *Nullpub_i*.

As a second attempt, a Tobit (or latent variable) model was specified. In this case, the distribution of publications is assumed to be partly continuous and partly discrete. The Tobit approach emphasizes that publications are just a proxy of an underlying variable, for example, the firm's attitude towards the basic research, *Brprop_it*. Such capability depends on the firm's characteristic variables and usually yields publications, even if several factors, such as small-scale R&D facilities, secrecy policies or other unobservable motivations prevent basic research from producing scientific publications. In other words, *Brprop_it* is a latent variable, while *Pub_it* is the observed empirical index. The Tobit model relies upon the following assumption, for $i \in I$, $t = 1990, ..., 1999$:

$$Brprop_{it} = \beta'x_{it} + \varepsilon_{it} \tag{5.3}$$

with $\varepsilon_{it} \sim N[0, \sigma^2]$; x_{it} is the vector of explanatory variables (see 5.4). In addition, *Pub_it* is related to *Brprop_it* in the following way:

$$Pub_{it} = Brprop_{it} \quad \text{if } Brprop_{it} > 0,$$
$$Pub_{it} = 0 \qquad \text{if } Brprop_{it} \leq 0.$$

In other words, a null value for $Brprop_{it}$ is the censoring level of the observations.

As illustrated above, vector x_{it} includes $Basepub_i$, $Nullpub_i$, and $Size_{it}$, which proxy, respectively, the presence of a knowledge stock in the pre-sample period, the size of that stock and the size of the firm. Furthermore, we used the variable $Wpub_t$ for the total number of world publications in the relevant technological fields and $Omkt_{it}$ for the liberalization year. In order to gain a greater flexibility, we included the product between $Omkt_{it}$ and $Nullpub_i$.

In synthesis, the vector of firm's variables will be, for $i \in I$, $t = 1990, ..., 1999$:

$$x_{it} = [Size_{it}, Wpub_t, Basepub_i, Nullpub_i,$$
$$Omkt_{it}, Nullpub_i \, Omkt_{it}] \tag{5.4}$$

After the estimation of the coefficients β in equations (5.2) and (5.3), it is possible to estimate the effects of any component of x_{it} on the conditional expected value of publications, λ_{it}, for any firm in the sample; λ_{it} will be, respectively for count and Tobit models (Greene, 1996):

$$\lambda_{it} = e^{\beta' x_{it}}, \tag{5.5}$$

and

$$\lambda_{it} = \Phi\,(\beta' x_{it}/\sigma) \cdot [(\beta' x_{it} + \sigma) \cdot \phi\,(\beta' x_{it}/\sigma) \,/\, \Phi\,(\beta' x_{it}/\sigma)] \tag{5.6}$$

with $\Phi(\cdot)$ normal distribution and $\phi(\cdot)$ normal density; $i \in I$; $t = 1990, ..., 1999$. As previously specified, in order to estimate the consistency of the 'announcement effect' we re-estimated equations (5.2) and (5.3) after replacing $Omkt_{it}$ with $Omkt1_{it}$ and $Omkt2_{it}$.

4.2 The Model for Applied Research

Model (5.2), which is based on the Poisson distribution, and model (5.3), based on the censored normal distribution, can be rewritten in order to describe the output of applied research. As previously stated, we measured this kind of output with the number of patents in a given year (Pat). In analogy to the basic research variables, the applied research variables are listed in Table 5.3.

In the Poisson model, Pat_{it} is a count variable and the likelihood that firm i in year t gets m_{it} patent is distributed as follows, for $i \in I$, $t = 1985, ..., 1999$:

$$\text{Prob}(Pat_{it} = m_{it}) = \frac{e^{-\mu_{it}} \mu_{it}^{m_{it}}}{m_{it}!} \tag{5.7}$$

where μ_{it} is the expected value of Pat_{it}; similarly to (5.5), μ_{it} is a function of the vector of explanatory variables.

Table 5.3   Variables in applied research models

Variable	Definition	Source
Pat	Number of patents in tlc technologies	USPTO
Wpat	Number of world scholarly patents in tlc technologies	USPTO
Size	Number of employees	OECD, 1990, 1993, 1995, 1997, 1999, Communications Outlook (Organization for Economic Cooperation and Development, Paris)
Basepat	Average yearly number of patents in tlc technologies before 1985	USPTO
Nullpat	Binary variable: *Nullpat* = 1 if *Basepat* = 0	USPTO
*Omkt**	Binary variable: *Omkt* = 1 from the year of liberalization of the firm's home country market to 1999	ESIS, ISPO project, European Commission

Note: * Similarly, *Omkt1* = 1 from one year before liberalization, and *Omkt2* = 1 from two years before liberalization.

In the Tobit model, Pat_{it} is the empirical index for the latent variable $Arprop_{it}$, that is, the firm propensity towards applied research. Such capability depends on the firm's characteristic variables, z_{it}, and usually yields patents, even if a range of factors may prevent firms from patenting.

In other words, $Arprop_{it}$ is a latent variable, while Pat_{it} is the observed empirical index. The Tobit model relies upon the following assumption, for $i \in I$, $t = 1985, \ldots, 1999$:

$$Arprop_{it} = \gamma' z_{it} + v_{it} \tag{5.8}$$

with $v_{it} \sim N[0, \rho^2]$ and z_{it} the vector of explanatory variables (see [5.9]). In addition, Pat_{it} is related to $Arprop_{it}$ in the following way:

$$Pat_{it} = Arprop_{it} \quad \text{if } Arprop_{it} > 0,$$
$$Pat_{it} = 0 \quad \text{if } Arprop_{it} \leq 0.$$

Again, we shall include in vector z_{it} the variable *Basepat$_i$*, together with *Size$_{it}$*, *Wpat$_i$*, and *Omkt$_{it}$*. *Basepat$_i$* is the average yearly number of patents granted to the firm over the five years before 1980. Furthermore we include *Nullpat$_i$*, which takes value 1 for firms that do not have any patents in the 1980–84 period, and its product with *Omkt$_{it}$*. The vector is therefore:

$$z_{it} = [Size_{it}, Wpat_i, Basepat_i, Nullpat_i,$$
$$Omkt_{it}, Nullpat_i \, Omkt_{it}] \tag{5.9}$$

The derivation of the conditional expected value of *Pat*, μ_{it}, is straightforward given by (5.5) and (5.6) for both the count and the Tobit models. Models (5.7) and (5.8) were re-estimated after replacing *Omkt$_{it}$* with *Omkt1$_{it}$* and *Omkt2$_{it}$* in order to test the anticipation effect.

5. RESULTS

Models (5.2) and (5.3) (publications) were estimated for the 1990–99 period, while models (5.7) and (5.8) (patents) for the 1985–99 period. Therefore, for models (5.2) and (5.3) we have 170 observations, while for models (5.7) and (5.8), 253 observations. Results from models (5.2), (5.3), (5.7) and (5.8) are listed, respectively, in Tables 5.4, 5.5, 5.6 and 5.7.

Let us start from the count model of basic research (5.2). If we look at the firms' characteristics, we see that all variables are significantly different from zero (confidence level equal to or larger than 0.99) with the exception of *Wpub* in the restricted version of the publication model, as shown in Table 5.4.[2]

The coefficients' signs in the extended model give us interesting hints. *Wpub* contributes positively to the expected value of the dependent variable, demonstrating that European PTOs have taken advantage of the broadening of the world knowledge base in that sector. The sign of the variable *Size* is positive, suggesting, as expected, that a greater dimension yields a more intense basic research activity. The coefficient for *Basepub* is positive, implying a direct relationship between the stock of knowledge of the firm and scientific activity. The coefficient of *Nullpub* is negative, implying that a null research activity in the pre-sample years heavily jeopardizes the firm's research capacity.

On average, the Tobit model (5.3) for basic research seems to encompass comparable estimation results even though the variables are less confidently different from zero in some cases (see Table 5.5).

Table 5.4 Results from count model of basic research

Observations: 170	Variable	Restricted model			Extended models								
		Coeff.	T-stat.	Confidence	Coeff.	T-stat.	Conf.	Coeff.	T-stat.	Conf.	Coeff.	T-stat.	Conf.
	Constant	0.671	1.98	0.95	-1.194	-3.19	0.99	-0.290	-0.80	0.57	-0.077	-0.22	0.17
	Wpub	0.001	0.02	0.01	0.206	6.72	0.99	0.097	3.37	0.99	0.086	3.02	0.99
	Size	0.009	12.39	0.99	0.006	7.94	0.99	0.009	11.63	0.99	0.009	11.92	0.99
	Basepub	0.087	20.43	0.99	0.146	22.02	0.99	0.137	19.98	0.99	0.124	20.06	0.99
	Nullpub	-2.278	-9.99	0.99	-2.848	-9.93	0.99	-3.069	-8.27	0.99	-4.424	-6.18	0.99
No lag	Omkt	-	-	-	-1.447	-13.19	0.99	-	-	-	-	-	-
	Omkt*Nullpub	-	-	-	2.040	4.80	0.99	-	-	-	-	-	-
One year lagged	Omkt1	-	-	-	-	-	-	-1.110	-10.41	0.99	-	-	-
	Omkt1*Nullpub	-	-	-	-	-	-	2.478	5.57	0.99	-	-	-
Two years lagged	Omkt2	-	-	-	-	-	-	-	-	-	-0.923	-9.25	0.99
	Omkt2*Nullpub	-	-	-	-	-	-	-	-	-	3.672	4.93	0.99

Table 5.5 Results from Tobit model of basic research

Observations: 170	Variable	Restricted model			Extended models								
		Coeff.	T-stat.	Confidence	Coeff.	T-stat.	Conf.	Coeff.	T-stat.	Conf.	Coeff.	T-stat.	Conf.
	Constant	-12.935	-1.02	0.95	-1.194	-3.19	0.99	-0.290	-0.80	0.57	-0.077	-0.22	0.17
	Wpub	0.691	0.63	0.01	0.206	6.72	0.99	0.097	3.37	0.99	0.086	3.02	0.99
	Size	0.079	2.94	0.99	0.006	7.94	0.99	0.009	11.63	0.99	0.009	11.92	0.99
	Basepub	1.682	6.11	0.99	0.146	22.02	0.99	0.137	19.98	0.99	0.124	20.06	0.99
	Nullpub	-14.588	-3.76	0.99	-2.848	-9.93	0.99	-3.069	-8.27	0.99	-4.424	-6.18	0.99
No lag	Omkt	–	–	–	-1.447	-13.19	0.99	–	–	–	–	–	–
	Omkt*Nullpub	–	–	–	2.040	4.80	0.99	–	–	–	–	–	–
One year lagged	Omkt1	–	–	–	–	–	–	-1.110	-10.41	0.99	–	–	–
	Omkt1*Nullpub	–	–	–	–	–	–	2.478	5.57	0.99	–	–	–
Two years lagged	Omkt2	–	–	–	–	–	–	–	–	–	-0.923	-9.25	0.99
	Omkt2*Nullpub	–	–	–	–	–	–	–	–	–	3.672	4.93	0.99

109

This is especially true for the extended publication models based on one- and two-year announcement effects; the significance of the *Omkt1* and *Omkt2* coefficients for firms with a non-null pre-sample publication base is rather small. Therefore, these variables might be excluded from the model. Nevertheless, the coefficient of *Omkt* is significant, testifying to an instantaneous effect of liberalization. Given the likelihood ratio test results, which will be discussed below (Table 5.8), we kept such variables in the model in order to parallel results obtained through the count model.

If we look at the count model of applied research (5.7), Table 5.6 reports that all the firm's characteristics have a significant explanatory power (confidence level equal to or larger than 0.99).[3] In addition, the variables show the expected sign, with the exception of *Basepat* in both the restricted and the extended models; quite surprisingly, other things being equal, a large historical patent stock influences negatively the current patenting activity.

Table 5.7 shows that the Tobit model (5.8) for applied research yields estimation results similar to the count model; however, in the case of patents, the liberalization effect is rather weak for firms with a null pre-sample patenting activity. Given the likelihood ratio test results, which will be discussed below (Table 5.9), we kept such variables in the model in order to parallel results obtained through the Poisson model. Analogously, in the case of patents, the announcement effect is rather weak for firms with a null pre-sample patenting activity.

It is to be underlined that liberalization does indeed significantly help to predict firm behaviour in both basic and applied research, in spite of the fact that Tobit models (5.3) and (5.8) show a weaker effect of liberalization for firms that were, respectively, more and less innovative in the pre-sample period.

Tables 5.8 and 5.9 illustrate the results of the log-likelihood test that we performed in order to verify the null hypothesis that the exclusion of variables related to market opening (*Omkt*, *Omkt*Nullpub*, *Omkt*Nullpat*) can be accepted for both basic (Table 5.8) and applied (Table 5.9) research. As clear, in all the extended models, *Omkt*, *Omkt1*, and *Omkt2* help, jointly with their cross-product with *Nullpub* or *Nullpat*, to explain the expected value of publications and patents to a significant degree, thus allowing us to reject the restrictions.

We can therefore confidently state that the liberalization event does influence the trend in the production of scientific and applied knowledge of the firms in our sample. More detailed comments are deserved on the question of the *sign* of liberalization effects, for both basic and applied research.

Table 5.6   Results from count model of applied research

	Restricted model			Extended models								
Observations: 253 / Variable	Coeff.	T-stat.	Confidence	Coeff.	T-stat.	Conf.	Coeff.	T-stat.	Conf.	Coeff.	T-stat.	Conf.
Constant	1.326	12.75	0.99	1.645	15.11	0.99	1.627	14.94	0.99	1.646	15.12	0.99
Wpat	0.081	21.69	0.99	0.056	10.62	0.99	0.056	10.73	0.99	0.051	9.97	0.99
Size	0.008	18.50	0.99	0.008	17.29	0.99	0.008	16.90	0.99	0.007	15.92	0.99
Basepat	–0.048	–9.31	0.99	–0.044	–8.45	0.99	–0.044	–8.51	0.99	–0.043	–8.38	0.99
Nullpat	–3.171	–34.01	0.99	–4.530	–22.68	0.99	–4.614	–20.97	0.99	–4.604	–19.48	0.99
No lag												
Omkt	–	–	–	0.220	3.20	0.99	–	–	–	–	–	–
Omkt*Nullpat	–	–	–	2.413	11.06	0.99	–	–	–	–	–	–
One year lagged												
Omkt1	–	–	–	–	–	–	0.262	3.97	0.99	–	–	–
Omkt1*Nullpat	–	–	–	–	–	–	2.302	9.77	0.99	–	–	–
Two years lagged												
Omkt2	–	–	–	–	–	–	–	–	–	0.393	5.94	0.99
Omkt2*Nullpat	–	–	–	–	–	–	–	–	–	2.103	8.40	0.99

Table 5.7 Results from Tobit model of applied research

Observations: 253	Variable	Restricted model			Extended models								
		Coeff.	T-stat.	Confidence	Coeff.	T-stat.	Conf.	Coeff.	T-stat.	Conf.	Coeff.	T-stat.	Conf.
	Constant	0.573	0.11	0.09	6.674	1.25	0.79	6.975	1.32	0.81	6.908	1.37	0.83
	Wpat	1.442	5.97	0.99	0.686	2.18	0.97	0.601	1.94	0.95	0.486	1.61	0.89
	Size	0.128	5.87	0.99	0.119	5.64	0.99	0.114	5.45	0.99	0.109	5.35	0.99
	Basepat	-1.221	-3.79	0.99	-1.032	-3.32	0.99	-1.030	-3.36	0.99	-1.007	-3.41	0.99
	Nullpat	-46.104	-11.96	0.99	-42.847	-10.41	0.99	-42.438	-10.01	0.99	-40.619	-9.52	0.99
No lag	Omkt	–	–	–	16.746	3.16	0.99	–	–	–	–	–	–
	Omkt*Nullpat	–	–	–	-4.730	-0.78	0.56	–	–	–	–	–	–
One year lagged	Omkt1	–	–	–	–	–	–	17.464	3.56	0.99	–	–	–
	Omkt1*Nullpat	–	–	–	–	–	–	-5.310	-0.94	0.65	–	–	–
Two years lagged	Omkt2	–	–	–	–	–	–	–	–	–	20.055	4.43	0.99
	Omkt2*Nullpat	–	–	–	–	–	–	–	–	–	-7.895	-1.49	0.86

Table 5.8 Likelihood tests for the basic research models

| | Count | | | | Tobit | | | |
| | Log likelihood, $\ln\hat{L}$ | | Likelihood ratio, v^* | | Log likelihood, $\ln\hat{L}$ | | Likelihood ratio, v^* | |
	Restricted model	Extended model	v	Restriction	Restricted model	Extended model	v	Restriction
No lag	−526.04	−429.55	192.98	Rejected (0.99)	−317.08	−311.14	11.87	Rejected (0.99)
One year lagged	−526.04	−462.89	126.30	Rejected (0.99)	−317.08	−313.23	7.69	Rejected (0.95)
Two years lagged	−526.04	−467.24	117.61	Rejected (0.99)	−317.08	−309.65	14.85	Rejected (0.99)

Note: * Degrees of freedom: 2; $v \sim \chi^2(2)$; $c = 10.60$ | $\text{Prob}[\chi^2(2) < c] = 0.99$; $c = 5,99$ | $\text{Prob}[\chi^2(2) < c] = 0.95$.

Table 5.9 Likelihood tests for the applied research models

| | Count | | | | Tobit | | | |
| | Log likelihood, $\ln\hat{L}$ | | Likelihood ratio, v^* | | Log likelihood, $\ln\hat{L}$ | | Likelihood ratio, v^* | |
	Restricted model	Extended model	v	Restriction	Restricted model	Extended model	v	Restriction
No lag	−713.00	−613.74	198.51	Rejected (0.99)	−392.67	−386.52	12.29	Rejected (0.99)
One year lagged	−713.00	−623.26	179.47	Rejected (0.99)	−392.67	−385.08	15.18	Rejected (0.95)
Two years lagged	−713.00	−626.57	172.85	Rejected (0.99)	−392.67	−382.30	20.74	Rejected (0.99)

Note: * Degrees of freedom: 2; $v \sim \chi^2(2)$; $c = 10.60$ | $\text{Prob}[\chi^2(2) < c] = 0.99$; $c = 5,99$ | $\text{Prob}[\chi^2(2) < c] = 0.95$.

The effects of liberalization, given its nature of shock, can be assessed as follows, both for the count and the Tobit models, respectively for publications and patents:

$$\varepsilon_{Pub} = \left(\frac{\hat{\lambda}_{Omkt = 1} - \hat{\lambda}_{Omkt = 0}}{\hat{\lambda}_{Omkt = 0}} \right) \tag{5.10}$$

and

$$\varepsilon_{Pat} = \left(\frac{\hat{\mu}_{Omkt = 1} - \hat{\mu}_{Omkt = 0}}{\hat{\mu}_{Omkt = 0}} \right) \tag{5.11}$$

We are especially interested in estimating the effect of liberalization for firms traditionally involved in R&D, other things being equal; accordingly, we shall estimate the expected impact on (5.10) and (5.11) after imposing the condition that each variable assumes the mean value computed from the set of firms with *Basepub* or *Basepat* larger than zero.

The six extended models for basic research evidence a negative impact of the liberalization event, for firms with a non-null publication base. Estimation of ε_{Pub} (that is, the relative variation of *Pub*, see 5.10) is as follows:

- for the count model: −76.4 per cent for the liberalization year, −67.06 per cent for the year before liberalization and −60.62 per cent for the two years before;
- for the Tobit model: −61.6 per cent for the liberalization year, −36.4 per cent for the year before liberalization and −33.5 per cent for the two years before.

These results confirm our hypothesis that the liberalization year narrows the absolute amount of resources dedicated to basic research, other things being equal.

On the other side, the six extended models for applied research evidence a positive impact of the liberalization date for firms with a non-null patenting activity. The relative variation of patents, ε_{Pat} (see 5.11), *ceteris paribus* and in absolute terms, is:

- for the count model: +24.62 per cent for the liberalization year, +30.01 per cent for the year before and +48.08 per cent for the two years before;
- for the Tobit model: +67.9 per cent for the liberalization year, +74.6 per cent for the year before and +93.8 per cent for the two years before.

Specifically, as far as patents are concerned, the 'announcement effect' seems to be particularly relevant. This can probably be explained by the augmented need to protect technological innovation when the market is opened up.

The two groups of results jointly witness an incentive for incumbents to decrease the level of basic activities coincidental with or in prospect of the forthcoming liberalization. We need to be very prudent in the interpretation of such results. We believe that the evidence presented is witness to the fact that the effect of an increase in product market competition is opposite in sign for the two components of R&D, and our conclusions cannot be stretched much beyond that. A few remarks are in order.

First, we do not claim that the process we described is inefficient. This will depend on which part of basic research activities is cut off. It may well be the case that only 'bad' basic research projects are abandoned and, if so, the process would be highly efficient. On the other hand, we cannot exclude that the reduction in the basic research effort implies that some valuable basic research project is abandoned. In order to answer this question, we shall need to measure research efficiency before and after liberalization, which is a matter for future research.

Second, we measured the change in basic and applied research for a single firm in each of the 17 countries (although by far the most important). We have no evidence that the dismissed quota of basic research was in fact outsourced either to the public research system or to other companies. In other words, nothing can be said, on the empirical side, about the effect of market liberalization on the overall amount of basic research activities at national level. Some descriptive evidence is presented in Table 5.10, where we calculated the trend in basic research for the most important nations included in our data set. In Table 5.10 we can observe that the evidence that increased competition actually affected basic research at a national level is very weak in three major countries (the UK, France and the Netherlands), while in Italy, Germany and some other smaller countries no clear pattern emerges. Therefore, we can argue that the decrease in tlc incumbents' basic research that follows liberalization is compensated either by the public system or by other firms performing basic research.

Unfortunately, at this stage of our research, we have no way of distinguishing between the part of basic research that is externalized to the public research system and the part outsourced to other firms. Rao suggests that a large part of telecom industrial R&D is being allocated to the software industry, and this could certainly account for an important part of the story (Rao, 2000). Unfortunately, data on public and corporate research spending in telecommunications are systematically missing in all OECD reports and databases, due to disclosure limitations, both for Europe and the US. This makes the empirical exercise rather difficult and different measures of research are to be found. Future research will address these aspects.

Finally, we want to make it clear that our model assesses the impact of liberalization on the basic and applied components of research both separately and in absolute terms. Our model allows us to conclude that competition has an opposite effect on the two components, when the two components are considered separately. Specifically, in our model we measured the variation in the absolute level of basic and applied research output, rather than the variation of the relative shares in firms' portfolio. However, Table 5.1 (Section 2) indirectly provides a rough indication about the change in the composition of firms' R&D portfolios, since the incumbents are shown to have maintained a relatively stable R&D expenditure and R&D/sales ratio over the years. As we anticipated, we interpreted this as an indication that the increase in applied research has occurred at the expense of basic research.

*Table 5.10   Basic research in selected European countries**

	BE	CH	DE	DK	ES	FI	FR	IT	NL	SW	UK
1988											1.00
1989										1.00	0.89
1990						1.00				1.09	1.07
1991						2.22				0.97	0.87
1992				1.00		1.87				0.96	0.95
1993				0.99		1.44				1.51	0.94
1994	1.00	1.00	1.00	0.69	1.00	1.66	1.00	1.00		1.38	0.96
1995	0.95	1.04	1.11	0.83	1.14	1.82	0.98	0.85	1.00	1.58	1.02
1996	1.12	1.11	1.14	0.59	0.96	1.97	1.08	1.12	0.86	1.38	1.02
1997	0.87	0.99	1.18	0.72	1.50	2.13	0.94	1.05	0.82	1.32	0.94
1998	1.22	1.03	1.11	0.91	1.79	2.40	1.07	1.16	0.76	1.50	0.93
1999	1.13	1.25	1.19	0.98	1.77	2.70	0.95	1.14	0.72	1.92	0.93
2000	0.96	1.52	0.92	1.07	1.53	2.19	0.84	1.12	0.77	1.59	0.75

Note: * Number of publications divided by world total (first year = 1).

Source: IEE/IEEE database.

6.   CONCLUSIONS

This chapter tried to shed some light on the role of market structure in determining the composition of R&D expenditure. Specifically, we studied the effect of an increased competitive pressure on the outputs of basic and applied research activities. Although the relationship between market structure and R&D has long been a crucial issue in economic literature, we believe that this specific matter should be investigated more thoroughly, and that its relevance should not be played down in any serious debate on the effects of market liberalization.

Our research question pertains to the balance between basic (long-term) and applied (short-term) activities. We claim that the effects highlighted by the many authors who studied the causal relationship between R&D and competition exert a different influence on the single components of research activities. Therefore, although we recognize that an increased competitive pressure would produce an ambiguous effect on the overall research intensity, we hasten to hypothesize that the effect on composition will be universal; that is, we should observe an increasing incidence of applied activities in the firms' research portfolios.

We tested this hypothesis in the telecom market, where we have a very clear example of institutional discontinuity generating increased product market competition, that is, market liberalization. We gathered data for 17 former tlc monopolists in those European countries where the telecom markets have been liberalized over the last decade. Measures related to patenting activity and scientific publications allowed us to empirically divide the incumbents' research activities into basic and applied research. We demonstrated that, coincidental with (or in anticipation of) the liberalization date, the incumbents, on average, drastically reduced their commitment to publication activities and remarkably increased their efforts towards patenting activities. We interpreted this as a clear indication of a mutation in firms' attitude towards applied research tasks, leading to a very different composition of their research portfolios.

It is here worth emphasizing that, though we are mainly interested in the effects of competition on R&D composition, our results may also shed some light on the indirect long-term effects of competition on the overall R&D intensity. A companion paper (Calderini, 2001) demonstrated that a sudden alteration in the balance between the two components of R&D, resulting from institutional discontinuity, may trigger, under certain conditions, a negative dynamic, leading to the complete loss of incentive to perform any R&D activity whatsoever.

The policy implications of our results are straightforward. The question is whether or not a sharp decrease in the total amount of basic scientific research carried on in-house may weaken the individual firms' (and industry's) capacity to sustain an appropriate rate of technological progress in the medium and long terms. The problem is that higher incentives to perform applied research may lead to an erosion of the resources needed for the firms (industry) to perform basic activities and to produce basic knowledge, a crucial intermediate output. In the short term, this might produce a beneficial effect in terms of competitiveness, since the exploitation of the existing knowledge stock will improve the innovative performance of the firm (industry). Nevertheless, in the medium/long term the depletion in the knowledge stock could negatively affect firms' (industry's) efficiency in performing their own applied activities.

This is a clear example of the static/dynamic efficiency trade-off, which should be given greater attention by policy makers.

One straightforward option would be to reallocate the basic research activities that are being dismissed by the industry to the public research system. Two arguments should be raised here. First, policy makers, in this historical circumstance, should seriously consider the adequacy of the public research system to sustain the extraordinary effort required to inherit the industrial basic research mission. We are doubtful whether policy makers in certain European countries could confidently assert that the national public research system has the resources and the skills to efficiently compensate for the missing quota of industrial basic research. Second, it is absolutely true that, as far as the direct results of research are concerned, the output of research is largely to be considered a public good and, as such, hardly appropriable and easily transferable. Nevertheless, if we consider the indirect results of performing basic research tasks, such as acquiring selection, prospection and absorption capacity, these latter are highly appropriable, idiosyncratic and, most important, not easily transferable. Therefore, even assuming that the public research system can efficiently take the place of in-house industrial research, it is debatable whether indirect results can be transferred to the industry and internalized by individual firms. The relevance of the argument lies in the fact that, for firms operating in countries that are not on the frontier of scientific research, this latter output (indirect results) is considerably more important than invention as such. The message is, therefore, that it could be rather risky to rely entirely on the public system to provide the national system of innovation with the appropriate stock of scientific knowledge. Policy intervention should be directed at guaranteeing that, even with a steep increase in competitive pressure, the information and communication industry could maintain a critical level of in-house basic research activity.

Finally, it is important to stress here that our analysis was limited to one specific kind of determinant, the liberalization process. Nevertheless, we believe that at least two other contingencies are bound to exacerbate the dynamics outlined in our chapter. First, the fact that liberalization in the European countries has very often been accompanied by privatization processes. Chapter 4 of this volume investigated this problem, and its conclusions seemed to point in the same direction as the results presented in this chapter. Second, both former monopolists and telecom carriers in general have recently spent enormous amounts of money on third-generation mobile phone spectrum rights. According to many commentators, this is bound to make many firms in the industry severely cash-constrained in the short term, thus exacerbating the tendency to favour investments that yield high returns in the short term.

The issue is crucial to policy makers. The negative effects (private and social) will become evident, by definition, in the medium/long term, when it might be too late to design any kind of policy aimed at mitigating the effects of a collapse in the industry's knowledge base. We address this comment to policy makers who operate in countries that are followers in the innovation race and that might, therefore, be tempted to direct their efforts uniquely to the exploitation of technological knowledge created elsewhere. This strategy is myopic and it is likely to lock the national innovation system into vicious trajectories.

NOTES

1. As Chapter 2 discussed broadly, we stylized R&D investments in two broad components: basic research activities, whose output is only loosely appropriable and whose returns are typically long term, and applied research activities, whose output is highly appropriable and whose returns are typically short term.
2. The goodness-of-fit of all the basic research count models (one restricted model and three extended models) is evaluated through the χ^2 tests on the set of explanatory variables. Computed χ^2 statistics are equal to 2203.38, 2396.36, 2329.68 and 2321.00 with, respectively, 4, 6, 6 and 6 degrees of freedom; the right-hand-side variables are jointly significant at any standard confidence level.
3. The goodness-of-fit of all the applied research count models (one restricted model and three extended models) is evaluated through the χ^2 tests on the set of explanatory variables. Computed χ^2 statistics are equal to 4694.94, 4893.45, 4874.41 and 4867.79 with, respectively, 4, 6, 6 and 6 degrees of freedom; the right-hand-side variables are jointly significant at any standard confidence level.

6. The Effects of M&As on the Innovation Performance of Acquired Companies

Mario Calderini, Paola Garrone and Giuseppe Scellato

---

1. INTRODUCTION

In this chapter we present an empirical study that will investigate the effects of acquisitions on the innovation performance of the target company.

In Chapter 3 we extensively reviewed the broad corpus of literature that in recent years has dealt with the problem of assessing the effects of the mergers and acquisition (M&A) processes on the companies' incentives to invest in innovation activities. In the following, we shall turn to the building blocks of such literature, highlighting the concepts that are most relevant with respect to our research hypotheses.

The core research question is whether the change in corporate structure determined by the deal would induce a more favourable environment for innovation in the target company. Such a research question is of the utmost importance in the specific information and communication technology (ICT) industry, which supplies high-tech input to downstream industries, spreading the effects of sector-specific technological change to a vast number of important industries.

Measuring the effects of acquisitions on innovation presents severe empirical problems. An analytical approach based on the comparison of *ex ante* and *ex post* performance of, respectively, the merging companies and the combined entity is certainly a straightforward empirical strategy, but its practical implementation is prevented by a number of specific problems.

A consistent estimation of the effects of a specific acquisition would require researchers to identify exogenous corporate events and to separate their effects from those directly linked to the change of the corporate structure following acquisition. The reason for this is mainly that acquiring companies are often fairly large corporations, very active in the market for corporate control; furthermore, their corporate strategies are very complex and articulated even in the short term. As far as the bidding company is concerned, it is therefore very difficult to separate the effects of several corporate combinations occurring almost simultaneously.

This consideration led us to tackle a specific aspect of the problem, namely the effect of the acquisition on the post-acquisition performance of the target company. Though this strategy limits our view to a specific aspect of the problem under investigation, it will enable us to obtain consistent evidence on a partial but significant aspect of the phenomenon within the merged entity.

Moreover, the impact of acquisitions on the innovation performance of the acquired company is extremely relevant when considering the implications in terms of local innovation systems. In fact, a reduction in the acquired companies' innovation efforts would result in a reduction of the spillovers' intensity on a local basis, with significant negative implications for local innovation systems.[1]

Although the empirical problem is far simpler when the analysis is limited to the target company, it should be noted also that the accurate assessment of the innovation performance of acquired firms presents severe methodological challenges. In particular, the choice of the target company as the unit of observation makes it necessary to identify and separate the contributions to innovation activities that are caused by a simple reallocation of research activities from the bidder to the target company, or vice versa. We shall tackle this problem in the remainder of this chapter. It is here worth anticipating that the literature on knowledge transfer and resource redeployment between merged companies suggests that the relevance of this specific issue should not be overplayed.

Before moving on to describe the empirical model used in the remainder of the chapter, we need to define the scope of our investigation. We used as a unit of observation the merger/acquisition process, excluding market-level determinants although, in principle, we cannot ignore the fact that changes in the market structure (through market concentration processes) may indeed exert their influence on the companies' incentives to innovate. The specific features of the acquisition processes considered in our empirical exercise, though, are such as not to imply significant changes in the market structure. The target firms we examined were, on average, small, with relatively small market shares; moreover, the markets such firms belonged to (that is, the ICT industries) were expanding rapidly in the period under investigation.

Our empirical strategy was based on the identification of two different samples, sharing many common features, but separated by the occurrence/non- occurrence of an acquisition event.

We drew the set of companies used in our initial sample from the initial public offerings (IPOs) that took place in the US during 1989–92.[2] In fact, such IPOs displayed a number of crucial features in relation to the objectives of our study. First, these were companies displaying a remarkable degree of homogeneity in terms of size and corporate governance. Second, the common nature of the listed companies induced similar incentives to signalling their innovation performance to the financial market, thus limiting the biases that are typical when using patents to measure the companies' innovation performance. Finally, the resulting sample turned out to be composed of small firms with relatively small market shares, thus allowing us to state that market structure effects were negligible with respect to specific acquisition effects. Importantly, such a choice allowed us to access a large number of company data through the public domain documents of the Securities and Exchange Commission (SEC).

As far as the problem of measuring the innovation performance is concerned, we used patents granted by the United States Patent and Trademark Office (USPTO) to estimate the innovation output of the target companies. An important remark is in order here: the corpus of literature we shall refer to in Section 3, when motivating our research hypothesis, is focused mainly on the acquisition's effects on R&D investments, thus concentrating on an *input* measure of the innovation process. This might appear to conflict with the use of patents in our empirical analysis. Nevertheless, it should be noted that some crucial contributions (Griliches, 1990; Scherer, 1965, among others) demonstrated that patents are actually to be interpreted as an intermediate measure of the innovation process, strictly correlated with R&D investments.

Moreover, the use of patents in the studies dealing with the effects of acquisitions on the innovation performance is increasingly popular (Hitt et al., 1991; Hagedoorn and Duysters, 2002b; Ernst and Witt, 2000; Ahuja and Katila, 2001). Finally, and most importantly, we wish to stress that the use of patents as a proxy for innovative activity presented a significant specific advantage in the context of our study. Patents guarantee a reasonable degree of traceability over time, when we are trying to assign patents to a single company's establishment. In this respect, they allow us to separate the contributions of the target company from the merged entity's overall patent output, according to a methodology that will be clarified in Section 3.

One minor and last comment about our choice of using patents as an innovation measure is related to the lack of reliable firm-level R&D expenditure data, due to the well-known R&D accounting problems.

At firm level, the correlation between patent output and innovation efforts may sometime be rather weak, but significant when year/sector-specific effects are accounted for. In our empirical exercise, we dealt with such critical issues, controlling for year/sector-specific effects, as clarified in the following section. Moreover, the comparative approach we adopted, confronting the relative performance of two different cohorts (that is, acquired and not acquired companies), was intended to minimize the distortion that might be induced by different approaches to patenting, know-how protection and commercial policies.

It is worth mentioning here that recent literature has thoroughly investigated the specific role played by patenting activities in M&As. The idea is that in the context of M&A processes, patenting should be interpreted as a strategic variable determined by a number of different factors, which are not simply related to R&D investments or research project productivity. Since there is no consolidated evidence about this specific aspect of the problem, we limited ourselves to mentioning the issue, leaving this aspect as a matter of unfinished business.[3]

In Section 2, we present our research hypotheses, which are the foundation of the empirical analysis developed in Section 3. In this latter section, we present the data set, the methodology followed to analyse the single mergers and the empirical strategy used to determine patent variables. In Section 4 we present the results and we try to assess the robustness of the methodology, while in Section 5 we discuss the results against the background of the conceptual framework set out in Chapter 3 of this book.

2.   RESEARCH HYPOTHESES

The literature survey presented in Chapter 3 of this book showed how the remarkable complexity of the acquisition processes is fully reflected in the heterogeneity and lack of coherence of empirical results.

A first reason for this is certainly the fact that the studies dealing with the relationship between acquisitions and innovation belong to very different streams of literature (managerial literature, resource based, industrial and innovation economics, finance) and focus on rather diverse aspects of the acquisition process. Nevertheless, such heterogeneity does not prevent us from highlighting a number of shared interpretations about the signs that are to be expected when empirically testing specific aspects of the relationship between acquisitions and innovation activity.

Second, some of the results reviewed in Chapter 3 appear to be heavily dependent on the absolute size of the deal, on the specific features of the merging entities and on the markets the companies operate in. The relatively small sample size did not allow us to control statistically for a specific deal's characteristics such as leverage, corporate governance or increased/decreased degree of diversification in the merged entity. An important caveat is, therefore, that our results may be conditioned either by an inadequate sample stratification or by a prevalence of a specific deal feature in our sample. We leave this issue to further extensions of the present work.

On the other hand, scholars have offered controversial evidence with respect to the effect on the innovation performance of the acquired/merged entity. Many different hypotheses coexist, suggesting opposite signs for the relationship between M&As and innovation.

Since we cannot rely on a consistent *ex ante* research hypothesis, we shall leave the problem to *ex post* empirical testing, in order to validate either of the two following hypotheses:

Hypothesis A
Following acquisition, the target company increases its innovation performance, as a consequence of the exploitation of new R&D scale and scope economies and an efficient resource redeployment process between target and bidder.

Hypothesis B
Following acquisition, the innovation performance of the target company decreases, as a consequence of decreased incentives towards innovation for both the managers and the key inventors of the target company.

We kept our research hypotheses deliberately generic, in order to be able to test for the effects that can be reasonably thought to be independent from the unobserved factors mentioned above (that is, leverage, corporate governance or increased/decreased degree of diversification in the merged entity). We can, therefore, concentrate on the specific hypotheses drawn from the literature reviewed in Chapter 3 and briefly summarized in the following.

Many recent studies focusing on scale and scope economies and on resource redeployment may be quoted in favour of Hypothesis A. As discussed in Chapter 3, the prevailing thesis is that, given a number of assumptions, the increased size of the merged entity is a potential source of efficiency (see Henderson and Cockburn, 1996; Ahuja and Katila, 2001). On the other hand, the studies that can be attributed to the *resource-* or *knowledge-based* literature present consistent evidence of super-additive properties of innovation input in the acquisition processes (see Capron et al., 1998; Ahuja and Katila, 2001).

On the other hand, three main lines of argument can be raised in favour of Hypothesis B. First, the hypothesis of a reduction in the innovation activity is supported by the idea that managers' commitment is diverted from innovation by the short-term objectives related to the management of the acquisition process itself. In particular, some recent contributions (Hitt et al., 1991; 1996) demonstrated that managers' behaviour during the turbulence preceding and following acquisitions is rather myopic and characterized by a substantial degree of short-termism (see Chapter 2). Furthermore, the increased size of the merged entity forces managers to resort to financial control in place of strategic control, thus exacerbating the short-termism problem. The short-term vision emerging in such circumstances is bound to be reflected in a less generous attitude towards R&D investments, which are, by their own nature, long term.

Second, the vast literature dealing with the relationship between R&D and the efficient allocation of property rights suggests that acquisitions may lead to a reduction in R&D investments in the acquired entity.

This is the case when three basic conditions hold: (1) when the acquired firms' innovation sources are as valuable as the acquiring company's; (2) when they are cash constrained; and (3) when they do not have a sufficient bargaining power towards the acquiring 'customers' (Aghion and Tirole, 1998). The specific features of the companies included in our sample make such hypotheses potentially relevant in the context of our study.

Third, acquisition processes have a profound impact on target companies' routines and on their single agents' behaviour. The difficult integration between companies characterized by different managerial cultures and/or management practices is indicated as the main source of failure for many mergers (see Chakrabarti, 1990; Cartwright and Cooper, 1993). On the other hand, the changes in the job environment and the uncertainty related to the acquisition process may negatively influence researchers' productivity (see Bommer and Jalais, 1999; Ernst and Witt, 2000); in extreme cases, the target company's key inventors are reported to have left the merged entity.

3. DATA SET AND METHODOLOGY

We built up our data set through a multi-stage process, starting by the definition of an initial large sample of firms that went public on one of the US stock markets during the years 1989–92. These companies belonged to the following industries (by SIC code): 357 (computer and office equipment), 366 (communication equipment), 367 (electronic components and accessories), 382 (laboratory apparatus and analytical, optical, measurement). Our selection of the relevant codes was aimed at describing, with a suitable degree of approximation, the ICT industry.[4] We opted for a three-digit level of detail, given the peculiar nature of the industry, characterized by overlapping technologies and rapid changes in the product variety.

The initial sample consisted of 115 firms: 40 belonging to the SIC 357 sector, 30 to 366, 30 to 367 and 15 to 382. Every firm included in the sample was characterized, at the time of the IPO, by firm-specific characteristics: price of share, total assets for the year before the acquisition and year of foundation.

On these bases, we singled out the companies that were subject to acquisition or merging processes over the years following the IPO. Thus, we could define two separate samples, one including the acquired companies and another consisting of companies that had remained in public hands all the way through to year 2001. The comparative analysis of the innovation performance of the companies belonging to the two samples is the building block of our empirical strategy.

The sample including the acquired companies was, furthermore, filtered according to additional criteria, defined in order to make our patent search as efficient as possible. Such criteria were the following:

- The acquisition process should have been concluded after the second term of year 1991 and before the first term of year 1998. In fact, if the acquisition process had stretched beyond the first term of 1998, it would have left us with too short a time period for assessing the impact of acquisition on the company's innovation performance. Moreover, since we used the patent application dates, the number of patents applied for after the first term of 1998 and already granted was very small at the time of our study.
- The acquired company should not have gone through any further acquisition processes (active and passive) over the two years following the acquisition under consideration. Otherwise, we would have had overlapping effects that would have made a correct estimation of the effects rather difficult.
- The geographical location (town) of the acquiring company's establishments should be different from that of the acquired company over the years preceding the acquisition.
- The acquiring company should not have acquired, in the same year of the acquisition, other companies in the same US state.
- The target company should not have returned to public ownership over the two years following the acquisition.

In Section 4 we shall discuss the effects of the application of such criteria on the results obtained. The final sample, grouping the acquired companies meeting all the specified criteria, consisted of 28 units of observation.

The remaining companies that had not been subject to any acquisition and that were still active in 2001 were included in the control sample.

Finally, both in the acquired companies' sample and in the control sample we excluded companies that presented a null patenting activity over the 1990–2000 period. This was for two reasons: first, measuring the variations in the innovative output would not be possible in the case of non-patenting companies; second, we preferred focusing on the acquisitions that were potentially technology related.

Table 6.1 summarizes the size of the different samples, which, at the end of the selection process, included, respectively, 19 acquired companies and 54 non-acquired companies. Tables 6.2, 6.3 and 6.4 illustrate the full list of acquisitions we considered. The tables allow us to identify several features that are shared by the vast majority of the examined deals.

Table 6.1   *Size of the different samples*

Industry	Initial sample	Acquired sample (with patents)	Control sample (with patents)
357	40	6	23
367	30	9	15
366	30	2	9
382	15	2	7
Total	115	19	54

Source: Our elaboration on SEC and USPTO data.

Table 6.2   *Acquisitions: merging companies' patenting activity*

Target	SIC	Patent	Bidder	SIC	Patents[a]	Patent ratio[b]	Deal date
Bay Networks	357	75	Nortel	366	1934	25.79	98/1
Computervision	357	9	Parametric Tech.	737	4	0.44	97/2
Supermac Technology	357	4	Radium	357	45	11.25	94/2
Soricon	357	5	Int. Verifact	357	9	1.80	95/1
Network General	357	3	Mcafee Associates	737	1	0.33	97/2
Adv. Logic Research	357	5	Gateway 2000	357	130	26.00	97/1
US Robotica	366	58	3com	357	557	9.60	97/1
Telebit	366	8	Cisco	357	368	46.00	96/2
Brooktree	367	48	Rockwell Int.	362	895	18.65	96/2
Micronics Computers	367	8	Diamond Multimedia	357	19	2.38	98/1
Zilog	367	93	Texas Pacific Group	357	160	1.72	98/2
Pulse Engineering	367	27	Technitrol	364	6	0.22	95/2
International Jensen	367	2	Recoton	367	28	14.00	96/2
Lannet Communications	367	2	Madge Networks	357	20	10.00	95/2
Electrocom	367	35	Daimler Benz	371	175	5.00	94/2
Mips Systems	367	17	Silicon Graphics	357	419	24.65	92/1
Bytex	367	1	Network Systems	357	7	7.00	93/2
Perceptive Biosystems	382	37	Perkin Elmer	382	272	7.35	98/1
First Pacific Networks	382	10	US Sterling Corp.	na	82	8.20	98/1

Notes:
a) Stock of patents granted in the 1990–2000 period.
b) Stock of bidder's patents/stock of target's patents.

Source: USPTO, SEC.

Table 6.3   Acquisitions: deal characteristics

Target	Bidder	Purpose[a]	Offer[b]	Foundation year
Bay Networks	Nortel	H	F	1986
Computervision	Parametric Tech.	H	F	1972
Supermac Technology	Radium	H	F	1988
Soricon	Int. Verifact	H	F	na
Network General	Mcafee Associates	H	F	1986
Adv. Logic Research	Gateway 2000	H	F	1984
US Robotica	3com	H	F	1976
Telebit	Cisco	H	F	1982
Brooktree	Rockwell Int.	H	N	1981
Micronics Computers	Diamond Multimedia	V	F	1986
Pulse Engineering	Technitrol	H	F	1957
Zilog	Texas Pacific Group	F	F	1984
International Jensen	Recoton	H	F	na
Lannet Communications	Madge Networks	H	F	na
Electrocom	Daimler Benz	V	F	1981
Mips Systems	Silicon Graphics	V	F	1984
Bytex	Network Systems	V	F	1980
Perceptive Biosystems	Perkin Elmer	H	F	1987
First Pacific Networks	US Sterling Corp.	F	F	1987

Notes:
a) Horizontal (H), Vertical (V), Financial (F).
b) Friendly (F), Neutral (N).

Sources: SEC, Mergerstat.

First, all the deals are likely to be technology related rather than motivated by market-share determinants.[5] Furthermore, they are horizontal, given that there is a systematic coincidence between the acquiring and the acquired company's SIC code.

Finally, all the acquiring companies are active in R&D and present a relevant patent stock. The ratio between the bidder's and the target's patent stock is favourable to the acquiring company.

In Figure 6.1, we illustrate the distribution in time of the examined deals. For the patent analysis, we used the USPTO database. The selection process and the attribution of patents to single companies before and after the acquisition event is the most critical issue. Two different approaches were used, one for the acquired companies' sample, the other for the control sample.

As for the latter, we limited ourselves to analysing the patenting activity on a semester basis, from the first term of 1990 to the second term of 2000.

Table 6.4 Acquisitions: merging companies' relative size

Target	Bidder	Bidder assets[a]	Target assets[a]	Price[b]
Bay Networks	Nortel	na	2 108 279 000	17
Computervision	Parametric Tech.	832 423 000	166 620 000	12
Supermac Technology	Radium	126 859 000	6 615 385	9
Soricon	Int. Verifact	na	1 433 555	5
Network General	Mcafee Associates	194 485 000	263 261 000	8
Adv. Logic Research	Gateway 2000	1 310 775 000	118 640 000	13
US Robotica	3com	1 525 117 000	990 959 000	13
Telebit	Cisco	3 630 232 000	27 401 000	10
Brooktree	Rockwell Int.	12 350 000	190 629 000	12
Micronics Computers	Diamond Multimedia	337 554 000	49 649 000	6
Pulse Engineering	Technitrol	84 755 000	5 182 797	10.5
Zilog	Texas Pacific Group	na	410 717 000	11
International Jensen	Recoton	168 997 000	141 887 000	na
Lannet Communications	Madge Networks	224 992 000	10 115 000	13
Electrocom	Daimler Benz	137 099 000	26 500 000	16
Mips Systems	Silicon Graphics	1 324 538 000	na	17.5
Bytex	Network Systems	305 481 000	na	8
Perceptive Biosystems	Perkin Elmer	1 094 715 000	133 951 000	7
First Pacific Networks	US Sterling Corp.	na	11 502 000	9

Notes:
a) Total assets ($) as appearing in the last income statement before the deal.
b) Price ($) of the target company's share at the time of IPO.

Source: SEC.

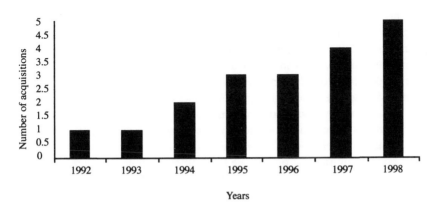

Figure 6.1 Trends in deals

In contrast, the analysis for the acquired companies' sample was far more articulated: first, we excluded the semester in which the acquisition had taken place, in order to avoid undesired noise related to the transition period; second, we tried to consider the different patent management policies implemented by the acquiring company after the acquisition period. We based our queries upon the following USPTO database variables: *Assignee Name*, *Assignee City*, *Inventor State* and *Application Date*. In fact, the attribution of patentable ideas developed in the target company may be inspired by very different criteria:

1. patents are attributed to the target company after the acquisition;
2. patents are attributed to the acquiring company (assignee name), but the address appearing on the patent front page is the target company's (it is therefore possible to identify the origin of the patented idea through the address of the assignee): in this case, the patent should be considered as an output of research activities carried on by the target company's establishments, the name of which no longer appears after the acquisition;
3. patents are assigned to the acquiring company (both assignee name and address);
4. a combination of the previous cases.

This was at the basis of our decision to exclude the acquisitions where the target companies were located in the same town as the bidding company's establishments. In fact, this situation would have made it almost impossible to attribute patents to the target company in situation 2.

Patents assigned to the bidding company's headquarters (situation 3), but generated by the research carried on by the target company, are the most critical aspect of the problem.[6] Since it is impossible to deterministically enumerate such patents, we resorted to the following hypothesis: we assumed that, in the two years following the deal, the percentage variation in the bidding company's patent numbers attributable to inventors residing in the same US state as the target company was entirely attributable to the acquisition under investigation. This is why we decided to exclude the companies that had concluded other acquisitions in the same US state where the target company had its seat.

The period we considered relevant as far as the measurement of the acquisition's effect was concerned spanned eight semesters, centred around the acquisition semester. This choice was the result of a trade-off between two contrasting factors: on the one hand, a longer time period would have made it very difficult to separate other exogenous effects on the company's patenting activity; on the other, a two-year period was a reasonable estimation of the interval potentially needed to abandon or to restructure any applied-research programme.

The total number of patents attributed to the target company, on a semester basis, can therefore be computed by one of the two expressions below, according to whether the semester considered precedes or follows the acquisition date.

$$P_{i,t}^{pre} = TP_{i,t} + CP_{i,t}$$

$$P_{i,t}^{post} = TP_{i,t} + CP_{i,t} + \Delta share \cdot SP_{i,t}$$

where i is the target company; TP the number of patents, per semester, with the *Assignee Name* equal to i's name; CP is the number of patents, per semester, with the *Assignee Name* equal to the name of the company acquiring i and the *Assignee City* equal to i's city; SP is the number of patents, per semester, with the *Assignee Name* equal to i's name and the *Inventor State* equal to i's state; $\Delta share$ is the change in the share of the acquirer's patents in i's state (based on the inventor's address) after the acquisition.

The use of CP in the pre-merger equation was motivated by the delay (18–36 months at USPTO) between the patent application date and the patent grant date. In this way, we were able to include in our computation the patents developed by the target company before the acquisition, but granted to the acquiring company only after the deal.

$\Delta share \cdot SP$ was the term that allowed us to compute the number of patents assigned to the acquiring company's headquarters, though developed at the target company's establishments..

Finally, in order to be able to compare patenting time series for companies with very different absolute levels of patenting activity, we weighted the variations in the company's patent numbers by the company's average level of patenting activity over the 1990–2000 period.

In conclusion, the variable Δp represents the percentage variation in patent applications in four semesters (centred on the deal's date), weighted by the company's typical patenting-activity level:

$$\Delta p_{i,t_i} = \left(\frac{1/4 \cdot \sum_{t=t_i+1}^{t_i+4} P_{i,t} - 1/4 \cdot \sum_{t=t_i-4}^{t_i-1} P_{i,t}}{1/21 \cdot \sum_{t \neq t_i, t=1}^{22} P_{i,t}} \right) \forall i \tag{6.1}$$

where t_i indicates the semester in which the acquisition took place and i indicates the target company; $P_{i,t}$ is the number of patents assigned to firm i at time t.

The main empirical difficulty with this approach was the need to compare deals that had taken place in different time periods. In fact, in the time period 1992–98 a number of exogenous variables beyond our control may have affected the incentives of the companies to patenting. Specifically, in the ICT sector, a number of technological breakthroughs might have substantially changed the technological regime, and, as a consequence, the overall industry's patenting activity. Therefore, we developed an analogous, corrected indicator at industry level, in order to account for sectoral trends over time.

$$\Delta p^c_{i, t_i} = \Delta p_{i, t_i} - \Delta p_{s, t_i} \quad \forall i \tag{6.2}$$

where $\Delta p_{i, t_i}$ is the indicator specified in equation (6.1) and $\Delta p_{s, t_i}$ is the same indicator at industry level, computed for the acquisition semester. As a result, $\Delta p^c_{i, t_i}$ is a time- and sector-adjusted indicator. In this way, we were able to aggregate and to compare data referring to different years and sectors throughout the sample.

It should be stressed that, in order to compute $\Delta p^c_{i, t_i}$, we had to identify those USPTO classes that are to be considered the core technological fields for ICT.

To this purpose, we implemented a procedure consisting of the identification of the following steps.

First, we singled out the patent classes where the companies belonging to both samples patented throughout the period. We then plotted, on a Pareto histogram, the frequency of each class and we considered all the classes recurring with a frequency of at least 1 per cent. The threshold level was selected in order to avoid considering classes where companies may have occasionally patented, but which were out of the core application fields of the industry.

Finally, it should be pointed out that this analysis was performed separately on the four SIC codes under investigation. In this way we were able to aggregate and also compare the deals taking place in different sectors and periods.

4.   MODEL AND RESULTS

Two alternative strategies were followed in order to test the hypotheses described in Section 2. First, we tried to understand whether the variation of the parameter $\Delta p_{i, t_i}$ (not corrected by sector and period) for the companies that were subject to acquisition processes was above or below the median value of the sample of non-acquired companies, in a specific semester. The result is illustrated in Table 6.5.

In Table 6.6, we analysed in more detail the median test for single companies. Although the empirical information that can be derived is not particularly strong, some interesting hints emerge from this table. First, acquired companies, in general, display a reduction or a smaller increase with respect to non-acquired companies. The second important observation is that the sector seems to be rather important in determining results. Values above the control sample's median are concentrated in SIC 366 and 382.[7] Overall, out of 19 observed deals, 14 show a patenting indicator below the control sample median value, while the remaining five are above. In Section 5, we shall discuss at greater length the possible interpretations of such results.

Table 6.5   Median test (by sector), number of acquired companies with $\Delta p_{i,t_i}$ above or below the control sample's median value

Sector	Below	Above
357	6	0
367	8	1
366	0	2
382	0	2

Table 6.6   Median test on single companies

Target	SIC	Deal	Δp	Median Δp in control sample	Result
Bay Networks	357	98/1	−2.660	−0.423	Below
Computervision	357	97/2	−1.160	0.000	Below
Supermac Technology	357	94/2	−0.286	0.125	Below
Soricon	357	95/1	−2.100	0.250	Below
Network General	357	97/2	−1.540	0.000	Below
Adv. Logic Research	357	97/1	−2.100	0.000	Below
US Robotica	366	97/1	0.724	−0.785	Above
Telebit	366	96/2	0.656	0.000	Above
Brooktree	367	96/2	−2.078	0.417	Below
Micronics Computers	367	98/1	−2.625	0.000	Below
Pulse Engineering	367	95/2	0.388	0.929	Below
Zilog	367	98/1	−0.846	0.000	Below
International Jensen	367	96/2	−5.250	0.470	Below
Lannet Communications	367	95/2	2.625	0.929	Above
Electrocom	367	94/2	0.150	0.589	Below
Mips Systems	367	92/1	−0.308	0.044	Below
Bytex	367	93/2	−5.250	0.000	Below
Perceptive Biosystems	382	98/1	−1.418	−1.833	Above
First Pacific Networks	382	98/1	−1.050	−1.833	Above

An alternative empirical strategy was aimed at analysing aggregately all the companies belonging to the four SIC codes we had previously selected. To this purpose, we used the corrected version of the patent indicator ($\Delta p^c_{i,t_i}$), defined in order to account for year's and sector's specific effects. The comparison between the control sample and the sample grouping the acquired companies was performed through a standard *t*-test. This was used in order to verify the null hypothesis that the two samples belonged to the same population or whether they were discriminated by specific factors (specifically the fact of the companies having been subject to acquisitions).

Given the small-sample problems related to the scarcity of data in certain sectors in our sample, we performed the *t*-test in two phases: first, we tried to analyse separately sectors 357 and 367, where we had a sufficiently large number of acquired companies in the samples; then, we tried to aggregate the four sectors. In Figure 6.2 we show the control sample's distribution, in order to qualitatively show that it is normally distributed. Consequently, we argued that it could be subject to a *t*-test. A similar test was performed for the acquired companies sample as well, with the same positive result.

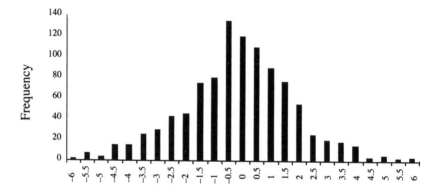

Figure 6.2 Distribution of Δp^c in the aggregated (4 SIC codes) sample

The null hypothesis that we wished to test was whether the two distributions had the same average value, against the adverse hypothesis that the average $\Delta p^c{}_{i,\,t_i}$ in the control sample was higher than the average value in the acquired companies' sample. In Tables 6.7, 6.8 and 6.9 we present the results of the tests, for increasing confidence levels.

The empirical test allowed us to demonstrate (with a 99 per cent confidence) that the acquired companies belonged to a population characterized by a lower average $\Delta p^c{}_{i,\,t_i}$. Only in the case of sector 367 did we limit our observation to a 95 per cent confidence level.

We therefore obtained more robust evidence that confirmed what had already been verified in the median value test.

The analysis showed that the aggregated $\Delta p^c{}_{i,\,t_i}$ distribution presents rather high variances, due to the presence of outliers in the control samples.

In order to limit the effects of such outliers on the overall significance of our mean estimation, we performed a further empirical test based on the median value, that is, Mood's median test. Here the null hypothesis was that the two samples belonged to the same population identified by its median value.

Table 6.7   t-test for sector 357

	Control sample 357	Acquired sample
Mean	−0.135	−1.538
Variance	2.612	0.787
Observations	299	6
DoF	6	
T-Stat	3.75	
H₀ rejected at 99% confidence level (99% critical value equal to 3.143)		

Table 6.8   t-test for sector 367

	Control sample 367	Acquired sample
Mean	0.175	−1.527
Variance	2.817	6.741
Observations	195	9
DoF	9	
T-Stat	1.948	
H₀ rejected at 95% confidence level (95% critical value equal to 1.859)		

Table 6.9   t-test for the four sectors (aggregated)

	Aggregated control sample	Acquired sample
Mean	−0.004	−1.167
Variance	3.198	3.809
Observations	702	19
DoF	19	
T-Stat	2.569	
H₀ rejected at 99% confidence level (99% critical value equal to 2.539)		

In Table 6.10 we provide the results for such a test. Clearly, the difference between the two median values belongs to the interval (0.13; 2.33) with a 95 per cent confidence. Since the interval does not include the null value, we can reject the null hypothesis that the samples belong to the same population and, since the interval is strictly positive, the control sample's median is higher than that of the acquired companies. Although the three empirical tests provide coherent and robust results, we need here to discuss a few sources of possible biases in our results.

Table 6.10   Mood's test on samples' median values

	Median value
Control sample	0.02
Acquired companies' sample	–0.75
Aggregated samples	–0.02
Median value difference (control–acquired)	0.77
H_0 rejected at 95% confidence level (95% critical value equal to 0.13; 2.33)	

In particular, given the specific way we had gathered the patent data, we selected only acquisitions where the bidding company had not owned, before the deal, establishments in the same US city as the target company. This is clearly a possible source of bias, if, as demonstrated by the literature that will be discussed below, geographical distance is indeed a major obstacle to the R&D integration between the acquiring and the target company.

Of 19 examined deals, only three are genuine cross-border acquisitions: one Canadian company and two European ones. Since recent literature has identified in the cultural and linguistic differences the major obstacles to R&D integration, in our specific case there seemed to be no plausible reason to believe that geographical distance had played a crucial role in determining a post-integration decrease in R&D efficiency.

A second important claim is that our empirical model cannot account for resource redeployment between target and acquiring companies. That is, the decrease in the innovation output of the acquired company might, in principle, be more than compensated by a contextual increase in the acquiring company. Concerning this latter topic, it is worth mentioning that the empirical literature has widely documented that, after the acquisition, the net flow of researchers is more often from bidder to target than from target to bidder. Moreover, this result is not dependent on the fact that the deal is cross-border or cross-state. Capron et al. (1998) presented an empirical analysis on the effects of resource redeployment after horizontal mergers. Data show a positive net flow from bidder to target (72 per cent) and from target to bidder (54 per cent). The smaller is the relative technological and innovative strength of the two companies involved in the deal, the more such a gap will be reduced. The relative strength of the pairs of companies in our sample can, as a first approximation, be evaluated through the relative patent stocks, as shown in Table 6.11.

It is clear that in most cases the bidder's patent stock is much more consistent than the target's: it is, therefore, plausible that the R&D resource redeployment goes from bidder to target companies. In conclusion, the decreases documented above in target companies' activity is not likely to be compensated by a symmetric increase in the acquiring entity.

Table 6.11   Relative technological and innovative strength (1990–2000)

Target	Patent	Bidder	Patent	Ratio B/T
Bay Networks	75	Nortel	1934	25.79
Computervision	9	Parametric Tech.	4	0.44
Supermac Technology	18	Radius	45	2.50
Soricon	5	Int. Verifact	9	1.80
Network General	3	Mcafee Associates	1	0.33
Adv. Logic Research	5	Gateway 2000	130	26.00
US Robotica	58	3com	557	9.60
Telebit	8	Cisco	368	46.00
Brooktree	48	Rockwell Int.	895	18.65
Micronics Computers	8	Diamond Multim.	19	2.38
Pulse Engineering	27	Technitrol	6	0.22
Zilog	93	Texas Pacific Group	160	1.72
International Jensen	2	Recoton	28	14.00
Lannet Communications	2	Madge Networks	20	10.00
Electrocom	35	Daimler Benz	175	5.00
Mips Systems	17	Silicon Graphics	419	24.65
Bytex	1	Network Systems	7	7.00
Perceptive Biosystems	37	Perkin Elmer	272	7.35
First Pacific Networks	10	US Sterling Corp.	82	8.20

A further possible problem is related to the fact that our empirical model estimated the acquisition effects in a two-year post-deal period, which may well be considered a short period, in terms of managerial decisions. The reason why we chose such a narrow time window lies in the fact that we needed to isolate a single acquisition in order to assess its effects without the patenting activity being disturbed by any other exogenous shock in the corporate structure.

In order to estimate the long-term effects of acquisitions on patenting activities, we selected a subsample of acquisitions and performed two more tests: a comparison with the control sample in the long run, excluding the short run, and a comparison with the control sample in the long run, *including* the short run.

The subsample consisted of the acquired companies for which we were able to verify that the conditions exposed in Section 3 had been holding all through the extended period. The resulting four companies we used in our estimation were studied both in the eight semesters after the deal (Table 6.12) and in only four semesters after the second year following the acquisition (Table 6.13); an indicator $\Delta p^{ext}_{i, t_i}$ was computed as in (6.1), after defining the post-merger interval from $t + 1$ to $t + 8$, and from $t + 5$ to $t + 8$, respectively. In three cases out of four, our data confirmed what had emerged in the model used to test the short-run effect. On the basis of available data, we are not able to provide any more robust analysis of the long-run behaviour of the model, although this seems a very important issue to be investigated in further research.

Table 6.12   Short- and long-run estimation (including eight semesters following acquisition)

Target	Bidder	SIC	Deal date	$\Delta p^{ext}_{i, t_i}$	$\Delta p^{ext}_{i, t_i}$ median
SuperMac Technology	Radium	357	94/2	−0.404	0.138
Pulse Engineering	Technitrol	367	95/2	1.125	0.837
LannetData	Madge Networks	367	95/2	0.000	0.837
Electrocom Automation	Daimler	367	94/2	−0.833	1.000

Table 6.13   Long-run estimation (including only semesters $t + 4$ to $t + 8$)

Target	Bidder	SIC	Deal date	$\Delta p^{ext}_{i, t_i}$	$\Delta p^{ext}_{i, t_i}$ median
SuperMac Technology	Radium	357	94/2	−3.208	1.134
Pulse Engineering	Technitrol	367	95/2	0.972	0.357
LannetData	Madge Networks	367	95/2	0.000	0.357
Electrocom Automation	Daimler	367	94/2	−0.750	0.239

5.   CONCLUSIONS

The results discussed in the previous section indicate that, after an acquisition, the innovative activity of the target company tends to shrink. When compared to a control sample of non-acquired firms, acquired companies show a contraction (or a smaller increase) in their patenting activity that is significantly larger. The result is confirmed both when the single sectors are examined and when the analysis is performed on aggregately on all sectors.

The theoretical arguments that inspired the hypothesis sketched in Section 2 are extensively reviewed in Chapter 3 of this book. In particular, we argued that the difficulties in exerting managerial control, in integrating different approaches to R&D management and the reduced incentives for target companies' R&D managers and key inventors were the main causes of such a decrease in patenting activities.

The companies examined in our study belong, in the vast majority, either to the same or to strictly related industries. A deeper analysis of the motivations leading to acquisitions, through the Securities and Exchange Commission's documentation, indicates that most of the deals were strictly horizontal ones, though finalized to acquiring competencies not especially related to the bidding company's technological core capabilities.

In general, product diversification and access to specific technological niches were the main objectives of the deals under observation. This last remark suggests that the problems related to R&D integration are probably the most important in determining the patent output contraction.

We suggest that the differences in the knowledge base and in the company's capabilities are at the basis of the lack of strategic coordination between the companies involved. This is confirmed by the observation of Figure 6.1, where the number of acquisitions displays an increasing trend, peaking in 1998. Analogously, our data show that, in the four semesters covering the years 1996 and 1997, the companies included in our acquired firms sample showed an above-average propensity to patenting, when compared with the respective industries' averages. The joint observation of such figures might well suggest that patenting activity worked out as a signalling device of technological capabilities. Alternatively, after the acquisition, the bidding companies might have exploited capabilities already existing in the target company, without fostering investment in the creation of new knowledge and capabilities. The specific case of SIC 366 seems to confirm the explanatory power of the last hypothesis; in this sector, where both acquisitions seemed to cause an increase in patenting activity, the acquiring companies (Cisco and 3Com) were characterized by strong innovative efforts and an intense acquisition activity. In this case, we suggest that the better performance in *ex post* patenting activity is attributable to the managerial skills that such companies displayed in integrating R&D routines, thanks to their customary engagement in such operations.

A further element of analysis is the company size. In our study, we used only one measure of size, namely the amount of fixed assets that the company reported in the SEC's filings just before acquisition. Although such a figure is characterized by relatively high variance (Table 6.4), it can be argued that the ratio between the bidder's and the target's total assets is such as to let us hypothesize a significant impact on the merged company's control practices. Once again, this would confirm one of the core hypotheses formulated in literature, namely that strategic managerial control is replaced by control devices based upon formalized performance indicators after asymmetric mergers; in turn, financial control is reported as a determinant of decreasing R&D efforts. In particular, the effect is stronger in the target entity, due to information asymmetries. The literature suggests that the difficulties in monitoring and controlling the acquired company's activities induce the bidding company to further reduce their financial support to the target's R&D activities.

The results presented in this chapter should be considered as a first approach to a complex and empirically difficult task. In particular, we expect to be able to shed more light on this problem by including more variables to specify the nature of the deal and some specific features of the acquiring companies.

On the other hand, patent analysis may convey valuable information when we set out to use patent applications in order to gain a better insight into the technological relatedness of the R&D output, through the analysis of technological classes and subclasses.

NOTES

1. The spatial dimension of technological spillovers is motivated in several studies by the importance of informal relationships and cultural and geographical proximity among the agents involved in innovation processes (Maskell and Malmberg, 1999). Therefore, geographical distance is deemed to be a major barrier to the diffusion of technological spillovers, while these are extremely relevant in geographically concentrated innovation systems (Jaffe and Trajtenberg, 1999; Maruseth and Verspagen, 1998).
2. We are grateful to Professor Jay Ritter, University of Florida, for allowing us to use his database on the US IPOs.
3. A good example of such a problem is the use of patents by the management of a public company as a signal to convey the value of R&D investments to shareholders (Wang et al., 2001). According to that hypothesis, if the change in corporate structure implies a shift from public to private ownership (reflected in a smaller degree of asymmetric information between ownership and control), one should expect a decrease in patenting activities due to a reduced need of using patents as a signalling device towards the shareholders. In this respect, in our specific application, the issue has to be considered negligible since all companies in the initial sample were acquired by public companies.
4. The list of relevant codes is drawn from the definition of the ICT sector given by the OECD report *Measuring the ICT Sector* (1998).
5. The most important pieces of information are drawn from the SEC's Defm 14-A module (including the plan that acquiring companies illustrate to the target company's shareholders) and from the Mergerstat database. Reliability is guaranteed by the friendly nature of the acquisition.
6. This situation actually occurred in only three out of 19 deals.
7. The control samples for sectors 366 and 382 were small (respectively nine and seven companies), because the majority of companies in those industries present no patenting activity. The poor empirical results may well be related to such a drawback.

7. The Organization of R&D Activities within Privatized Companies

Federico Munari

1. INTRODUCTION

This chapter documents and analyses six privatization cases drawn from four industries – steel, telecommunications, electricity generation and automotive – and two countries – Italy and France – with the aim of identifying in greater detail the changes brought about by privatization and liberalization processes in the organization of R&D activities. In Chapter 4, we showed that the divestiture by the state following privatization may lead to a significant decrease in the levels of R&D investments, even relatively to industry trends, and highlighted the impact of prior restructuring undertaken by the government. However, the switch from the public to the private sector may make a profound impact not only at the macrolevel of investments, but also at the microlevel of structures, processes and researchers' attitudes. Given the peculiarities of the state as a principal, expectations or manifestations of changes of its presence in the company could lead to a deep reformulation of the mission of the agent's mandate and, consequently, of R&D goals and organizational processes. Ultimately, all these changes are likely to make an impact on the firms' innovative outcomes, in terms of both private and social returns stemming from research activities.

In this chapter we adopt a multiple case-study approach in order to better understand the evolution of corporate R&D units within privatized companies, by focusing on four primary areas of intervention in the management of technology and innovation: the mission of R&D units; the size of R&D units; the composition and funding of the R&D portfolio; and the valorization of research outcomes. To this purpose, we analysed the experiences of the corporate R&D units of Telecom Italia, Ilva and Enel in Italy, and France Télécom, Usinor and Renault in France. We decided to focus our attention on Italy and France because, in both countries, state-owned enterprises (SOEs) had historically shaped the development of the industrial and economic systems, until the late 1980s and the early 1990s, when widespread privatization and deregulation programmes led to a substantial retreat of the direct presence of the state from the economy. Moreover, in those countries, SOEs had made a fundamental contribution in directing and characterizing the evolution of the national innovation systems, in many cases by creating and maintaining the national capabilities in industries of strategic importance for the country to secure an international lead. In the case of Italy, up until the mid-1990s, the R&D expenditures of the two main state-owned conglomerates, Iri and Eni, accounted for approximately 30 per cent of the overall Italian research expenditure in industry. Moreover, the entry and permanence in most of the technologically advanced sectors – such as power generation and telecommunication equipment, oil extraction and refining, microelectronics, aeronautics and military production – were largely promoted by public enterprises, given the endemic reluctance of the Italian private sector, both industrial and financial, to promote capital-intensive and long-term projects (Malerba, 1993; Bussolati et al., 1996). Turning to France, from the early post-war years public enterprises acted as 'national champions' in different industries of strategic importance for the nation, such as electrical power production, telecommunications, aerospace, electronics, and petroleum (Chesnais, 1993). The French national system of innovation has largely developed around the alliance and intersection between the state R&D facilities and the public and/or private business enterprises constituting the core of French industry. Given these peculiarities, it is easy to comprehend how privatization processes, in both countries, profoundly contributed to the redesign of the role of the state within the innovation system, and had a dramatic impact on the mission and the internal configuration of R&D facilities, which once acted as national laboratories for the whole country.

The rest of the chapter is organized as follows. In Section 2, we briefly present the main features of the privatization programmes undertaken in Italy and France over the last two decades. In Section 3, we present empirical evidence from our six case studies, and in Section 4 we discuss the similarities emerging in the patterns of the changes affecting the R&D mission, scale, composition and outcomes, determined by privatization and liberalization efforts. Finally, we discuss a few open questions concerning the relation between the changes in ownership and industry structure following the privatization processes and the R&D activities at firm level.

2.   THE PRIVATIZATION PROGRAMMES OF FRANCE AND ITALY

In Italy and France, SOEs have historically played a pivotal role in a wide variety of industries up to the late 1980s and, with higher intensity, since the early 1990s, when both countries undertook broad privatization programmes that radically reduced the role of the state as a major owner of productive assets. In France, following the example of the United Kingdom, a first wave of privatization was realized by the Chirac government in the 1986–88 period, when 14 state enterprises were privatized (all of them totally, except for the partial sale of Elf Acquitaine and Crédit Local de France) in both the industrial and the service sector (de Bandt, 1998). In the 1993 parliamentary elections the conservative party again won a majority again, and the new Balladur government launched another privatization programme, continued under the Juppé administration, involving the total or partial selling of many important groups, such as Renault, Usinor, Pechiney, Rhône-Poulenc, Total and Elf Acquitaine in the industrial sector, and BNP and AGF in the service sector. Although the French privatization programme was among the most prominent worldwide over the last two decades, it almost completely ignored the public utilities, which still remain totally under state ownership (as in the case of Eléctricité de France [EDF] and Gaz de France), with the sole and partial exception of France Télécom, whose $7.1 billion initial public offering (IPO) in October 1997 represents the largest French privatization ever. A peculiarity of the French experience concerns the procèdures adopted in the public offers, which were substantially different from the 'public company model' previously developed in the United Kingdom and driven by the priority to create widespread share ownership. In the French case, prior to the sale to the public, the government generally identified and established a hard core (the so-called *noyau dur*) of national shareholders, usually banks or insurance companies, in order to promote the joint objectives of creating stability in the corporate governance and of retaining national control on the privatized companies.

In Italy the process of privatizing public enterprises began in the early 1990s, largely imposed by the necessity to reduce the excessive Italian public debt. A first and fundamental step was made in 1992, when the Amato government announced a plan to sell off the vast majority of the state-owned companies and transformed the four main state-controlled agencies – Enel (electricity), Eni (petrochemical), Ina (insurance) and Iri (a large and diversified conglomerate) – into public limited companies, in order to create the preliminary conditions for their sale. The different governments that followed over the decade continued to promote the policy of privatizations as a way of reducing the public debt, speeding up the development of the stock market and improving efficiency within the economy. Among the wide and diversified set of companies sold over this period, we can recall the privatization of the steel companies under the Ilva group (from 1994 to 1996); those of Ina and Imi in the financial sector (1994–96); the placement of different tranches of the Eni group (from 1995 to 1998); the privatization of Telecom Italia

(1997) and, more recently, the partial privatization of Enel (1999) and Finmeccanica (2000). This effort has produced significant results in terms of generated revenues, totalling more than $122 billion, so that Italy established itself in second place after the UK in terms of global proceeds generated by the selling of state-owned enterprises in the 1979–99 period, and gained first place in the 1992–99 period (see Table 7.1).

Table 7.1   Privatization programmes in the main European countries (1979–99): public offers versus private sales (US$ millions)

	1992–99			1979–99		
	Public offer	Private sale	Total	Public offer	Private sale	Total
United Kingdom	24 500	23 300	47 800	136 400	28 600	165 000
Italy	94 500	22 787	117 287	98 500	23 700	122 200
France	50 400	12 700	63 100	62 000	12 700	74 700
Germany	29 300	31 700	61 000	32 930	33 300	66 230
Spain	48 800	4 100	52 900	51 700	4 220	55 920

Source: Adapted from Gros Pietro et al. (2001).

As to the procedures adopted, the Italian experience of privatizations combined several characteristics of the two previous models: the public company adopted in the United Kingdom and the *noyau dur* pioneered in France. In fact, various structural constraints, such as the relative limitations of the Italian stock market, the lack of domestic institutional investors and the small number of national publicly-held or private companies of significant size, precluded a direct replication of either of the previous approaches. For these reasons, the choice was to adopt a 'mixed model' envisaging the simultaneous use of a public offer and of a stable group of shareholders (between 20 and 30 per cent of the capital), which was generally smaller than the average French one. However, it should be stressed that the most recent evolution of the Italian and of the French models has led to a higher degree of convergence between the two (Gros Pietro et al., 2001).

3.   CASE STUDIES

In this section we discuss the experiences of the corporate R&D units of six companies privatized in Italy and France, in four different industries: Telecom Italia and France Télécom in the telecommunication industry, Ilva and Usinor in the steel industry, Enel in the electricity generation industry and Renault in the automotive industry. The cases were chosen to differ not only with respect to location and industry, but also to timing, extent and the kind of political choices made by the governments about the degree of residual participation, the extent of market liberalization, or the acceptance of foreign competition and bidding. In this phase we looked for high variability in the characteristics of the companies investigated and in their institutional and competitive context, in order to identify other factors that might have had an impact on the organization of R&D activities, quite apart from the change in the shareholder base.

For each company, we first conducted several interviews with their R&D managers and then collected further evidence through a detailed analysis of their annual R&D reports, in order to better identify the main changes that had occurred over time and their possible determinants. In documenting and analysing the changes that had affected the organizations studied after privatization, we decided to highlight four dimensions that are particularly critical in the management of R&D activities. These dimensions are:

- the overall size of the R&D organization;
- the composition of R&D activities;
- the funding of R&D activities;
- the valorization of R&D outcomes.

3.1   From the Cselt to Telecom Italia Lab

The idea of constituting a research facility within Stet[1] following the examples of other industrialized countries goes back to 1955. At that time, the telephony service in Italy was provided by five operators covering different geographical areas, their interconnection being directly guaranteed by ASST (Azienda di Stato per i Servizi Telefonici), a state-owned agency. This solution, adopted by the Italian government in 1925, aimed at avoiding the creation of a single telephone operator under a monopolistic regime, but proved to be highly problematic from a technological perspective, especially with regard to the planning of the telephony network and the coexistence of systems based on different technological standards. For this reason, it was decided that the new research centre should support Stet and its subsidiaries in the process of strategy formulation, in the definition of technological standards and in the specification of telecommunication systems and methods, by carrying on related research activities. To this purpose, the Csel (Centro Studi e Laboratori, that is, Centre and Laboratory for Telecommunication Studies) was established in Turin and assigned the original mission of concentrating and coordinating all the research activities previously undertaken independently by the different national telecom operators.

In December 1964, the research centre was renamed Cselt (Centro Studi e Laboratori Telecomunicazioni) and officially inaugurated as an independent corporation fully owned by Stet, with the mission of conducting research, development and service activities to support Stet and the different subsidiaries of the group. Since then, Cselt has witnessed a continuous growth in its personnel, passing from the initial 100 units up to a peak of more than 1 200 in 1997.

The 1990s were a period of serious turmoil for the Cselt and the whole Telecom Italia Group (as Stet was renamed in 1997), due to several competitive, institutional and technological discontinuities: the opening up of the telecommunication market to competition, the privatization of Telecom Italia in 1997, the successful takeover bid by Olivetti/Tecnost in 1999, followed by the one led by the Pirelli group in 2001 (see note 1), the upsurge in the Internet diffusion and the convergence between communications and information technologies.

In order to face those changes, and especially the pressures posed by the liberalization process of the Italian telephone market, the Cselt was subject to a major restructuring, beginning in 1999 and centring on the switch of resources and priorities from the infrastructure technologies sector to service and applications, the increased focus on development activities, and the search for efficiency improvements and cost reduction (Cselt Annual Report, 1999).

In April 2000, the new management instituted after the takeover operated a major reorganization of the group, emphasizing the entrepreneurial and commercial independence of the business units, and more radically stressing the emergence of a new role for research and innovation activities. While the Cselt was formerly a corporate-level function under the strategy and innovation unit, following the reorganization it was incorporated in a newly-established company of the Telecom Italia Group, called Telecom Italia Lab. Since 1 March 2001, Telecom Italia Lab has combined the group's venture capital activities, the Cselt research laboratories in Turin, and other research facilities of the group into one single unit operating as a profit centre, whose mission is the identification, development and use of new technologies to develop innovation in the field of the information and communication technology.

Within this context, the research activities of the Centre have gradually been focused on the development of new services and applications (such as Internet data and services offered through fixed or mobile networks; applications and services based on advanced vocal technologies; and call centre and interconnection services), whereas the research efforts in the fields of network infrastructure and hardware have been gradually reduced. In contrast, the Cselt research portfolio, until the early 1990s, had largely been focused on the evolution of the telecommunication infrastructures and linked mainly to network renewal plans: the Network Division, originally within Sip and then within Telecom, was traditionally the main financial source for the Cselt, but in more recent years the share of funding provided by this division has decreased steadily, only partially compensated by the increased commitment of Tim, the mobile phone company of the Group. For the same reasons, the budget portion funded by Italtel and Sirti, the equipment manufacturing companies that were formerly part of the Telecom Italia Group,[2] was consistently reduced over the same period. Also the sale of the Centro Tecnologie Ottiche (Optical Technologies Centre) to Agilent, operated by the Cselt in 1999, must be ascribed to the decision to reduce commitment in hardware technologies and to focus on the fields related to software, services and applications.

Consistent with the new logic, the scope of the research portfolio and the budget composition reflected a gradual shift towards a tighter integration with the needs of the Telecom Italia Group business units. An internal classification schema traditionally distinguishes two classes of projects, that is, the *strategic research activities*, funded by the corporate, oriented to medium-term projects in revolutionary technological fields and directed to nurture core technological competencies; and the *commissioned activities*, based on contracts stipulated with internal clients according to a customer–supplier logic. During the 1980s, about 50 per cent of the budget was allocated to the first class of projects, whereas in recent years this share has been set to 30 per cent (26.7 per cent in 1999), with a contextual increase of the budget portion covered by the business units up to 62.8 per cent in 1999. Overall, Cselt revenues steadily increased at an average annual rate of 17 per cent during the 1990s, reaching a peak of 295.1 billion lire in 1997, and stabilized in the following two years, respectively to 277.3 billion lire in 1998 and 291.1 billion lire in 1999.

The competitive and institutional discontinuities of the most recent years have also had a consistent impact on the size of the centre's R&D personnel: after thirty years of continuous growth, culminating in a maximum of 1 243 units in 1997, between 1998 and 1999 its total employment was reduced to 1 149, mainly because of the dismissal of the Centro Tecnologie Ottiche and the downsizing of the staff personnel (the ratio of researchers to total personnel had increased, between 1990 and 1999, from 73 per cent to 78 per cent). However, in 2001 Telecom Italia Lab launched an ambitious recruiting programme. It is interesting to notice that over the same period the personnel dismissal phenomenon, which was very limited at the beginning of the 1990s, had been sharply increasing since 1996 (57 dismissals in 1998 and 48 in 1999, about 5 per cent of total employment), mainly because of the opening up of the market to competition and the transfer of employees to competitor telephone carriers.

Turning to the recourse to external sources of technology, Cselt has built and developed over time a wide network of relationships with external institutions, such as universities, public laboratories, manufacturers and international carriers, very often within research programmes sponsored by the Italian government or by the European Union, in order to identify and utilize new opportunities and to exploit synergies with different institutional actors. With regard to the relationships with the telecom manufacturing companies, the decision to favour the core business of telecommunication services and to divest manufacturing led to a weakening of the mutual dependence between Telecom Italia and Italtel and Sirti, and to stipulate partnership agreements with international telecom equipment manufacturers, such as Lucent, Cisco and Ericsson. In contrast, the cooperation with the research facilities of foreign telecom carriers has of late entered a critical phase, largely due to the increasing level of mutual competition, which redefined the cooperation agreements in a tighter organizational, technical and legal framework, for instance with regard to the attribution of the intellectual property rights. On the other hand, the number of collaborations with Italian and international universities has consistently risen. These are generally classified into two different categories: research contracts aiming at specific results (31 in 1999) and research grants (six in 1999) for long-term projects entrusted to high-level academic teams operating in the scientific fields of interest to the company.

Finally, one of the main reasons leading to the birth of Telecom Italia Lab was the need for a stronger and more effective valorization of their research results. The synergy between the research capabilities and the venture capital activities led, in 2001, to the first spin-off created by researchers of the group, called Loquendo and deriving from the traditional area of excellence in the field of voice recognition. Telecom Italia Lab carried out many direct investments in companies operating in the ICT sector, as well as many investments in venture capital funds as a means of entering new markets and of gaining access to deal flow. The first effort in this area was the creation of the venture capital fund Fintech, as a joint venture between Mediocredito Centrale and Telecom Italia, focused on financing early-stage initiatives in the field of information and communication technologies. Moreover, the protection of intellectual property rights and the exploitation of research results have become a major concern in recent years. Consistent with the role of Cselt as a cost centre, scant attention was paid in the past to the commercialization of its technological capital (only 1.5 billion lire of revenues, stemming from licensing activities in 1998, while the revenues from research activities commissioned by extra-group subjects amounted to 4.6 billion lire), as demonstrated by the lack of a unit responsible for the marketing of research results. As a consequence, the protection of intellectual property tended to be underestimated, except within some areas (voice/multimedia, radio, microelectronics). To this purpose, a project was started in 2000 in order to facilitate the propensity of researchers to patent and the commercialization of the technologies of the centre.

3.2 From CNET to France Télécom R&D

The Centre National d'Etudes des Télécommunications (National Centre for Telecommunication Studies – CNET) was created in 1944 within the Direction Générale des Télécommunications (DGT) of the French Ministry of Post and

Telecommunication, as an interministerial body with the mission to 'undertake, or to organize the undertaking of, research requested by the various ministerial departments and public services' (CNET, 1995). In a country undergoing reconstruction and modernization after the devastation of the Second World War, the main priorities were identified as recovering from the technological deficiencies of the French industry and providing the telecommunication ministry with the necessary equipment to modernize its network, in particular by focusing the research efforts on the fields of transmission and switching. CNET's efforts and results in research and development over the years, further pursued by manufacturers, were critical for France in helping it catch up in telephone technology and in enabling it to set up one of the most highly digitalized network in the world.

In order to better adapt to an economic environment that was undergoing major changes driven by internationalization and deregulation processes, in 1991 the former DGT was renamed France Télécom and given the status of an independent public operator. CNET was integrated into France Télécom as the public operator research centre, and given the responsibility 'for covering every aspect of communication technology and passing on research results which may be of general interest to other ministerial departments, the scientific community and French industry' (CNET, 2000). A second major restructuring took place in 1996, with the transfer of CNET to the development business unit and the adoption of a formal organizational structure that more closely mirrored that of France Télécom business divisions. The new priority was identified as the strengthening of the relationships between researchers and the market demand, by encouraging a closer cooperation with sales and marketing departments from the very beginning, and through the adoption of a multidisciplinary approach. As a consequence of the tighter integration in France Télécom, CNET activities were increasingly reoriented towards the communication services, the Group core business, at the expense of the network and component technologies, which were gradually moved or delegated to equipment manufacturers, universities or public laboratories. For instance, partnership agreements were signed with Alcatel to perform collaborative research in the field of optoelectronics, following the transfer of CNET's upstream research activities in optoelectronics components to the CNRS (National Research Foundation) in February 1998. Under the same logic, research activities in the field of microelectronics are now being performed within a partnership with ST Microelectronics and the Cea-Leti.

In October 1997, about 20 per cent of France Télécom shares were put on the market, approximately 18 months after the beginning of the process, in the summer of 1996. Both the French and the international offerings were largely oversubscribed and concluded with almost Ffr 40 billion revenues (US$6.7 billion), which was France's largest equity offering. Moreover, in 1998 the

French telecommunication services and infrastructure were fully deregulated, in line with EU policy. These changes spurred a major change in the role and nature of the R&D facilities within the company. In March 2000, after a survey made among its employees, CNET changed its name to France Télécom R&D. An internal document of the company clearly explains the motivations behind this choice:

> In use since its creation, the name CNET (Centre National d'Etudes des Télécommunications) today no longer reflects the reality of its mission, especially after the continuous evolution of the 1990s. The name 'France Télécom R&D' better translates its progressive mutation and reflects the continuity of the changes already implemented: a statutory change (from public to private), the reorientation of its activities (less fundamental research, more applied research), international ambitions and locations, activities centered on the needs of the France Télécom Group and its subsidiaries in France and abroad.

Consistent with this new mission, over the last few years France Télécom has adopted various measures to link its R&D division more tightly to the needs of its operating units. For instance, so-called *ingénieurs d'affaires* are now operating within the R&D departments, acting as market gatekeepers in managing the relationships with the operating units: more precisely, when a new project is commissioned, they become the interface between the business unit marketing group and France Télécom R&D. Moreover, France Télécom R&D started to recruit not just engineers and scientists, but also people with different backgrounds and competencies, such as marketing experts, ergonomists, designers or sociologists, in order to spread a new culture and a new language, better suited to understanding business and customers' needs. These different competencies are generally integrated within cross-functional project teams in order to develop new applications and services in a more effective and rapid way.

Another major priority was identified as the valorization and exploitation of the research portfolio through three main avenues: the creation of start-ups; the promotion of venture capital initiatives to finance new enterprises; and a policy of licensing agreements and patent sale. In 1998, the Centre inaugurated a very ambitious policy of nurturing spin-offs, with the goal of creating eight start-ups per year, by offering assistance and support to researchers wanting to exploit entrepreneurial opportunities. This led to the launch of almost 20 spin-offs generated from France Télécom R&D since March 1998, which are now employing several hundred people. The most successful stories among them are probably those of Algety and Highwave: in May 2000, Algety Telecom merged with the American start-up Corvis, which joined Nasdaq in July 2000, whereas Highwave was put on France's *Nouveau Marché* in June 2000.

Then, in order to provide funding to telecommunication and information technology start-ups, also outside the company borders, in 1998 France Télécom set up a venture capital structure, Innovacom, which has already funded more then 240 companies in the telecommunication and data sector, besides establishing a unit in Silicon Valley, in order to more closely monitor the evolution of the most promising technologies in the field. Finally, greater attention was paid to the protection and exploitation of the intellectual capital of the company, incorporated in a portfolio of more than 3 700 patents, assigned both in France and abroad. With regard to this, it is interesting to observe that the old CNET in many cases did not demand any royalties for transferring its patented technologies to other French companies operating in the ICT sectors, given its role as a national research laboratory. In contrast, over the last two years France Télécom R&D has led a very active policy of intellectual property transfer, for instance through actions aimed at enhancing the researchers' involvement in protecting intellectual property and by the creation of a team of specialized patent engineers, or through the set-up of a specialized sales team and the development of brokerage and distribution agreements to intensify the licensing and sale of patents. Those actions led to a consistent leap in the number of patents requested in 1999 (149 patents and 77 software products were registered in France) and to an increasing trend in the revenues generated by intellectual property transfer (Ffr 130 million in 1999).

3.3   CSM

The Centro Sviluppo Materiali (Centre for Material Development, from now on CSM) began its activities in 1963 as a joint initiative promoted by major Italian steel and mechanical corporations. Its mission was to promote and coordinate research activities in the areas of metallurgy and steel production, and to become a centre of excellence in the associated fields for the country as a whole, proactively promoting a technology transfer towards industry and a knowledge transfer towards universities. In 1982, following a wider restructuring of the state-owned portion of the steel industry, CSM formally became part of the public industry sector with the specific mission to strategically support the needs and requests of the different firms being part of the government-controlled conglomerate Finsider, spanning from the production of special steel in Terni to the heavy duty continuous casting plants of Genoa, Bagnoli and Taranto.

The new mission of CSM was to maintain the knowledge base of the technical disciplines related to the Finsider core business, and to provide specialized support to the innovation needs of the different operating companies. These goals were further reinforced in 1988, when the Finsider group went through a re-engineering round, with the establishment of Ilva as a more focused operating group in the steel business, setting aside the financial perspective that had inspired the previous restructuring. As a consequence, CSM became an independent corporation, 90 per cent controlled by Ilva, and was structured in technical departments along three key areas of business (steel-making processes, metallurgy of structural steel, metallurgy of special and transformed steel) and three key areas of technological attention (corrosion and surface protection, system engineering, new materials).

The central labs, located near Rome, became the reference point for the so-called 'strategic projects', characterized by a medium/long-term horizon, with a planned duration of five years on average, partly addressing the specific needs expressed by internal customers, but also targeted towards a more general knowledge–development objective and therefore, sometimes, co-financed by national or European public research funds. Projects in this category were aimed, for example, at the definition of radically new blast furnace technology, the reconfiguration of casting processes, the production of coloured steel alloys and the like.

A second class of projects, whose coordination and operative responsibility were still retained, generally, by the central units – although with the increasing importance of localized laboratories – were the 'technological assistance projects', which were shorter in duration (between one and three years) and usually more applied in their nature and expected results. Projects within this group were activated to address the specific implementation needs of a well-identified internal client. Finally, the third set, called internally 'service maintenance', grouped all the projects commissioned by one specific client to subcontract technological assistance at plant level. Typical activities included laboratory testing, process consulting and quality certification.

The underlying philosophy of articulating research projects along a loose basic/applied development span was retained over the years and can still be found in the now privatized CSM. What has changed significantly over the years and after the privatization of Ilva is the proportion of CSM's revenues generated by an internal captive market, the overall size of CSM and the distribution of the revenues associated with the different classes of projects described. Between 1992 and 1993, after another major crisis in the steel industry and the redefinition of national production quotas within the EU, Ilva was steered towards a complete privatization of its activities. The privatization process was completed in 1996 with the divestment of Dalmine, sold to Techint-Banca di Roma. Following these changes, CSM became an independent company operating in the business of promoting and selling its research capabilities to the steel industry, thus apparently returning to its original mission, dating back to 1963, when it had been founded.

Several differences characterized the new competitive arena. First of all, CSM's revenues in earlier years had been primarily dependent on an internal captive market, with a large share of R&D projects used as an indirect way of financing long-term activities without specifically allocating a portion of the budget to a generic entry such as basic R&D activities. Moreover, despite the large number of laboratories and the availability of sophisticated testing equipment, the testing activities had been formerly largely undeveloped. The funding from external sources was connected with public financing programmes, rather than with specific service requests advanced by the private sector. Finally, several local units were divested as dedicated laboratories, together with the manufacturing plants with which they were associated, as for example was the case with the Taranto facilities.

The need to shift convincingly towards a more market-focused approach and a significant restructuring of the existing activities was perceived as crucial by the top management, in order to create the financial and operating conditions necessary to promote a subsequent privatization of CSM. As a consequence of the privatization of Ilva, the total CSM turnover decreased, between 1993 and 1995, by nearly 30 per cent, from 110 billion lire to 80 billion lire. Using several legal measures, such as early retirement, the total employment was reduced from 587 to 390 units. Meanwhile, the now privatized steel producers decreased their quota of projects from 90 per cent to about 50 per cent in later years, with a substantial shift in the composition of their portfolios towards more applied projects of shorter duration and with better-defined industrial targets. In 1993, the CSM budget allocated 63 per cent of its resources to long-term projects, 25 per cent to medium-term projects and the remaining 12 per cent to qualified testing and technical assistance. In the three-year strategic plan following its separation from Ilva, the targeted proportions for 1996 were set to 41 per cent, 35 per cent and 24 per cent respectively.

The new CSM, albeit dramatically affected by years of restructuring, has now found a coherent way of acting in the market of industrial research by working along two main strategic directions. First, it has invested in some areas of application of its internal competencies outside the steel industry, which still remains the core activity, though is not likely to be further expanded in the future. Second, its strategic objective was to tap into different markets to support long-, medium- and short-term projects, targeting three different subjects: first, national and international research funds, in order to promote fewer applied and more extended projects; second, large operating companies, to support their direct needs with qualified technical competencies for applied and development projects; and, third, small and medium-sized firms, to exploit its testing capacity by promoting the access to sophisticated laboratories and equipment.

3.4   Irsid

The decision to create a research institute in the field of steel making was undertaken in 1946 by Corsid (Comité de la Sidérurgie), the association of the major French steel companies: as specified by the founding report, the new centre would carry out applied research in the interest of the national steel industry, positioning its activities between pure academic research and technical research undertaken by private companies. With this mission, Irsid (Institute de Recherche de la Sidérurgie) was created in Paris in 1946, operating under the Ministère de l'Industrie et de la Recherche, initially funded by the different steel companies in proportion of their revenues. The crisis that hit the industry between 1970 and 1980 led to a massive concentration in the French steel industry, which regrouped around two companies: Usinor and Sacilor. In 1981 the French government took over a majority interest in these, which were still facing serious economic difficulties, through the conversion of prior debt for equity. In 1986 the state, which now held about100 per cent of both companies, decided to merge them in a new group, Usinor Sacilor (later, in 1997, the group adopted a simplified corporate name, Usinor). The completion of the nationalization of the French steel industry had important implications for the role and mission of Irsid, as acknowledged in the company book presenting the history of the centre:

> The state acknowledges the central role of French steel research. The underpinning logic is straightforward: if France wants to place itself in the global steel market, it is necessary to invest heavily in research, in order to bridge the gap separating France from its main competitor. Progressively, Irsid has emerged as the most appropriate structure to answer these imperatives.

The restructuring led to a redefinition of the boundaries between Irsid and the internal research laboratories located near the production plants of Usinor Sacilor. Irsid became the central R&D organization (CCR, Centre Commun de Recherche) of all the branches of the group (flat steel, stainless steel, long products, heavy plate) and was put under the authority of the research director of Usinor Sacilor. It was assigned the mission to undertake common research work on the fundamental processes and proprieties that were common to all of the group products and on more long-term studies, whereas the division-level laboratories would focus on the development of new products and processes. After this reorganization, a major supplementary research effort was launched, and Irsid consistently increased its budget and personnel, which rose from about 680 units in 1986 to 880 in 1992.

However, at the beginning of the 1990s the steel industry faced a major crisis worldwide, so that the European Union was forced to set up a restructuring plan of the industry, contemplating significant employment cuts. In 1993, still under the presidency of François Mitterrand, the right won the parliamentary elections and the newly appointed prime minister, Edouard Balladur, immediately announced a new and ambitious privatization programme. A law passed in the same year declared that almost all the nationalized companies operating in competitive sectors, including Usinor Sacilor itself, would be privatized.

In such a turbulent context, the company, which was incurring substantial losses, decided to reorganize its R&D structure in order to reduce its fixed costs in that sector, and to increase its research yields. The restructuring contemplated a consistent downsizing of Irsid, mainly through its concentration from three locations into a single site located north of Metz, in the Lorraine area. Moreover, it was decided to reduce the company's commitment in those fields that were of exclusive interest to its single branches, and to transfer the relative personnel to the divisional research laboratories. As a consequence of these changes, the Irsid personnel scaled down to 490 units in 1994.

In July 1995, all the Usinor Sacilor shares owned by the state and Crédit Lyonnais (which had become a 20 per cent shareholder in 1991, simultaneous with an increase in capital) were sold on the Paris Bourse with a public offer that concluded with 2.2 more applications than available shares. A group of stable shareholders, including industrial companies, service suppliers and financial institutions, held 15 per cent of Usinor's shares, after privatization. After the major discontinuity of 1994, Irsid's size stabilized over the following years, slightly decreasing to 551 personnel units in 1999. Following a more general restructuring of the Usinor Group, aimed at strengthening its market orientation, in 1999 a new reorganization of the R&D structure was undertaken, based on the appointment of a corporate director of R&D, directly responsible for all laboratories, and on the introduction of a tighter internal market logic for R&D activities. According to that philosophy, for research to be closer to the company's businesses it should answer directly to the requests advanced by the operating divisions, which in turn should be free to use either internal or external technology suppliers. However, about 20 per cent of the R&D budget is still directly financed by the head office, in order to identify the possible breakthroughs in process technologies and to maintain and expand the core technological competencies necessary for future development. Under the new scenario, the main role became, for Irsid, that of improving Usinor competitiveness through full process control and knowledge of the fundamental mechanisms and features common to the group's products.

Moreover, a clear shift towards the outsourcing of R&D was introduced, under the principle of 'mutualization' of research efforts, in order to exploit benefits such as spreading risks, pooling resources, leveraging R&D funds and speeding innovation. According to such a philosophy, Irsid has intensified its collaborative research work with its clients' R&D laboratories (that is, automobile, electronic appliance and packaging industries), with the scientific community and with the industrial world (suppliers, steel production equipment manufacturers, other steel producers), especially through European programmes or within bilateral agreements.

3.5   Enel's R&D

The nationalization of the Italian electricity industry in 1963 profoundly affected not only the operating activities, but also the organization and structure of R&D work in the field. The aggregation of the different areas of business (production, transmission and distribution) and of almost all the formerly private facilities operating in the country generated a national monopoly characterized by a remarkable critical mass. R&D activities were identified from the beginning as a central priority, directed to 'improving the productive performance and reliability of the generation, transmission and distribution facilities, solving the problems related to the integration between the facilities and the environment, and generally increasing the quality of the service offered' (Galbani and Paris, 1994). But the newly nationalized Enel had to define the characteristics and the structure of its R&D function, given its heritage of previous market structures, where the fragmentation on the production side had resulted in the emergence of three different research companies: Cise, Cesi and Ismes.

Considering the strategic priority assigned to R&D activities, they were organized as one of the Direzioni Centrali, directly reporting to the Enel board, and recruiting from among its several electricity companies a group of researchers who were familiar with the structures then used as a model to design the new organizational arrangements, namely EDF in France, and the Central Electricity Board and the Electricity Council in the UK. The three research companies already active in the Italian electricity industry were incorporated by Enel, which technically became their sole shareholder. Their independent legal form, however, remained unmodified until the most recent changes of the late 1990s.

In addition to Cise, Cesi and Ismes, five different areas of research were identified in the 1960s, and as many internal departments were established. Each of these departments operated one or more second-level units, specializing in relevant areas of research within the more general competencies of the department. For example, the Department of Automatics was focused on the definition of mathematical models for the distribution network stability and for the general programmeming needs of transmission and distribution flows. Its three units specialized in systems, data manipulation and transfer, and equipment and control procedures.

In 1992, as a preliminary step to a subsequent privatization of Enel and the end of its monopoly, as requested by the EU for 1999, when Enel was targeted to decrease its production share by 30 per cent, the company was transformed into a private corporation controlled by the Ministry of Treasury. After several reorganizations during the following years, which time and again reallocated part of its resources among the different areas and modified some organizational labels of the R&D units, the changes introduced by the new top management in 1996 tried to impact in depth an area of Enel activities employing about 1 300 people, without including Cise, Cesi and Ismes, generating a turnover of about 600 billion lire.

One of the main areas of intervention was the redefinition of the internal classification schema used to distinguish among different kinds of projects. Following the fiscal and accounting separation of the production, transmission and distribution activities into three divisions, later to become independent companies, the R&D unit was restructured as a corporate-level area of services, characterized by three main areas of activity. First came the development and advancement of technical knowledge, directed towards maintaining and nurturing specific competencies in the core business of the company, by promoting corporate-funded projects. The second area should support the operating companies in their development projects, offering dedicated technical consultation through projects directly commissioned by the interested internal customers. The third set of activities was to leverage the available testing laboratories' capacity by offering dedicated technical services both to the internal divisions and to the external market.

Although still envisaged as a valuable asset to support corporate and business division activities, the R&D unit was also encouraged to exploit its competencies in the outside market. Before these changes, which were introduced only in the second part of 1997, the outside contracts represented only about 16 per cent of the total R&D budget, coming from the participation in EU (or Italian) research funding programmes and from specialized technical assistance to external partners, while corporate-funded projects accounted for 60 per cent of the budget. The changes in the definition of the classes of projects to be performed were also accompanied by a restructuring of fund allocation procedures to the departments. For the first class of projects it was established that only 20 per cent of the budget would be financed with corporate funds, which would be awarded to a number of proposals to be selected by a central innovation committee on the basis of their potential applicability and compatibility with the company core business. For the second class of projects, the single R&D departments would have to shop around inside the company for clients interested in their competencies. For the third class of projects, those departments proving best equipped with laboratory capacity would have to develop some commercial ability to start tapping into the external market. Together, these three classes of projects were intended to cover the remaining 80 per cent of the budget, with some differences among the departments, depending on the availability of laboratories and testing facilities. This new reality profoundly contrasted with the former allocation system, based on projects and areas of research. Projects had been characterized by a well-defined set of activities, with clearly defined goals and an expected end. In contrast, the various areas of research had identified one or more fields of interest where researchers were involved, regardless of a specific focus or target. Previously R&D had been considered essentially as a fixed staff cost, to be funded somehow by the operating activities. With the new structure, however, the economic viability of R&D would be determined mainly by its own capacity for providing a high-quality and specialized service, to be purchased at a specific cost by the operating divisions.

In February 1999 the Electricity Act presented by the Italian government defined the new structure of the electricity industry, based on the unbundling of the generation, transmission and distribution activities, and on the division of generation assets of Enel in different independent companies, to be subsequently sold on the market in order to create a competitive environment. Then, in October 1999, 31.74 per cent of Enel shares were floated on the stock market, with a public offer that involved about 3.83 million private and institutional investors and generated revenues of 31 045 billion lire.

In order to adjust to the new competitive context, shaped by the liberalization of the electricity sector, over the period from 1998 to 1999 Enel undertook a radical internal reorganization, leading to the creation of different business units, each aiming at optimizing the provision of the core services and at exploiting new business opportunities in order to counterbalance the progressive reduction in the presence on the electricity market. R&D activities and organization were dramatically affected by these changes. It was decided that only those research activities that directly impacted on the competitiveness of the company should be performed by Enel, and consequently only the so-called 'competitive research', regarding power generation and employing about 200 people, had to be retained within the group. In contrast, all the research activities regarding the electricity system at large (the so-called 'system research') – including the distribution and transmission network, environment, renewable sources, energy efficient utilization – were assigned to Cesi, thus creating an independent research company of about one thousand employees. Starting from January 2000, Cesi incorporated most of the former Enel R&D personnel and facilities, and its ownership is now diffused among the major firms operating in the Italian electricity generation business, with Enel still holding more than 50 per cent of the shares.

To guarantee appropriate efforts in the research activities regarding the electricity system, the Bersani Law stated that this kind of research, performed by Cesi, should be partially funded by means of a fee taken from the electricity bills, at least as a temporary solution to preserve the continuity of the R&D facilities of the former monopolist. To this purpose, the law established the constitution of a fund for system research, fed by the companies selling electricity in proportion to their utilization of the system (that is, as a proportion of their revenues) and specified that the results of the research projects so funded should remain public, although the operational details – for instance with regard to issues of intellectual property rights and technology transfer – were not specified.

3.6 The Renault Research Department

The establishment of a research department within Renault is relatively recent and goes back to the creation, in 1976, of the Direction des affaires scientifiques and techniques (Department of scientific and technical activities), almost a century after the birth of the company in 1898. Before, research within Renault had been carried out by its many different operational departments, as witnessed by the several hundred patents registered by the company since its very early years (the fame and fortune of Renault began in 1898, when the founder, Louis Renault, invented the direct drive system; the relevant patent was filed a few months later). In 1976, Renault created a research department in order to establish a bridge towards the knowledge and technology generated by universities and other major research facilities: the new centre was initially intended to operate as an open window on academic research. Originally, the new research department was set up as an autonomous organization, physically separated from the rest of the company, and, in keeping with its mission, was headed by a representative from the French academic system. For more than two decades, it was granted wide autonomy to pursue its essentially free research, but, despite coming up with a substantial number of new ideas and inventions, only a few of them were actually put into production and incorporated in new products, processes or services. As the research and operational sectors tended to behave as two separate worlds, only 10 per cent of the projects undertaken by the research units led to results that actually reached the commercialization stage (Beuzit, 2000).

This way of operating was felt to be increasingly inappropriate for facing the challenges posed by globalization and the heightened competition which has shaken the automobile industry over the last decade. The 1990s were also characterized by the beginning of the company's privatization process. The motor group was partially privatized in November 1994, when the government reduced its holding from 80 per cent to about 53 per cent, with a public offer at a value of Ffr 165 per share. A stable core of shareholders was constituted, including Elf Acquitaine, the Lagardère Group, BNP and Rhône-Poulenc, which together retained about 5 per cent of the company shares. The following year, state ownership decreased below 50 per cent, with the private placement of about 6 per cent of the capital to a core of companies which reinforced the *noyau dur* of Renault.

To face the new pressures posed by the competitive environment, a major restructuring of the research department was undertaken in 1998, with the aim of strengthening the integration with the operational organization and making a more effective contribution towards attaining the strategic targets set by the company. First, a new research director was appointed: for the first time, the position was given to an engineer with experience in industry (he had headed the Clio project launched in 1992), rather than to a scholar from academia or from the public research sector. Then, research was made part of the vehicle engineering department, and all its personnel (340 units in 1999, a number that has remained more or less stable over the last decade, reaching a peak in 1995 with 369 units) were moved to the Technocentre, the new structure located at Guyancourt, south-west of Paris, fully operational since 1998, where Renault brought together in a single site all the people and all the facilities involved in research, design and development activities. More than 7 500 people are now operating at the Technocentre, including 1 000 representatives of suppliers and equipment manufacturers, in a cross-functional environment which is expected to enhance communication, speed and creativity.

In this new context, it was decided that two types of research were to be performed at Renault: the first one, essentially incremental in its nature and representing the core of the innovative work of the company, would take place within the teams in charge of the development and industrialization of new vehicles, and it would be carried out by the operational sectors. The second type of research would be focused on technological discontinuities and it would be carried out by the research department, whose mission was now threefold: to help attain the strategic objectives of the group, by transposing into research projects the main themes of the overall company plan (such as protection of the environment, active security, driver/passenger comfort, and so on); to introduce innovations into new products and services; and to develop knowledge and expertise in new technologies of interest for the group, essentially through the recruiting and training of new personnel.

A major effort was undertaken to effectively bring the innovations developed by the research unit from the experimental to the development stage. The budget for the research department is currently allocated at 30 per cent for long-term research activities (which are freely chosen, but which should follow the overall strategy of the company), and the remaining 70 per cent for projects run on behalf of the operational departments. Most of these projects directly involve the operational staff, especially in the areas of vehicle engineering, mechanical engineering and marketing, in order to foster the exchange of communication and knowledge from the early stages of the innovation process. Moreover, to facilitate the transfer and integration of research results with the development and manufacturing stages, the research engineers who have run the projects from the beginning will see it through to the end (the turnover of research personnel was equal to 20 per cent in 1999). As a consequence of the new way of operating, the technology-transfer indicator, measuring the percentage of research activities that is transferred into products and services sold on the market, is now about 50 per cent (Beuzit, 2000). Another indicator that has been increasingly used to evaluate the performance of the research department – the production of new patents – shows a clear trend upward over the last few years and points to a greater attention being paid to the protection and exploitation of intellectual property: the number of patents applied for in France and generated by Renault's research department has been steadily increasing, from an average of 32 in the 1990–94 period up to the peak of 106 new patents in 1999 (72 in 1998).

4.   DISCUSSION[3]

The six firms analysed above operated in different countries and industries, were subject to a different degree of privatization and by various processes, and were affected by different degrees of market liberalization and regulation. However, they presented many similarities regarding the changes characterizing the corporate R&D policies and organizations since the state divestitures occurred. In this section we analyse those changes along four dimensions that are particularly critical to the management of R&D activities:

- the role and mission of the corporate R&D organizations;
- the size of the corporate R&D organizations;
- the composition and funding of the corporate R&D portfolio;
- the valorization of research results.

4.1   A New Mission for R&D

In all cases, privatization has led to a clear redefinition of the nature and the strategic role of R&D activities within the company, as clearly shown in Table 7.2, reporting the mission assigned to the corporate R&D centres before and after state divestment. Under state control, the mission of the R&D units in most cases was explicitly to pursue national interest goals, such as those of strengthening the technological base of the country and supporting its economic growth. Generally speaking, therefore, the attitude towards R&D activities within the government-controlled companies is likely to be more permissive with regard to R&D's possible contributions to the public good, favouring not only business-specific objectives, but also broader national goals. As a consequence, under state control the R&D units investigated tended in many ways to operate like national laboratories, partly guaranteed by the availability of secure and stable funding. This was especially true for those public utilities operating in a monopoly regime, consistent with the belief that it was part of the public nature of the organization to sustain a sizeable R&D programme.

Table 7.2   The mission of corporate R&D units before and after privatization

	Mission	
	Before privatization	After privatization
Telecom Italia Lab	'The company founded the "Centro di Ricerca e Laboratori" with the aim of monitoring systematically the technological developments and the most useful applications for the technical and economic interests of the country'.	'A centre of strategic importance for the identification, development and integration of innovative solutions for new ICT services, which become competititve key factors and value generating components for the Telecom Italia Group'.
CSM	'To promote and coordinate research activities in metallurgy and steel production and to provide a centre of excellence in these fields for the country as a whole, proactively promoting technology transfer to the industry and knowledge transfer to the universities'.	'An independent company operating in the business of promoting and selling research capabilities to the steel industry'.
Enel R&D	'To support studies and research projects promoting the technical and scientific progress of the Italian electricity system, and the increased efficiency and reliability in electricity production, transmission and distribution'.	'To contribute directly to company competitiveness focusing on innovative solutions for the sustainable production, transmission and distribution of electricity'.
France Télécom R&D	'To cover every aspect of communication technology and pass on research results that may be of general interest to other ministerial departments, the scientific community and French industry'.	'One mission: to innovate in the present to build a winning future for France Télécom through the value of its research'.
Irsid	'The state acknowledges the central role of French steel research... If France wants to place itself in the global steel market, it is necessary to invest in research'.	'The main role of Irsid is to enhance the competitiveness of Usinor.'
Renault R&D	'The research unit was created to establish a bridge towards external research institutions: it was intended to be a window on academic research'.	'Today its mission is threefold: to help attain the strategic objectives of the group; to introduce innovation into new products and services; to develop knowledge in new technologies'.

Sources: Company reports CSM, Cselt, Enitecnologie, Enel, CNET-FT R&D, Irsid (various years). For Renault R&D: Beuzit (2000).

In contrast, following privatization the company has no longer any implicit or explicit interest in promoting public welfare or the general good of the industry, by carrying out research programmes that may well go far beyond its own immediate business needs. Accordingly, there emerges a new role for R&D: that of directly contributing the generation of added value for the business units and for the company's final customers, as we can see from all the quotations reported in Table 7.2. The shift from social objectives to more business-oriented ones is particularly evident in the cases of France Télécom R&D – the former CNET – and of Irsid in France, which were both created at the end of Second World War as public research centres with the goal of supporting the technological and economic growth of the national industries. Only many years later – Irsid in 1986 and CNET in 1991 – were they incorporated into Usinor and France Télécom as corporate R&D centres, and recent restructuring actions have explicitly stressed that their only mission is now one of generating value for the company.

Thus, under the pressures of profit-oriented new shareholders and of more competitive markets, R&D is increasingly turning into an investment that must be justified by the additional returns it generates. All the organizations investigated adopted different communicative and symbolic actions in order to define their new priorities and to stress the need for a major cultural change. For example, in the cases of France Télécom and Telecom Italia, the decision to change the name of the corporate R&D centres after privatization was motivated mainly by the desire to emphasize the new orientation towards the market and to clearly stress the discontinuity with their former nature of public laboratories. The redefinition of the R&D role and mission we have so far described bears important implications on both the scale and the composition of R&D activities, as will be highlighted in the following subsections.

4.2   The Scale of R&D Activities

The most evident and striking phenomenon that characterizes all the cases examined regards the reduction in resources devoted to R&D that closely precedes or follows the divestiture of the state. At the time of the divestiture, and sometimes in the run-up to the sale, R&D facilities were affected by substantial restructuring, which in some cases (CSM and Enel) was extremely dramatic, even involving the reconsideration of the very existence of the R&D units within the companies. Such a restructuring can be captured by observing the decreasing levels of R&D personnel and of the R&D budget before and after privatization, as reported in Table 7.3.

This phenomenon needs to be carefully interpreted in terms of its possible determinants and main outcomes, both from the company and the public point of view. As suggested by the studies into the effects of corporate restructuring on R&D investments (Hall, 1990a; 1994), the crucial question is whether the resulting reduction affects activities and projects of potential long-term value for the company (projects cut in an effort to reduce costs and achieve quicker results), or if it is just the result of the elimination of waste and inefficiencies leading to a better use of resources. In the latter case, rationalization should be considered positive for the company, since it ultimately leads to higher economic returns for each currency unit invested in R&D, whereas in the former case it risks weakening the company's technological capabilities in the long run, and should therefore be considered not optimal, even though it may lead to apparent efficiency gains in the short run. Moreover, it is important to reflect on the potential effects of the observed reduction, at both the private level of the company and at the social level of the collective good. Since the seminal contributions of Arrow (1962) and Nelson (1959), many studies have highlighted the gap existing between the private and social rates of returns on R&D activities – the latter being significantly higher – a phenomenon that can lead to substantial risks of underinvestment in research activities by private firms (Mansfield et al., 1977; Romer, 1990).

Table 7.3   The reduction in R&D resources after privatization[a]

R&D unit	R&D personnel		Researchers/ Total R&D personnel		R&D budget[b]	
	Pre	Post	Pre	Post	Pre	Post
Telecom Italia Lab	1 206	1 183	78%	79%	255	284.60
CSM	550	340	80%	91%	98.97	68.7
Enel R&D	960				2.2%	1.8%
France Télécom R&D	4 300	3 700			3000	
Irsid	802	526	33%	41%	367	280
Renault R&D	327	357	59%	62%		400

Notes:
a) The values reported in columns 'Pre' and 'Post' refer to average values for the three years preceding and the three years following privatization.
b) R&D budget data are expressed in current billions of lire for the Italian companies and in millions of French francs for the French ones. For Enel it refers to R&D/Sales ratio.

Sources: Company reports CSM, Cselt, Enitecnologie, Enel, CNET-FT R&D, Irsid, Renault (various years).

It should be stressed that, in itself, the analysis of the six cases does not permit any generalization, but it can help to define some possible complementary explanations, summarized in Figure 7.1, which future research should investigate in more depth. As a first explanation, adopting a public choice theory perspective (Buchanan, 1972; Niskanen, 1971) we may suggest that the reduction observed is largely due to the elimination of the inefficiencies inherent in public enterprises. This was certainly true for all the cases analysed, since the contraction of the R&D personnel concerned mainly the administrative positions, so that the ratio of researchers to total personnel generally increased. The same data suggest that a process of reskilling of the human capital generally accompanied the restructuring. Those observations are consistent with the more general results of the literature on the economic effects of privatization, which showed, on average, higher productivity levels in the use of resources after divestiture (Megginson et al., 1994; D'Souza and Megginson, 1999), as well as with the studies documenting a higher administrative burden in public research laboratories than in private ones (Bozeman and Loveless, 1987; Emmert and Crow, 1988).

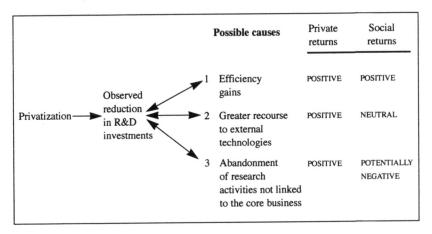

Figure 7.1   Explaining the reduction in R&D investments after privatization: causes and consequences

As a second explanation of the reduction observed, the cases examined suggest a greater recourse to external sources of technology, mainly involving activities which are important and valuable for the company, but that can be equally well, or even better, performed by external subjects, to be acquired and integrated at a later stage. In this case, it is not necessary for the privatized company to keep performing such activities in-house, as they can be more effectively performed by other public or private sources, which can benefit, for example, from economies of scale or specialization. In the case of the utilities in the sample, this was the case for the research activities regarding hardware systems and components, which were progressively delegated to the equipment manufacturers. Both France Télécom R&D and Cselt, for example, historically undertook research on hardware technologies – for example in the fields of microelectronics or optoelectronics – which, in more recent years, have gradually been abandoned and left to the telecommunication equipment manufacturers, in order to concentrate resources on more service and application-oriented activities. In this case, rationalization can be interpreted as a positive factor from the company point of view, if we assume that it possesses the absorptive capability needed to successfully integrate and use the technologies provided by external sources (Cohen and Levinthal, 1990). At the same time, it can be regarded as neutral from the social point of view, since the abandoned research activities continue to be undertaken by other actors.

Third, the reduction in R&D investments may be ascribed to the abandonment of research activities which are not directly linked to the companies' core business, but derive from historical diversification processes driven by social or political objectives under state ownership, such as the aim of supporting national industries in crisis or the country's underdeveloped areas. In this case, at least from the private (the company's) point of view, rationalization should be considered as a positive factor, since it focuses the allocation of limited resources on the firm's core activities. However, a critical situation arises when the abandoned R&D activities, of limited interest for the company at least in the short term, but important in a more general sense for the industry or for society as a whole, are not undertaken by other subjects. In this case their abandonment can have a negative impact on the social welfare. A typical situation of market failure then emerges, and the intervention of the state should be requested, in forms differing from ownership and control. The experience of the Enel group in Italy provides a very interesting example of this kind of risky situation, with the decision of the former monopolist to focus its R&D effort on the field of electricity generation (the so-called 'competitive research'), abandoning the so-called 'system research', regarding the environment, the transmission network or the final use of electricity. To this purpose, the crucial task for policy makers becomes one of identifying the most appropriate instrument of industrial policy, different from ownership and control, in order to address the peculiar kind of market failure emerging from privatization and liberalization processes and to counterbalance the risks of underinvestment in those R&D activities that are crucial to social welfare.

Moreover, it is important to stress that both our interviews and the companies' annual reports strongly emphasized the impact of liberalization in explaining the rationalization process, particularly in the case of public utilities that had acted in a monopolistic regime under state ownership. Changes in the ownership structure are, therefore, only one among the many factors leading to a change in the managerial incentive system and, hence, in the decisions on how to allocate the resources, which are also generally contingent upon competition and regulation (Vickers and Yarrow, 1988). In the regulated monopolies (telecommunication and energy), tariffs tend to be set on a 'cost-plus' basis, so that R&D expenditures are essentially regarded as fixed costs. As the intensity of competition increases, R&D becomes more and more an investment that must be justified by the additional return it is likely to generate. The discipline of the markets implies that managers are increasingly obliged to ask themselves what returns they are getting, or are likely to get, from their R&D expenditures. Moreover, the market itself determines the benchmark for defining the kind of returns that the company must get on its R&D investment, depending on market-determined tariffs and revenues.

Finally, the cases investigated clearly showed that restructuring was more profound and dramatic in those companies operating in low-technology industries (steel and energy), where there are fewer possibilities of reshaping competition by generating new technological breakthroughs, whereas in the high-tech industries (telecommunication) the change was definitely milder and more gradual, thus suggesting that the level of technological opportunities in the industry can strongly influence managers' decisions to reduce, or not, their R&D commitment.

4.3   The Composition and Funding of R&D Activities

Long-term research becomes extremely vulnerable in the restructuring process following privatization. When they were under state ownership, all the organizations studied clearly used to allocate substantial funds, probably excessive if compared with industry averages, to long-term research projects and to make huge commitments to scientific and downstream activities that were often loosely coupled with the direct needs of their main businesses. After the divestiture by the state, all the companies reduced the allocation of resources to long-term activities and defined a more balanced allocation towards applied research and development. The pressures of competition further encouraged such a shift: basic science studies became less numerous and were scaled back in scope to match more closely the areas of core competency. In the cases of Cselt and France Télécom R&D, for example, in recent years a lot of emphasis has been put on the development of new services and applications as a way of confronting increasing levels of competition and of standing out from the new competitors. In this sense, newly privatized firms were forced to conform to a more general cycle in industrial R&D in the 1990s, characterized by a steadily increasing focus on development issues at the expense of longer-term fundamental or basic research (Roberts, 1995,

2001; Rosenbloom and Spencer, 1996). The cases suggest also that external relationships typically become a way of substituting for the traditional internal base, especially in those areas affected by a long-term or fundamental orientation. In general, most of the companies analysed tend to rely increasingly upon external organizations for basic research activities, in particular to universities, as a way of maintaining an open window on new scientific and technological development.

Moreover, the pre-privatization era was typically characterized by a predominance of corporate-level funds, in line with a view of R&D as a fixed cost and with the belief that it was part of the public nature of the organization to sustain a sizeable programme of R&D. All the organizations studied illustrate a clear shift towards an increase in the portion of the budget funded by the operating units and the creation of an internal market among the research divisions and the operating units. Moving the budget towards the business units has the advantage of providing a good market test for the selection of research projects, of facilitating technology transfer and of leveraging business-unit resources, but it can lead to substantial risks of missing future technological opportunities by pursuing an excessively short-term outlook. However, none of the managers interviewed expressed any concern that this reorientation might undermine the technological capabilities of the firm in the long run. Changing the balance of the R&D budgeting is only one of the options that argues in favour of turning research more toward products and services: all the organizations studied have implemented different organizational solutions to strengthen their links with the business divisions. For example, in the last two years, all the organizations have adopted various measures to link more tightly their R&D division to the needs of the operating units, such as cross-functional teams, boundary spanning roles, inter-functional career paths, or incentive systems based on technology transfer indicators.

4.4 The Valorization of Research Results

Both the interviews and the analysis of the annual reports highlighted, in all of the cases, a drive to get an economic return from research results. As stated above, mostly during the pre-privatization period, the funding of R&D activities was almost exclusively an internal issue and there were almost no incentives to exploit the research results commercially. On the other hand, as the national interest goals disappeared after privatization and the intensity of competition increased with the opening-up of the market, the effective valorization of the technological capital became a major concern.

As to this point, a privileged area of intervention regarded the protection and commercialization of intellectual property rights, which partially emerged also from an examination of the data on patent productivity reported in Table 7.4:

the number of patents assigned per researcher in most of the cases increased in the period following privatization, suggesting that patent productivity had not been slowed down by the dramatic restructuring that in general affected the R&D units, but in many cases it had increased. It should be stressed that the companies studied may have simply been conforming to a more general trend in the industry, given that the attention to the protection of intellectual property rights has increased dramatically in many countries and industries in the last decade (Jaffe, 2000). However, from our case study it emerged quite clearly that, under state ownership, less attention was paid to the control mechanisms against information leakage and know-how spillovers, as a consequence of the R&D organizations' status as national laboratories. As a consequence of the mandate to diffuse the results of their own technological base in order to contribute to the national wealth, within public-owned enterprises such laboratories were less concerned with the tight and exclusive control and appropriability of their innovative outcome. Acting as national laboratories, these institutions had a mandate – implicit or explicit – to inter-act with other national research institution, such as universities, research agencies, equipment providers, and to diffuse their knowledge base.

Table 7.4   Patent productivity before and after privatization

Corporate R&D unit	Assigned patents		Patents per researcher (*100)	
	Pre	Post[a]	Pre	Post[a]
Telecom Italia Lab[b]	7.33	9	0.77	0.96
CSM	38	36	8.6	11.4
Enel R&D				
France Télécom R&D	147	149	3.4	4
Irsid	20.33	12	7.5	5.5
Renault R&D	32	55	16	25

Notes:
a) The reported values in columns 'Pre' and 'Post' refer to the average values for the three years preceding and the three years following privatization. Patents data refer to the total number of patents assigned to the companies.
b) For Telecom Italia Lab, they refer to the number of patents assigned at the USPTO.

Sources: Company reports CSM, Cselt, Enitecnologie, Enel, CNET-FT R&D, Irsid, Renault (various years).

The role of leader and nurturer emerges in its highest form in the case of CNET, whose policy was that of involving industrial partners, from very early stages, in the development process, and often to transfer to them the property rights of the inventions. As a consequence, at the beginning of the 1990s, CNET held less than 10 per cent of all the French patents in the telecommunication area, while the manufacturers held about 80 per cent (Chesnais, 1993). This policy has consistently changed over the years following privatization, when different actions have been adopted to increase the researchers' propensity to patent and the firm's capabilities to commercialize their research results. In some cases, the change in priorities and orientation was also reflected in the characteristics of the incentives and in the systems adopted for rewarding researchers, as these shifted towards more market-oriented models that are typical of the privately-owned enterprises. The number of patents produced thus becomes a direct and objective indicator to measure the productivity of the research personnel and the effectiveness of the process of developing new inventions of potential economic value.

Moreover, both France Télécom and Telecom Italia have introduced, over the last few years, different actions to favour the scientists and engineers who decided to set up their own business, as a way of more effectively exploiting the research conducted in their laboratories, at the same time promoting the rapid development of their technologies. The creation of start-ups can bring consistent advantages to the high-technology-based industries, such as accelerating the introduction on the market of the related products or technologies, enabling the group to make early use of the products or services developed by the new companies, and generating positive deal flows. In this sense, both companies have identified as a strategic priority the exploitation of the potential synergies stemming from the integration of their traditional research capabilities in the fields of communication and information technologies with the ability to identify and fund new business opportunities through corporate venture capital activities.

5.   CONCLUSIONS

The results of this study make it possible to clarify the processes of organizational change taking place within the R&D units of companies facing privatization and liberalization processes, a topic so far largely ignored in the literature. The six cases analysed suggest that privatization represents a significant break in the way R&D activities are considered and managed. The most striking effect we highlighted regards a substantial restructuring and scaling-down of R&D facilities following the change in their mission towards a more direct contribution to the creation of value for the company and the new private shareholders. We argued that this rationalization can be explained mainly by a reduction in inefficiencies and overhead resources and by the abandonment of projects not directly linked to the core business of the firms, but in some cases this can lead to situations of market failures and research underinvestment in terms of social good, with the result that a state intervention may be required to counterbalance such risks. The organizations studied also showed a clear shift towards increasing the proportion of the budget funded by the business units and towards the creation of an internal market for R&D. This generally made the companies focus on those technological capabilities more directly meeting their business needs, while increasingly prompting them to access external sources of innovation, especially for longer-term activities. In addition, the cases showed an increased orientation towards the economic exploitation of research results after privatization, with more attention being paid to issues of intellectual property protection and commercialization, which may bring to a rise in the number of patents produced per researcher.

Of course, these changes do not occur overnight, but they typically require a long and sometimes difficult restructuring process that can last several years and generally starts well before the company is actually sold. The experiences of the organizations studied showed that this is indeed a very difficult and risky task for the management, in particular with respect to two aspects: the importance of reskilling the human resources employed in the R&D units in a way that could best match the restructuring process, and the need to effectively communicate the reasons for change, and to adequately motivate the research personnel to face this challenge. A main challenge to be addressed within the R&D units is one of a cultural nature, a matter of shifting from one set of norms and values typical of the public sector to a new one, oriented towards the creation of value for the company and its private shareholders. Consequently, it becomes important to invest an adequate amount of time and resources to communicating and disseminating the new set of priorities, for example by adopting high-profile symbolic actions such as the change in the purpose of the R&D unit or of its name, as in the case of France Télécom and Telecom Italia.

Finally, both the Italian and the French companies seemed to share many commonalities in the processes of organizational change that occurred around privatization. However, although it is not possible to draw any definitive conclusion as to the potential differences in the private and the social long-term consequences of privatization in the two countries, an interesting observation can be made from the comparison of the experiences of Telecom Italia and France Télécom, in particular with respect to the consequences of the diverse governance structures emerging after the sale. Telecom Italia faced several difficulties in the post-privatization period, leading to the undervaluation of the stock value and to the hostile takeover successfully undertaken by Olivetti, largely due to the weaknesses of the stable core of shareholders that had been constituted and to the disputes arising between the management and the principals (there were three different CEOs in the period between the public offer and the takeover). It is likely that all these uncertainties may have delayed the actions necessary to restructure the company, also as far as R&D activities were concerned. Our evidence suggests that, for privatization to deliver improvements in firm performance, a fundamental precondition is the creation of effective corporate governance structures. The literature on privatization has already stressed that the speed and effectiveness of the restructuring process necessary to adapt to the new environment are likely to be highly dependent on how SOEs are privatized, in particular with regard to the government's residual ownership after privatization, to the kind of private capital they attract, and to the degree of ownership concentration (Dyck, 1999; Megginson et al., 1994; Ramamurti, 2000). In particular, these considerations highlight the importance of considering how the different forms of governance and ownership systems may influence management incentive to promote innovation and their ultimate consequences in terms of entrepreneurial and innovative outcomes. In this sense, the relationship between corporate governance mechanisms and structures, on the one hand, and innovation on the other hand appears to be an area rich with fruitful opportunities for researchers, in particular with respect to European or non-US countries and in the specific case of firms facing privatization processes.

NOTES

1. Stet (Società Torinese Esercizi Telefonici) was formed in 1933 as a finance company under the state-owned conglomerate Iri, to take over control of the three private Italian phone companies demerged from Sip Elettrica (Stipel, Timo and Telve), which were then facing deep financial crisis. In the 1950–58 period Stet incorporated the two remaining major local telephone companies, Teti and Set. In 1964 Stet unified the five local operators in the newly-established Sip (Società Idroelettrica Piemontese) and undertook a relevant plan of renewal and modernization of the national telephonic network.

    In 1994, Telecom Italia was formed as an operating unit of Stet, by merging four Italian telecommunication companies, including Sip. In 1997, after the merger of the holding Stet and its operating unit Telecom Italia and the approval by the Italian Parliament of the law establishing the Telecommunication Authority, approximately 35 per cent of Telecom Italia shares were sold through a public offer concluded with 2.2 more applications than the available shares, generating revenues of about 26 000 billion lire, thus resulting in the largest single privatization operation ever carried out in Europe. A core group of shareholders was formed equivalent to 6.6 per cent of the share capital, with the goal 'to ensure stability of control, with a plurality of actors and no dominant position'.

    However, the corporate governance structure that emerged from the privatization proved to be extremely weak and unstable, and in 1999 the company was subject to a hostile takeover led by Olivetti/Tecnost. In February 1999, Olivetti launched a public tender offer for 100 per cent of Telecom Italia's share capital and three months later its takeover bid was successfully concluded, obtaining 51.02 per cent of Telecom Italia's share capital and the total control of the company. In July 2002, the Italian tyre and cable maker Pirelli, in a deal with the Benetton family's Edizione Holding, took over as the controlling shareholder of Olivetti, giving it effective control of Telecom Italia as well.

2.   During 2000, Telecom Italia implemented a wide-ranging divestment of participation in companies operating in non-strategic businesses. In December, it sold 80.1 per cent of Italtel, the company specializing in manufacturing and communication device systems, to a group of investors led by Clayton, Dubilier & Rice Inc. and by Cisco Systems. In November 2000 it sold 49.095 per cent of Sirti to a group consisting of Techint, Stella International, 21 Investimenti Interbanca and 3I, under a public offer that generated revenues of 314 billion lire.

3.   This section is based on Munari (2002).

PART III

The Economic Value of R&D Activities

8. A Meta-analytic Study of the Relationship between R&D Investments and Corporate Value

Raffaele Oriani and Maurizio Sobrero

1. INTRODUCTION

The theoretical and empirical work presented in the previous chapters examined in detail several different aspects of the relationship between corporate governance, market structure and innovation activities. All the contributions were developed under the assumption that the technological knowledge created through R&D investments represents the engine of innovation both for the firm and for the economic system in general. As a consequence, the previous chapters were focused on the input side (R&D levels and investments), as indirect measures of the actual final output (innovations exploited in the market), and of its economic impact.

A stream of empirical literature drawing from the fields of industrial organization and financial economics, however, has coped with these questions extensively, investigating the relationship between measures of the firm's technological capital, based on R&D investments, and the performance of the firm, measured by stock market indicators (see Hall, 1999a, for a review). Different methodologies were adopted. Some focused on the levels, analysing the relationship between the capitalization of R&D or patents and the firm's market value at a given time (Griliches, 1981; Cockburn and Griliches, 1988; Jaffe, 1986; Hall, 1993a, 1993b, among others), whereas others observed the long-run stock returns associated with R&D-based measures (Pakes, 1985; Lev and Sougiannis, 1996, 1999; Chan et al., 1999, among others) or short-term market value adjustments following corporate announcements on R&D activity (Chan et al., 1990; Woolridge and Snow, 1990; Doukas and Switzer, 1992, among others).

The application of different methodologies to the problem of market valuation of R&D investments led to results that not always coincide. In fact, even though all the analyses generally show a positive effect of technological assets on firms' market value, some further questions have not yet found a clear answer. First, the market valuation of R&D investments is erratic. In particular, equilibrium models based on hedonic regression show that the rate of return to R&D activity seems volatile over time and across industries or technological clusters (Cockburn and Griliches, 1988; Jaffe, 1986; Hall, 1993a, 1993b). Second, it is not certain that market valuation fully reflects future benefits from R&D investments. In this respect, the authors who analysed the relationship between R&D capital and stock returns found that, after controlling for several firm-specific characteristics (such as size and market-to-book ratio), R&D-intensive companies have higher returns, suggesting that the R&D capital could be systematically underestimated (Lev and Sougiannis, 1996, 1999; Chan et al., 1999). In addition, all the studies are based on US data, with the exception of a few studies on British companies (Green et al., 1996; Toivanen and Stoneman, 1998; Blundell et al., 1999), while no comprehensive analysis exists for other European countries, where the structure of financial markets is significantly different.

This and the following chapters will complete the analysis of the relations between corporate governance, market structure and innovation by founding theoretically and examining empirically the effects of the R&D activity on the firm's economic performance. This chapter presents a meta-analysis of the empirical literature linking R&D investments and firm performance and assesses the magnitude of the reported coefficients against three potential moderating factors: the time window used in the study, the reliability of the independent variable and the reliability of the dependent variable. Applying the Hunter and Schmidt correction procedures on all the published studies and using hedonic models to estimate the impact of different corporate assets on the firm's market value, we shall show that such a relationship is consistently positive. Significant differences in the size of the effect emerge, however, depending on the period of observation, while the concerns commonly raised on empirical indicators such as Tobin's q or R&D investment measures find no empirical support. Chapters 9 and 10 will build on these results to further examine how privatization processes and dedicated funding sources, such as stock markets focused on highly innovative start-ups, intervene to mediate these relationships.

2.   THEORETICAL BACKGROUND

The study of the relationship between innovation-related investments and firm economic performance is characterized by specific problems related to the measurement of the phenomena observed. Such measurement problems are strictly connected with the resolution of wider theoretical issues. In this section, therefore, we shall start by discussing the theoretical frames lying behind alternative measurement choices, focusing first on the measurement of technological knowledge, and then moving to the use of market value as a measure of a firm's economic performance. We shall then present the different classes of models used in empirical studies to test such theoretical assumptions, focusing in particular on a subset whose evidence will be drawn together in the empirical section.

2.1   The Measurement of Technological Knowledge

The concept of knowledge capital is broad and difficult to define from an empirical point of view. There are, indeed, different types and levels of knowledge that it would be virtually impossible to aggregate into one single index (Griliches, 1995). Moreover, such knowledge is embodied in different instruments, such as people, procedures and systems (Leonard-Barton, 1992), and, furthermore, it is seldom codified (Nonaka and Takeuchi, 1995; Zander and Kogut, 1995). Nevertheless, if the definition of comprehensive measures for this complex and intangible asset can sound too presumptuous, it is possi-ble to assess the contribution of identified investments in advancing the state of knowledge in some given areas. In particular, we can refer to R&D activity, which is one of the main internal sources of knowledge cre-ation. Consistently with this interpretation, Griliches (1995) defined the following formal relationship between a firm's stock of technological knowledge and R&D investments:

$$K = G \left[W(B) \, R, \, \mathrm{v} \right] \qquad (8.1)$$

where K is the current level of technological knowledge, $W(B) \, R$ is an index of current and past R&D expenditures and v is a set of unmeasured influences on the accumulated level of knowledge. From this perspective, R&D invest-ments will add value if they are able to generate an intangible asset, that is the stock of technological knowledge (Griliches, 1981). Accordingly, under the assumption of a linear aggregation function with a constant depreciation rate, a measure of a firm's technological knowledge can be more precisely computed as the capitalization of present and past R&D expenditures in the following way (Griliches and Mairesse, 1984; Hall, 1990b):

$$K_t = (1 - \delta) \, K_{t-1} + R_t \qquad (8.2)$$

where K_t is the R&D capital at time t, R_t is the amount of annual R&D expen-diture at time t and δ is the depreciation rate of the R&D capital from year

$t - 1$ to year t. The use of (8.2) to capitalize R&D investments is needed because the generally accepted accounting principles (GAAP) require R&D costs to be written off as expenses when incurred because of the lack of a clear link with subsequent earnings (Lev and Sougiannis, 1996). The use of a depreciation rate is justified by the decay of knowledge over time (Argote et al., 1990) and by the loss of economic value due to advances in technology. Most of the studies analysed in this chapter used a constant annual 15 per cent depreciation rate (Jaffe, 1986; Cockburn and Griliches, 1988; Hall, 1993a, 1993b). Other studies adopting a different approach that is not reviewed in this chapter used an estimation procedure that allows industry and time-specific economic depreciation rates to be determined (Lev and Sougiannis, 1996, 1999)[1] Moreover, some studies also used the annual R&D investments as an alternative to the R&D capital (Cockburn and Griliches, 1988; Hall, 1993a, 1993b; Hall and Vopel, 1996), because of the persistence over time of R&D investments at firm level shown by previous empirical research (Hall et al., 1986).

However, the use of R&D-based measures does not definitively answer the questions related to the measurement of technological knowledge. Some problems still persist. First, the quality of corporate financial reporting on R&D activity and intangibles in general is often inadequate for economic analysis purposes (Lev, 2001). R&D investments become, from this perspective, a source of greater information asymmetries, as confirmed by the evidence that insider gains are larger for R&D-intensive firms (Aboody and Lev, 2000). Second, national accounting laws often do not require the corporations to disclose the amount of their annual R&D expenditures. For example, in the European Union, the United Kingdom is one of the few countries where quantitative disclosure of R&D investments is compulsory, while in France, Germany and Italy there is only an obligation concerning R&D qualitative information (KPMG, 1995; Belcher, 1996).

Finally, there is a problem related to the nature of R&D investments that would exist even if the reporting were effective. R&D investments are not an output, but an *input* measure of innovation processes. In addition, the link between R&D activity and firm performance is quite fuzzy, because it is very difficult to assign R&D inputs and outputs to specific products at firm level (Hall, 1999a). In fact, the significance of innovation for competition primarily depends on its capacity to influence the firm's resources, skills and knowledge (Abernathy and Clark, 1985). Only secondarily is there an effect on the firm's products and processes (Clark, 1987). Moreover, the outcomes of R&D projects are highly uncertain (Abernathy and Clark, 1985; Dixit and Pindyck, 1994; McGrath, 1997; Huchzermeier and Loch, 2001). In particular, Encaoua et al. (2000) distinguished among three types of uncertainty that are relevant to the analysis of profits from R&D investments: technological uncertainty (related to the attainment of a discovery and its transformation into viable industrial and commercial projects); strategic uncertainty (arising from the fact that a company allocating funds to a specific R&D project is never sure that it will be the first mover and will benefit from it); and market uncertainty (concerning the actual presence of buyers for the innovation).

Several studies considered patent-based measures of technological knowledge in order to overcome these problems. However, the use of the raw count of the firm's patents has a very low explanatory power, as the value of the patents has a very skewed distribution, many patents having no value and very few patents being of great worth (Griliches et al., 1987). Some recent analyses have tried to correct this shortcoming by weighing the count of patents through the number of forward citations the patents receive by following patents (Hall et al., 2000; Bloom and Van Reenen, 2000). In fact, any patent cites the previous patents that represent the prior state of the art. Therefore, the number of citations a patent receives can reasonably be considered an indicator of its technological strength (Jaffe et al., 2000).

However, these studies are very recent and their small number makes them unsuitable for a meta-analytic investigation. Therefore, we shall focus on the analyses using R&D-based measures, which represent a broader field of study. From this perspective, the testing of their limits in representing firms' knowledge stock becomes another important aim of our meta-analysis.

2.2 Measurement of a Firm's Economic Performance

In order to empirically test the relationship between technological knowledge and a firm's economic results we first have to choose a performance indicator. A possible approach is to consider the relationship between innovative activities and measures of accounting profits (for example, McEvily and Chakravarthy, 1999). Nevertheless, these methods have limits embedded in the very nature of the accounting indicators. First, the existence of uncertain time lags between R&D investments and the subsequent effects on the firm's economic performance can cause accounting measures not to gauge the effects beyond the considered time horizon (Hall, 1999a). Second, the accounting rate of returns significantly depends on the different accounting practices and standards and, even when properly determined, it is seldom representative of the *economic* rate of return (Fisher and McGowan, 1983). Finally, accounting criteria underestimate the value of R&D investments, stemming mostly from the creation of future growth opportunities (McGrath, 1997).

Alternatively, it is possible to use methods relating measures of technological knowledge to the market value of the company. According to valuation theory, the market capitalization of a firm is the sum of two elements: the net present value of the cash flows expected from the assets in place and the net present value of the cash flows stemming from investment opportunities the firm is expected to undertake in the future (Myers, 1977; Woolridge and Snow, 1990; Berk et al., 1999; Jagle, 1999). Therefore, the use of market-based indicators theoretically allows an assessment of the effects of R&D investments both on the cash flows from assets in place and on the creation of new growth opportunities for the future. Consistently, stock-market-based measures of economic performance have the fundamental advantage, compared to accounting measures, of being forward looking (Hall, 1999a; Bharadwaj et al., 1999). In particular, Tobin's q, that is, the ratio of the market value of a firm's assets to their replacement cost, presents several especially attractive theoretical features: it implicitly uses the correct cash flow risk-adjusted discounted rate, it imputes equilibrium returns and it minimizes the distortions due to tax laws and different accounting standards (Lindenberg and Ross, 1981; Montgomery and Wernerfelt, 1988).

Tobin's q has also, however, several limitations, which are essentially related to the calculation of the market value of corporate debt. In fact, the Tobin's q numerator is the total market value of the firm, given by the sum of the market value of equity and the market value of debt. However, while a firm's equity is traded on stock markets and the data on its valuation are available daily, there are no comparable measures for *debt* valuation, because not all firms issue bonds on the financial markets. Some studies based on US data tried to define some proxies based on the information drawn by the US corporate bond market (for example, Hall, 1990b). However, these measures are unsuitable for capturing firm-specific risk factors affecting the value of corporate debt. Other studies on UK data just add the outstanding value of debt to the market capitalization of the firm (Blundell et al., 1992, 1999), as European corporate bond markets are of a much smaller size than in the US.

The use of market-based measures of performance clearly requires some assumptions on the way financial markets work. In particular, it builds on the statement of stock market informational efficiency, implying that security prices fully reflect all the information available (Fama, 1970, 1991). Fama (1970) identified three distinct degrees of market efficiency, corresponding to different relevant information subsets: the weak form, where the information set consists only of historical prices; the semi-strong form, where prices adjust to other information that is, obviously, publicly available, such as public announcements or the like; and the strong form, where some given investors have access to all of the information relevant for price determination. These definitions imply the precondition that information has no cost. However, it is possible to give a definition of market efficiency even in the presence of costly information. In this case, security prices reflect all the available information to the point where the marginal benefits of acting on information do not exceed the marginal costs (Jensen, 1978). Even though the debate is still open, there is robust empirical evidence supporting the efficiency hypothesis (Fama, 1970, 1991; Woolridge and Snow, 1990).

The assumption of market efficiency has several important implications for our analysis. In particular, it justifies two fundamental conditions that the studies analysed in this chapter build on. First, the market capitalization of a firm can be considered a reasonable proxy of its value. Moreover, it changes if – and only if – the stock market receives new (either general or firm-specific) information that modifies investors' expectations about the cash flows from its current and future assets (Pakes, 1985; Woolridge and Snow, 1990). Consequently, if R&D investments create an intangible capital likely to generate current and future cash flows, they will affect the market valuation of the firm (Griliches, 1981). Second, stockholders agree that all decisions, including investments involving long-run pay-offs, should be evaluated according to their contribution to the market value of their residual claims (Fama and Jensen, 1985). Therefore, managers are constrained by the stock market to make investment choices aimed at the maximization of the corporate value. Under those conditions, it is possible to assume that both its R&D programmes and its other investment policies are maximizing the present value of the firm's future cash flows (Pakes, 1985; Hall, 1993b).

2.3 Empirical Approaches

Several authors have already tested the effects of different types of investments in innovation on firm-level performance measures based on the stock market. In a recent study, this set of contributions has been analysed and divided into three groups according to the estimation methodology adopted (Oriani, 2002). The first group examined the relationship between R&D investments and their contemporary or subsequent stock returns, trying to verify whether the stock market had correctly evaluated the corporate innovation activities. From this perspective, if the assumption about market efficiency discussed in the previous subsection holds, and the market does indeed provide a correct valuation of the expected cash flows stemming from a firm's current and future activities, in a given time the excess rate of return should equal the percentage increase in the discounted value of those cash flows caused by the arrival in that time of new information on corporate activity (Pakes, 1985). Therefore, the possible negative or positive abnormal returns are due to the previous mispricing of several corporate assets, R&D investments included (Lev and Sougiannis, 1996, 1999; Chan et al., 1999).

The second group was based on the event study methodology, broadly used for the analysis of strategic and investment decisions (McConnell and Muscarella, 1985; Mohanram and Nanda, 1996; Chan et al., 1997; Das et al., 1998; Bajo et al., 1998, among others), which relates corporate announcements of R&D programme revisions to the stock returns in the days preceding or following the announcement. From this perspective, under the assumption of naive investor expectations about the firm's R&D expenditures, that is, a forecast of no change from the previous fiscal year, new information implying a change in R&D plans should lead to a revision in expectations about future earnings and hence to a change in stock price (Woolridge and Snow, 1990; Chan et al., 1990).

Finally, the third group of studies focused on the analysis of the relationship between different measures of a firm's knowledge capital and market value at a given moment in time, in a way more similar to the theoretical and empirical observations developed in the following sections. Therefore, this is the stream of literature we decided to concentrate on.

The studies analysing the relationship between knowledge stock and market value implicitly or explicitly assumed that a firm is evaluated by the stock market as a bundle of tangible and intangible assets (Griliches, 1981; Hall, 1999a). In equilibrium, the market valuation of any asset results from the interaction between a firms' demand for investment and the market supply of capital for that specific asset (Hall, 1993b). It is possible to represent the market value V of firm i at time t as a function of its assets (Hall, 1999a):

$$V_{it} = V\left(A_{it},\ K_{it},\ I^1{}_{it},\ \ldots,\ I^n{}_{it}\right) \tag{8.3}$$

where A_{it} is the book value of tangible assets, K_{it} is the replacement value of the firm's technological knowledge and $I^j{}_{it}$ is the replacement value of the jth intangible asset (with $j = 1, \ldots, n$). If single assets are purely additive, it is possible to express the market value of the firm as a multiple of its assets (Griliches, 1981):

$$V_{it} = b\left(A_{it} + \gamma K_{it}\right)^\sigma \tag{8.4}$$

where b is the market valuation coefficient of firm's total assets reflecting its differential risk and monopoly position; γ is the relative shadow value of the knowledge capital to tangible assets, and the product $b*\gamma$ is the absolute shadow value of the knowledge capital. In practice, $b*\gamma$ reflects investors' expectations on the overall effect of K_{it} on the discounted value of the present and future earnings of the corporation, while γ expresses the differential valuation of the knowledge capital relative to tangible assets.

Expression (8.4) is the base of the model known, in literature, as the 'hedonic model'. The assumptions leading from the general form of equation (8.3) to the linear specification of equation (8.4) were formally described by Hall (1993b, Appendix A). In particular, the author considered the necessary condition that the firm maximizes the present value of the future profits of its various tangible and intangible capitals (Hall, 1993b, p. 319), which, as discussed in the previous subsection, holds when the assumption of efficient financial markets is made.

Taking the natural log of both sides in (8.4), and assuming constant returns to scale ($\sigma = 1$), it is possible to write:

$$\log V_{it} = \log b + \log A_{it} + \log(1 + \gamma K_{it}/A_{it}) \tag{8.5}$$

If we subtract $\log A_{it}$ from both sides of (8.5), we shall obtain the following expression:

$$\log(V_{it}/A_{it}) = \log b + \log(1 + \gamma K_{it}/A_{it}) \tag{8.6}$$

The ratio V_{it}/A_{it} can be considered a first proxy of Tobin's q. The estimation of (8.6) allows us to assess the average effect of a currency unit invested in R&D on the market value of the firm. Hall and Kim (2000), Hall et al. (2000) and Bloom and Van Reenen (2000) estimated expression (8.6) through non-linear least squares. Other authors applying the same model used the approximation $\log(1 + x) \approx x$, so as to obtain the following equation, estimated through ordinary least squares (Griliches, 1981; Jaffe, 1986; Cockburn and Griliches, 1988; Hall, 1993a):

$$\log(V_{it}/A_{it}) = \log b + \gamma K_{it}/A_{it} \tag{8.7}$$

Some studies used the same approximation, but they moved from (8.5), so that the dependent variable is $\log V_{it}$ (Hall, 1993b; Hall and Vopel, 1996):

$$\log V_{it} = \log b + \log A_{it} + \gamma K_{it}/A_{it} \tag{8.8}$$

In both (8.7) and (8.8), however, the purpose of the estimation is the determination of γ, that is, the differential valuation of K_{it} relative to A_{it}. Moreover, the intercept $\log b$ is the same and has the same meaning (market valuation of all the firm's assets).

Note that some authors referred to an additive function slightly different from (8.4), which can be expressed in the following general linear form (Hirschey, 1982):

$$V_{it} = \alpha + \beta A_{it} + \gamma K_{it} + \sum \lambda I^j_{it} \tag{8.9}$$

Dividing both sides of (8.9) by A_{it}, we shall obtain the following functional form, where the dependent variable is again a proxy of Tobin's q (Chauvin and Hirschey, 1993):

$$V_{it}/A_{it} = \alpha \cdot 1/A_{it} + \beta + \gamma K_{it}/A_{it} + \sum \lambda I^j_{it}/A_{it} \tag{8.10}$$

Finally, some studies subtracted A_{it} from the firm's market value, so as to obtain a regression equation of the following kind (Connolly et al., 1986; Connolly and Hirschey, 1988, 1990; Green et al., 1996):

$$(V_{it} - A_{it})/A_{it} = \alpha \,(1/A_{it}) + \beta + \gamma K_{it} + \sum \lambda I_{it} \qquad (8.11)$$

3. EMPIRICAL ANALYSIS

3.1 The Sample

To review the empirical results of the relationship between a firm's R&D investments and its market value, we proceeded in three steps. We began by retrieving
all the studies cited by a survey on this subject published by Hall in 1999 as an
NBER working paper (Hall, 1999a). We initially selected all the studies that,
according to the classification of Oriani (2002), discussed in the previous section,
were included in the third group, analysing the relationship between levels of
knowledge capital and market value. For these studies, we recorded information
concerning the theoretical framework, the estimation model used, the relevant
dependent and independent constructs, their operationalization and the sample
size; the magnitude and significance level of the results was recorded, including
detailed information about the covariates. After this initial approach, we retrieved
11 studies, nine of which have already been published in refereed journals, one is
published in a book, and one is still under working paper format, albeit released
by primary-level research institutions.

   We then followed a 'snowball strategy', looking at all the papers cited in
the retrieved studies. We finally made an electronic search on Abi-Inform of
the articles published in the major international management and economics
journals from 1976 to 2001. In our search, we used an informed set of key-
words derived from the previous steps. These two steps allowed us to retrieve
12 more studies, eight of which have been published in refereed journals and
four are still under working paper format. The selection process led to a final
sample of 23 empirical studies examining, under different approaches, the
relationship between a firm's R&D investments and market value. For the
meta-analysis conducted in this chapter, we then retained only a subset of the
initial sample, as described in the following subsection.

3.2 Methods

Meta-analytic procedures are used to transform literature reviews from purely qualitative realms into quantitative ones. Each study reviewed is treated as
an observation: allowing the comparison or the combination of the empirical
evidence emerging from the studies reviewed, using the reported significance
level or effect size as a starting point (Hunter et al., 1982). The first purpose
of any meta-analysis is to differentiate the overall variance observed in the
reported results, in order to screen out study-specific variance (Hunter and

Schmidt, 1990). After any spurious source of variation has been screened out, meta-analysis can be used essentially for three purposes (Rosenthal, 1991, p. 1): (1) to help summarize the evidence emerging from several studies investigating the relationship between two or more variables; (2) to isolate a set of moderators and verify their overall impact on the relation under study; and (3) to generate hypotheses by clustering the examined studies along variables not directly observed or measured. In this chapter we focus on the first two steps. We begin by investigating the cumulative evidence on the relationship between a firm's market value and the level of its R&D investments. We then examine the effects of three moderators: the time window in which the observations were collected within every single study; the reliability of the independent variable; and the reliability of the dependent variable.

Despite its merits, however, meta-analysis suffers from some substantial and computational limitations (Hedges and Olkin, 1985; Rosenthal, 1991), among which three are particularly relevant in our case. First of all, to fully benefit from all the potential outcomes of the meta-analytic techniques, experimental studies with reported effect size estimates are needed. While the use of experiments is fairly common in certain disciplines (that is, experimental psychology), social sciences often focus on levels of analysis where experiments are unfeasible. Our area of interest being exactly such a case, we are dealing with non-experimental studies, where different covariates are often included. Since we have to accept the non-experimental nature of firm-level studies, we are rather limited in any meta-analysis involving the comparison and combination of effect sizes. Obtaining indicators by screening out the effects of the covariates might be impossible, depending on the type of results reported. In addition, the presence of difference covariates in the various studies reviewed might increase the magnitude of the problem (Rosenthal, 1991, chapter 2). Second, the same theoretical constructs are frequently operationalized and measured in different ways. The effect that the weaknesses in construct validity and in reliability might have on the observed results is a common concern among meta-analysts.

To cope with these two important potential limitations affecting any case of meta-analysis, we worked in three ways. First, we applied very conservative selection criteria in the identification of the studies analysed. In particular, among the studies on knowledge capital and market value reviewed in the previous subsection, we chose only those applying the hedonic model and hence based on the aggregation function (8.4) because, as explained below, this function has more suitable characteristics for the meta-analysis procedure. After that, as K was operationalized by different constructs (see the discussion in Section 2), we selected only the studies using the R&D capital, calculated according to (8.2). Second, in order to evaluate the extent to which the variance in the observed results could be driven by differences in the study characteristics, we corrected all the observations for their sample size, and different levels of reliability in the dependent and independent variables. Third, we computed the amount of variance due to sampling error and subtracted it from the total variance in the corrected observations, to obtain the true variance in the corrected observations. Each analysis was then based on the true variance in the corrected observations.

A third criticism often made of the meta-analytic studies concerns their being based on biased data sets, since published studies are only a fraction of all the studies performed on a certain topic (the so-called 'file-drawer problem'). Typically, the objection is that studies reporting non-significant results are seldom published. While there is accordance on the other problems of meta-analysis discussed, this specific point is still being strenuously debated (Hunter and Schmidt, 1990; Rosenthal, 1991). On the one hand, it is argued that unpublished studies remain so because inherent methodological flaws make their results unreliable and account for the weakness of their findings. On the other hand, one might argue that deviants of well-established 'paradigms' are more likely to meet with a certain resistance within the scientific community, and therefore are less likely to be published.

Both positions focus on the possible reasons for the presence of a high number of unpublished studies. Whatever these reasons are, however, one would like to estimate their potential impact on the external validity of the results of the meta-analysis. Rosenthal (1991, pp. 103–9) proposed to address this issue by calculating how many studies reporting unimportant results, or even results contradicting established theoretical predictions, need to be lying in a drawer awaiting publication, for the conclusions reached by the meta-analysis to be invalidated. The higher the number of unpublished studies needed to invalidate such conclusions, the smaller the selection bias, and the greater the generalizability of their results (see also Hunter and Schmidt, 1990, chapter 13). In this analysis we use the file-drawer test applied to effect size estimates to assess the external validity of the presented results.

3.3   Data Coding

Meta-analyses usually focus either on the directionality and significance of the effects or on their magnitude. In either case, one needs to recover from each of the analysed studies a measure of association between the variables of interest. Bivariate correlation coefficients are normally used, while procedures also exist for dichotomous comparisons relying on d-values. The use of regression slopes and intercepts, in contrast, is more controversial (Hunter and Schmidt, 1990, pp. 202–6).

First of all, while correlations are attenuated by unreliable measures of both the independent and the dependent variables, raw score regression slopes and intercepts are attenuated only by measurement error in the independent variable. Moreover, regression slopes and intercepts are usually not comparable across studies, unless all studies used exactly the same scales to measure both variables. Finally, slopes and intercepts can be very difficult to interpret, due to arbitrary choices in the scaling of the variables.

All these limitations strongly suggest relying on correlations, even when examining studies using regression models, collecting the relevant information from the correlation matrix which should normally be reported. In our case, however, very few of the studies examined reported simple bivariate correlation coefficients. The very stringent selection procedure used in the definition of the final sample, and our focusing only on the studies based on function (8.4) and on the estimation equations (8.7) and (8.8), however, offered the opportunity of overcoming all the above-mentioned concerns about the use of regression slopes. First, all the studies had used exactly the same indicators, measured on identical scales, both for the dependent and for the independent variables. Second, the slope coefficient we were interested in, K/A, as previously discussed, did not suffer from scaling problems likely to affect its interpretability. Our slope coefficient measured, in fact, the amount of currency units by which a firm's value increases (or decreases) as a consequence of an investment of a single currency unit in R&D activities relative to an investment in tangible assets. Third, due to the functional form used to derive the final specification, the intercept had its own specific meaning in the estimation model (that is, the amount of currency units by which a firm's value increases or decreases as a consequence of an investment of one currency unit in any kind of assets). The K/A slope can then be interpreted as a correlation coefficient, and an analysis of the effects of measurement errors in the dependent variable becomes meaningful again.

For each study, therefore, we recorded the slope coefficient associated with the K/A term in the hedonic regression estimation equation. Whenever more than one analysis was performed on the same functional relationship within the same study and on the same sample, we first determined the slope coefficient associated with each indicator, and then calculated their average (Rosenthal, 1991, pp. 27–8). For example, a standard procedure in economic research is to present and to estimate different functional forms associated with the model being developed, and then compare the emerging results. In this case, we considered each estimate as a single set of results and combined them all (Hunter et al., 1982, chapter 5). Analyses on different samples performed within the same study, however, were treated as fully replicated designs, and therefore as independent observations. Table 8.1 reports a list of all the samples used, together with their main characteristics.

Table 8.1   The studies examined in the meta-analysis

Study	Sample size	Period of observation
Griliches, 1981	1 091	1968–74
Jaffe, 1986	864	1973–79
Jaffe, 1986	432	1973–79
Cockburn and Griliches, 1988	722	1980
Hall, 1993a	24 333	1973–79
Hall and Vopel, 1996	3 968	1987–91
Blundell et al., 1999	3 211	1972–82
Gambardella and Torrisi, 1999	356	1988–97
Hall et al., 2000	17 111	1976–84
Hall et al., 2000	19 628	1979–88
Hall et al., 2000	15 605	1985–92

3.4   Statistical Tests

We conducted all the tests in accordance with the procedures presented and discussed by Hunter and Schmidt (1990). The ultimate goal was to obtain an estimate of the true relationship between a firm's market value and its R&D investments, starting from the slopes reported in the studies examined. Each slope needs to be weighted for its sample size, here measured by the number of observations included in the regression model. As all the studies were longitudinal, if they had been based on balanced panels, the sample size would have been the product of the number of firms analysed and the number of periods of observation for each firm. Unfortunately, all the studies were based on unbalanced panels. As a consequence, we had to take the total number of observations reported in the regression models considered as a measure of the sample size for each study. Then, we could calculate the standard deviation of the observed slopes, in order to estimate the variability in the relationship observed. Such variability, however, could be the sum of different components: the true variation in the population, the variation due to sampling error, or the variation due to measurement error. Before proceeding any further in the analysis, to assess the impact of the effects of moderators on true variation, it was therefore important to eliminate the influence of the random variation of the values reported by the studies examined, and also the systematic variation due to measurement problems.

We obtained the results of the analysed studies in five steps. These steps were common across all the different analyses performed, while the calculations changed according to the research question of interest. Table 8.2 reports and describes the formula used for each calculation.

Table 8.2   Statistics used and computation methods

Statistic	Computation	Notes
Average observed slope (AOS)	$\sum \beta_{oi} n_i \big/ \sum n_i \ (i = 1 - s)$	β_{oi} = slope reported by study i n_i = sample size of study i s = total number of studies examined in the meta-analysis
Sampling error variance in uncorrected slope (SEVUS)	$(1 - \mathrm{AOS}^2)^2 \big/ \sum n_i \ (i = 1 - s)$	Amount of variance among observed slopes due to random error if no correction for artifacts is applied
Uncorrected slope variance (USV)	$\sum n_i (\beta_{oi} - \mathrm{AOS})^2 \big/ \sum n_i \ (i = 1 - s)$	Total amount of variance among the study not correcting for artifact influence
Attenuation factor (A_i)	$a_{i1} \ a_{i2} \ a_{i3}$	Total artifacts correction factor with: a_{i1} = reliability of the independent variable in study i a_{i2} = reliability of the dependent variable in study i a_{i3} = attenuation factor for sample size of study i, calculated as $1 - [1/(2n_i - 1)]$
Average corrected slope (ACS)	$\sum (n_i \beta_{oi}/A_i) \big/ \sum n_i A_i^2 \ (i = 1 - s)$	Average effect size obtained by meta-analysis after correcting for artifact influence
Sampling error variance in corrected slope (SEVCS)	$\sum (\mathrm{SEVUS} n_i / A_i) \big/ \sum n_i A_i^2 \ (i = 1 - s)$	Amount of variance among corrected slopes due to random error after correction for artifacts is applied
Corrected slope variance (CSV)	$\sum n_i A_i^2 (\beta_{oi} - \mathrm{ACS})^2 \big/ \sum n_i A_i^2 (i = 1 - s)$	Total amount of variance among the slopes after correcting for artifact influence
Sampling error corrected variance of corrected slope	CSV − SEVCS	True variance among the slopes after correcting for artifact influence and random variance

First, we computed the average uncorrected slope coefficient, as the average of all the slope coefficients reported by the studies examined, weighted by the study's sample size calculated as described above. Second, we calculated the raw uncorrected variance of all the slope coefficients examined. Third, we calculated, for each study, the attenuation factor, so as to take into consideration the effect of measurement errors in the dependent and independent variables. This third step was repeated four times, considering four possible levels of reliability for each study: 0.7, 0.8, 0.9 and 1. Fourth, we calculated both the average sample slope and the slope variance, corrected for artifact influence. Before any analysis could be made, however, it was still necessary to eliminate from the variance calculated in the previous step the amount of variance due to sampling error. The fifth and last step, therefore, consisted in the calculation of the slope variance corrected for sampling error, resulting from the difference between the slope variance corrected for artifact influence and the sampling error variance, calculated on the average sample slope corrected for artifact influence.

The slope variance corrected for sampling error was used to calculate confidence intervals for the average sample slope corrected for artifact influence. Confidence intervals were then used to assess statistically whether the relationship between a firm's market value and its R&D investments was different from zero, and the effects on this relationship of three moderators: the time window in which the observations were collected within every single study; the reliability of the independent variable; and the reliability of the dependent variable.

Finally, to address the 'file-drawer problem' we followed the procedure recommended by Rosenthal (1991, pp. 103–9). The purpose was to estimate the number of unretrieved studies averaging null results that should exist if the results obtained from the retrieved studies were due to chance alone. Traditionally, meta-analyses consider as unretrieved studies those that are still unpublished. The procedure, however, can logically be extended to consider the generalizability of the results, which might also be affected by the sampling criteria used. The file-drawer test, therefore, also becomes a way of controlling for the possible biases introduced by our decision to exclude some papers (as we explained above) and to avoid including other journals in our analysis.

Technically speaking, we needed to calculate the number of unobserved studies averaging null results to bring the magnitude of the effect size observed to a negligible level. In our case, scaling such a value according to the measurement unit shared by the variables considered in the analysis, we were interested in computing the number of unobserved studies reporting null results necessary to bring the value of the average corrected slope to 1. In this case, in fact, it would make no difference whether we invest a currency unit in R&D activities or in any other tangible asset. Given k, the number of the studies reviewed, β_μ the average corrected slope, modified the formula presented in Hunter and Schmidt (1990, p. 513) to compute x, the number of studies to be exceeded in order to invalidate the results of the meta-analysis was as follows:

$$x = k\,(\beta_\mu - 1) \qquad \text{File-drawer test} \qquad (8.12)$$

4.   RESULTS

Table 8.3 reports the results of the meta-analysis for R&D investments and market value, as well as the changes in the different values of interest for different levels of the moderators considered in our analysis. The overall results considering all samples and all observations indicate a rather strong support for a systematic relationship between the two variables. The average corrected slope is equal to 1.6978, and the 95 per cent confidence interval varies between 0.96 and 3.3, indicating not only that the true population slope is always positive and well above 0, but also that the market values 1 dollar (or 1 euro) invested in R&D activities generally more than 1 dollar (or 1 euro) invested in any other tangible assets.

A change in the reliability of the indicators used to estimate the relationship (that is, Tobin's q and the reported level of R&D investments) has, as we expected, an impact on both the average corrected slope and the corrected slope variance. These changes are reflected in the 95 per cent confidence interval, which at $a = 0.9$ varies between 0.11 and 3.67, at $a = 0.8$ varies between 0.12 and 4.12, and $a = 0.7$ varies between 0.14 and 4.71. So, while the average corrected slope increases to 1.89, 2.12 and 2.42 respectively, and the confidence intervals do not include 0, thus confirming that the true population slope is always positive, the number of cases in which the market does not pay a premium for R&D investments with respect to investments in other physical assets increases.

When we split our sample on the other moderating factor previously identified, that is, the timing of the observations examined in the empirical studies of our meta-analysis, we find another interesting result. The average corrected slope is equal to 2.66 for studies based on observations collected before 1980, with a 95 per cent confidence interval ranging between 2.17 and 3.15, and it is 1.18 for studies based on observations collected after 1980, with a 95 per cent confidence interval ranging between 0.26 and 2.1. These results confirm the anecdotal evidence reported by Hall (1999a) about the inter-temporal variation of the shadow value of R&D activities, showing that, before 1980, R&D investments systematically created a much greater value than investments in physical assets, while after 1980 this spread has been appreciably reduced and R&D investments are in many cases undervalued.

Table 8.3 Observed and corrected slope and variance values by different levels of moderators[a]

	Sample size	No. of samples	AOS	ACS	USV	SEVCS	SECVCS	95% confidence interval	File-drawer test[b]
Overall	87 321	11	1.6977	1.6978	0.6683	0.0004	0.6679	0.9587 : 3.2996	7.6758
Reliability									
0.9	87 321	11	1.6977	1.8864	0.6683	0.0005	0.8246	0.1065 : 3.6663	9.7504
0.8	87 321	11	1.6977	2.1222	0.6683	0.0006	1.0436	0.1198 : 4.1246	12.3442
0.7	87 321	11	1.6977	2.4254	0.6683	0.0009	1.3632	0.1370 : 4.7137	15.6794
Time									
Before 1980	30 653	6	2.6612	2.6615	0.0692	0.0072	0.0619	2.1737 : 3.1493	9.969
After 1980	56 312	5	1.1764	1.1765	0.2184	0.0000	0.2184	0.2605 : 2.092	0.8825
Time and Reliability 0.9									
Before 1980	30 653	6	2.6612	2.9572	0.0692	0.0089	0.0765	2.4153 : 3.4992	11.7432
After 1980	56 312	5	1.1764	1.3072	0.2184	0.0000	0.2697	0.2894 : 2.3250	1.536
Time and Reliability 0.8									
Before 1980	30 653	6	2.6612	3.3269	0.0692	0.0113	0.0968	2.7172 : 3.9366	13.9614
After 1980	56 312	5	1.1764	1.4706	0.2184	0.0000	0.3413	0.3256 : 2.6157	2.353
Time and Reliability 0.7									
Before 1980	30 653	6	2.6612	3.8022	0.0692	0.0148	0.1264	3.1054 : 4.4990	16.8132
After 1980	56 312	5	1.1764	1.6807	0.2184	0.0000	0.4458	0.3721 : 2.9893	3.4035

Notes:
a) For column notations please refer to Table 8.2.
b) Number of studies reporting null results needed to bring average corrected slope coefficient to 1.

These conclusions are robust even after correcting the timing effect for possible errors of measurement in the dependent and independent variables. When reliability coefficients are estimated at 0.9, 0.8 and 0.7 levels, the confidence interval widens, as expected, both for the studies based on observations collected before 1980, and for the studies based on observations collected after 1980. While in the first group we can also observe a sensible change on the average market premium on R&D investments, the overall situation does not change as much in the second group, where in many cases the slope is still smaller than 1, although always greater than 0.

Table 8.4   Comparison of average corrected slope coefficients

Effect	Group 1	Group 2	t-test	Significance level
Reliability effect				
	Overall	Reliability 0.9	0.15	ns
	Overall	Reliability 0.8	0.32	ns
	Overall	Reliability 0.7	0.51	ns
Time effect				
	Before 1980	After 1980	6.39	<0.001
Time and reliability effect				
	Before 1980	Before 1980 $\alpha = 0.9$	0.80	ns
	Before 1980	Before 1980 $\alpha = 0.8$	1.67	
	Before 1980	Before 1980 $\alpha = 0.7$	2.63	
	After 1980	After 1980 $\alpha = 0.9$	0.24	ns
	After 1980	After 1980 $\alpha = 0.8$	0.39	ns
	After 1980	After 1980 $\alpha = 0.7$	1.57	

Table 8.4 reports a comparison between the different groups of observations illustrated in Table 8.3, based on the average corrected slope only. The differences in magnitude of the coefficients are mostly not significant at conventional levels, suggesting that the greater impact of the changes in the different moderators presented above is reflected in changes in the corrected slope variance, and, as a consequence, in the confidence interval. The important point in the analysis, considering that the slope coefficients preserve their original measurement unit, is not to rule out a 0 value, but rather to rule out a value smaller than or equal to 1. Any time the *K/A* coefficient is smaller than one, it means that one currency unit invested in R&D activities is valued by the market less than a corresponding amount invested in tangible assets. Only after ruling out this possibility, are we interested in assessing the magnitude of the coefficient.

These observations are confirmed by the file-drawer tests reported in the last column of Table 8.3, which indicate that, without considering any time effect, the number of unretrieved studies reporting null or contrasting results that would be needed to invalidate the conclusion of a positive and greater than 1 K/A coefficient is quite large, compared to the number of studies already reviewed. However, when the time effect is considered, we notice that, while this number remains high for the studies based on observations made before 1980, it drops appreciably for the studies based on observations made after 1980. Possible errors of measurement in the dependent and independent variables also have a considerable effect, especially for the studies based on observations made after 1980, although the absolute number remains small. When reliability coefficients are estimated at 0.9, 0.8 and 0.7 levels, the file-drawer test gives values approximately equal to 1, 2 and 3 respectively.

5. DISCUSSION AND CONCLUSIONS

The extent to which investments in innovation have a positive effect on firms' economic performance has attracted scholarly research and practitioners' attention since the seminal works of Schumpeter. Empirical analyses have therefore been conducted over the years, using different methodologies and displaying different levels of analysis.

With the increasing importance of financial markets as a source of financing for economic activities, the extent to which investors are sensitive to innovation activities has become a critical area of attention for both managers and stockholders. The relationship between the market value of a firm and its R&D investments has therefore emerged as a growing research area, where economic, accounting and strategic management perspectives have converged, using a variety of tools and approaches in order to assess the existence, the directionality and the magnitude of such a relationship.

In this chapter we first discussed some measurement issues related to the more general problem of assessing firm-level innovating activities and performance, focusing on the conceptual and empirical meaning of these two constructs. We then introduced the three theoretical and empirical approaches under which all the studies appeared so far can be classified, and examined with special care the approach based on the seminal contribution of Griliches (1981), considering the firm as a bundle of assets and estimating the marginal effect of knowledge-based assets incorporated in R&D investments. This stream of research was the first to test empirically the theoretical arguments developed, and attracted growing attention over the years, leading to a constant improvement of the research design and to the attempt to widen the geographical sources of the data outside the US market. Moreover, such an approach is also particularly interesting in the light of the debate on the notion of the firm and of the sources of competitive advantage that has characterized the strategic management literature of the last decade, and it is heavily based on the role of intangible assets.

The rest of the chapter was then dedicated to a quantitative meta-analysis of a significant sample of studies drawing on the same research tradition, performed following Hunter and Schmidt's (1990) procedures, described at length in their application to this specific case in the research design section. Considering the amount of available empirical evidence, the practical and theoretical importance of the subject, and the evolution of financial markets all over the world, a formal cumulative analysis of the results can offer several insights. First, it can give an informative assessment of the level of agreement among the studies conducted so far. Second, it can screen out from the various estimates the effect, if any, of several measurement problems usually discussed. Third, it can test whether the variance among the results is random or whether it is due to some moderating effect. Finally, it can offer specific and stimulating insights to the scholars interested in continuing this line of research, by suggesting unexplored paths and underlining possible inconsistencies, while avoiding inefficient replications on findings already robust and systematic.

The results presented in this chapter encompass all these four lines of enquiry. First, our results show that an overall analysis of the results offer convergent and robust evidence of a positive relationship between R&D investments and the market value of a firm. More specifically, we can state not only that the true population slope is always positive and well above 0, but also that the market generally values 1 dollar (or 1 euro) invested in R&D activities more than 1 dollar (or 1 euro) invested in any other tangible asset. Moreover, random error is always a negligible proportion of the total variance observed.

Measurement errors in the dependent and independent variables, however, might introduce a significant bias both upward and, more importantly in our case, downward, increasing the number of cases where the market values 1 dollar (or 1 euro) invested in R&D activities less than 1 dollar (or 1 euro) invested in any other tangible assets. This is a first important observation for any future research, and some attempts to refine the calculations of the value of the outstanding debt are an example of practical attempts to mitigate such issues.

While measurement errors affect the confidence interval, but do not generate significant differences in the average corrected slopes, accounting for the time period in which the observations used in the analysed studies were made helps to explain the true variance observed. At all levels of reliability in the dependent and independent variables, in fact, the average corrected slope is always greater than 2.5 for the studies based on observations collected before 1980, while it ranges between 1.18 and 1.68 for the studies based on observations collected after 1980. These results confirm the anecdotal evidence reported by Hall (1999a) about the intertemporal variation of the shadow value of R&D activities, showing that R&D investments before 1980 systematically created a much greater value than investments in physical assets, while after 1980 the spread has been appreciably reduced and R&D investments are, in many cases, undervalued. All these results are robust and have strong external validity, according to the estimates obtained from the file-drawer test.

Our analysis suffered from certain limitations, directly connected to some of the results obtained. First of all, we focused our attention on only one of the three research traditions linking economic performance and R&D investments at firm level, that is, on financial markets. Moreover, within this set of studies we considered only a specific subsample, so as to eliminate the possible computational problems arising from the considerable differences in the estimation models used. Future research should address the evidence available from the other two research traditions and find appropriate strategies to incorporate all the possible models in the meta-analysis. Moreover, while accounting for one important moderating factor (the time window of the observations used in the study examined), we left out many other factors, such as the estimation technique used, the type and amount of the covariates included in the models, or the presence of interaction effects involving the K/A coefficient. Additional efforts in extending the coding procedures of the studies will provide important information to further extend the analysis of the true variance observed so far. Finally, all the studies except one had used US-based samples, although an increasing number of studies based on European data are being presented at conferences, with results generally aligned with the ones obtained in the US, but also with some differences, usually explained by the specific features of the different stock markets. A closer analysis of such studies using the meta-analytic framework developed in this chapter will allow us to evaluate these conclusions more carefully.

Despite all these limitations, the points raised in our chapter are of interest to different research communities and offer important indications on a topic whose relevance is directly connected to the theory and practice of technology and innovation management. Considering the evolution of several decision-making tools, emphasizing the role of opportunity-increasing investments to leverage on the existing competencies in order to enhance future competitive opportunities, the value attributed to such signals by the market can represent a critical opportunity to raise the funds necessary to develop and commercially exploit the new inventions. Discussions about the value-increasing or -destroying activities, therefore, cease to be based upon a generic jargon to classify investment decisions, and become a powerful heuristic instrument to be directly related to the expected evaluation expressed by shareholders and investors, and also for highly intangible activities, such as those related to the development of innovation.

NOTE

1. More precisely, the authors run a regression model where the dependent variable was the annual operating income and the independent variables were the lagged values of total assets and advertising expenditures, and a vector of past R&D investments.

9. R&D and Market Value: The Case of Privatized Companies

Federico Munari and Raffaele Oriani

1. INTRODUCTION

In this chapter we examine the relationship between privatization, R&D investments and a firm's market value. Although there is a broad literature on the impact of privatization on a firm's performance, almost no attention has been paid, so far, to evaluating its consequences on the economic gains stemming from R&D activities. In the previous chapters we documented that state divestiture may negatively affect long-term investments such as research and development, especially when coupled with the contemporaneous opening up of the market to competition. Building on these findings, it seems important to assess whether the decreasing levels of R&D efforts are mainly driven by the abandonment of low-return research projects and by efficiency gains in the use of resources, or by the more generalized reduction of potentially valuable innovative projects in a search for more short-term, low-risk results. In the former case, the reduction of R&D investments might be justified by their increased productivity, while in the latter it may lead to negative consequences for the long-run performance of privatized firms.

We contend that the literature on the relationship between innovation and market value (Griliches, 1981; Hall, 1999a) may provide a fruitful contribution to address this question. Given the forward-looking nature of market valuation, the prices of newly-privatized firms may be expected to incorporate the expected effects of R&D outcomes on their future performance. Indeed, if the transfer of ownership to the private sector progressively leads to higher productivity of innovative projects, we expect the relationship between R&D investments and market valuation to increase over time after the public offer. To explore this issue, we used data from a sample of 38 firms – including 19 privatized firms, which were matched, at the country and industry levels, with 19 publicly-held firms – and proceeded in the following way.

We first integrated, at a theoretical level, the field of study concerning the economic performance of privatized companies with the one analysing the relationship between a firm's knowledge assets and its market value. We then made an exploratory analysis to highlight the potential areas of interest for future empirical research on this topic. In particular, we dealt with three main issues. First, in line with the evidence provided in the preceding chapters, we compared the R&D investment behaviour of privatized firms with the control group of publicly-held companies, in order to gauge whether a state divestment impacts on the incentives to promote R&D activities. Second, we used Tobin's q, defined as the ratio between the market value and the replacement cost of a firm's assets, to explore the dynamics of the market valuation of privatized firms *vis-à-vis* the publicly-held firms included in our control group. Third, we analysed whether the stock market value of newly-privatized firms is consistent over time with the expectation of increasing economic returns from knowledge assets brought by the change in ownership.

The rest of the chapter is organized as follows. In Section 2 we first provide theoretical explanations to justify our expectations of higher private pay-offs to innovations following privatization. We then discuss the literature on the financial market valuation of firms' knowledge assets, and explain why market value may be a useful indicator to assess the expected economic performance of a firm's R&D activities after privatization. In Section 3 we describe the sample used in the empirical analysis and the technique adopted to build the industry-matched control group. In Section 4 we present first exploratory evidence on the relationship between R&D investments and Tobin's q following privatization, both over time and in comparison with our control group. In the final section we draw preliminary conclusions from the empirical analysis and discuss the main implications for future research.

2.   BACKGROUND

2.1   The Effects of Privatization on the Economic Returns to R&D Activities

The results of both the econometric study examined in Chapter 4 and the case study described in Chapter 7 suggest that privatization can be followed by a consistent restructuring and scaling down of the R&D facilities of former public enterprises, especially when the transfer of ownership is accompanied by the contemporaneous opening up of monopolistic industries to competition. The econometric study showed that, after controlling for inter-industry differences, privatization processes negatively affect different measures of R&D commitment. The same study also documented a significant increase in the number of patents assigned to the companies of the sample following privatization, even after controlling for more general trends within the respective industries. Such an increase does not impact negatively on the average patent quality, as measured by the number of citations received by following patents.

However, R&D expenditures, and somehow patents as well, are essentially 'input' rather than 'output' measures of innovative activity. Therefore, the previous evidence on the dynamics of R&D investments and patenting activity did not fully address the question of how privatization actually impacts on the innovative and economic performance of the company.

As already indicated in Chapters 4 and 7, it is possible to advance two different but interrelated arguments, implying that privatization may be associated with higher *private* economic gains stemming from R&D activities. First, building on the gap between private and social returns from R&D activities as identified in the seminal works by Nelson (1959) and Arrow (1962), we can argue that the attitude towards R&D activities within state-owned enterprises (SOEs) is likely to be oriented towards fulfilling general national goals of generating and diffusing knowledge as a public good, rather than addressing exclusively business-specific objectives. In fact, at least theoretically, SOEs should pursue goals that differ from simple profit maximization, such as those of promoting social welfare by limiting or resolving possible situations of market failures (Vickers and Yarrow, 1988). In contrast, after privatization the company has no further obligation to act in the interest of public welfare and can focus on the maximization of its private returns, for example by abandoning or outsourcing those R&D activities falling outside its core business. Sometimes the change in ownership also fosters a greater entrepreneurial orientation in the recognition and exploitation of business opportunities (Frydman et al., 1998). Therefore, the issues of the valorization and exploitation of the technological capital become major concerns after privatization, and several organizational solutions targeted to improve their effectiveness are, then, typically undertaken, as suggested by the cases investigated in Chapter 7.

Second, the reduction in the level of R&D investments may be interpreted as a consequence of overall efficiency gains in the use of resources, rather than as a shift in the objectives and in risk propensity. Public choice theory (Niskanen, 1971) views SOEs as inherently inefficient, since managers are held to account for political objectives rather than financial performances. Moreover, compared to publicly-held companies, they lack effective control mechanisms to discipline managers' effort and behaviour and to solve agency problems, such as the threat of hostile takeover or the possibility of linking firm performance and managers' compensation and turnover (Cragg and Dyck, 1999). According to the property rights theory (De Alessi, 1987; Vickers and Yarrow, 1988) privatization produces a better alignment of managerial incentive with financial performance, resulting from the increased incentive of private owners to supervise the management. In this respect, some authors have especially stressed the role of capital market scrutiny (Dewenter and Malatesta, 2001). From this perspective, both the observed reduction in R&D expenditures and the surge in patenting can be ascribed to the elimination of wastes or slack resources and to the higher productivity level of R&D operations.

Ultimately, these two different lines of reasoning may lead to opposite conclusions about the possible consequences of privatization for *social* welfare in the long run. However, they converge in suggesting that *private* economic returns stemming from innovative activities are likely to increase after state divestment. Following privatization, the firm not only could focus on those R&D activities most important and useful for its own business needs, but in the long term it should be able to manage them in a more efficient way. In other words, we should expect that, *ceteris paribus*, any currency unit invested in R&D by the privatized company produces higher economic pay-offs compared to what used to happen under state ownership. These theoretical expectations are perfectly in line with the results provided by previous empirical studies on the general economic consequences of privatization processes at the firm level, which generally showed productivity gains, efficiency improvements and higher profitability after divestiture (La Porta and Lopez de Silanes, 1999; Megginson et al., 1994 and 2000; Dewenter and Malatesta, 2001).

However, it is likely that changes in the firms' innovative and economic performance after privatization will not occur instantaneously, but they will probably take some time to be implemented. Indeed, a major drawback of the economic literature on the consequences of state divestment resides in the fact that privatization is usually interpreted as a discrete event, and in the underlying assumption that it should immediately lead to increased performance. In contrast, the organizational change processes induced by the transfer of ownership from state to market, which are far from being immediate and smooth, are still largely unexplored in literature (Cuervo and Villalonga, 2000). The exit of the state as a principal or sole owner of a company in fact generally induces consistent changes in the firm's strategic orientation, organizational structures and processes, and cultural values, which in turn affect its performance. These changes are implemented by the firm's management, usually newly appointed, and are largely driven by the new goals and incentives brought about by the modified governance structure and by the different contextual framework. Cuervo and Villalonga (2000) suggested that, by considering organizational and contextual variables, it is possible to open up the 'black box' between privatization and performance and to explain the variance generally observed in post-privatization consequences.

One first, important, advantage of adopting 'organizational lenses' in the study of privatization derives from the observation that organizations do not adapt instantaneously to a different institutional context, but are characterized by substantial inertia and tend to change slowly (Nelson and Winter, 1982; Hannan and Freeman, 1984). Firms develop through an incremental process of recombination of their existing resources and capabilities that is highly dependent on initial conditions (Kogut and Zander, 1992). Early stages of privatization are thus, generally, still characterized by residual conformity to the norms and routines of the public sector, even though they increasingly prove to be obsolete and unfit as sources of competitive advantage in the new environment. In such circumstances, both from an institutional and an individual point of view, there is a search for a new identity and new rules, and two different templates coexist: the old public sector one and the new private sector one. Thus, the adoption of a private sector template does not take place at a definite point in time, but through an incremental and progressive process of experimentation, being sometimes highly conflictual and uncertain (Johnson et al., 2000).

With specific regard to the case of R&D activities, the above-mentioned considerations suggest that, in the early period following privatization, path dependencies may still negatively affect the efficiency of R&D operations. However, the returns to R&D activities are likely to increase over time, as the efficiency pressures brought about by the new private ownership diffuse through and become established throughout the organization. Empirically, this implies that it is necessary to estimate the evolution of R&D performance for a consistent time window after the divestiture in order to fully capture the expected benefits. In the next subsection we shall discuss the potential contributions of the literature on innovation and market value (Hall, 1999a) to the analysis of the private returns to R&D activities within firms subject to privatization processes.

2.2 Tobin's q and the Assessment of R&D Performance in Newly-privatized Firms

The market value of the firm can be a useful indicator to assess the expected economic performance of the firm's R&D activities after privatization for at least two reasons. First, market value is a forward-looking measure expressing the stock market expectations about firms' future performance (Hall, 1999a). Second, as shown by previous empirical literature applying the hedonic method, it is possible to assess the specific effect of different technology-related assets, including R&D and patents, on the market value of the firm (see Hall, 1999a for a review).

In particular, some scholars have used Tobin's q to infer the value of the firm's stock of knowledge (among others Griliches, 1981; Cockburn and Griliches, 1988; Hall, 1993a, 1993b; Blundell et al., 1999; Hall et al., 2000). Theoretically, in the long-run equilibrium Tobin's q should be equal to 1. In fact, if it should exceed unity, firms would find it convenient to invest until equilibrium is re-established because the value of the rents generated from the assets would be higher than their replacement cost. In the opposite case, the firms would divest their assets until the equilibrium is reached again. However, as the financial market reacts to new flows of information more rapidly than the real market does, in the short run Tobin's q can differ from unity (Lustgarten and Thomadakis, 1987).

There is also a measurement problem that causes the value of Tobin's q to differ from 1. In fact, as corporate reports provide very poor information on intangible assets, in practice Tobin's q is often calculated as the ratio of the market value of the firm to the book value of its tangible assets, even though the growing importance of intangible assets in the firm's value is broadly recognized.[1] This implies that, *ceteris paribus*, Tobin's q is more likely to exceed unity when intangible assets become a larger fraction of the firm's total assets (Bond and Cummins, 2000).

The determinants of Tobin's q were clearly shown by the studies analysing the impact of the stock of knowledge on the market value of the firm. In particular, some of those studies adopted the following 'market value equation'[2] (Griliches, 1981; Jaffe, 1986; Cockburn and Griliches, 1988; Hall, 1993b):

$$V = b \, (A + \gamma \, K) \qquad (9.1)$$

where V is the market value of the firm (equity plus total debt), A is the book value of net tangible assets, b is the market valuation coefficient of the firm's tangible assets, K is the 'book' value of the firm's stock of knowledge and γ is the relative shadow value of K to A. It is possible to rewrite equation (9.1) in the following way:

$$\frac{V}{A} = b \left(1 + \gamma \, \frac{K}{A} \right) \qquad (9.2)$$

where the ratio V/A is a form of Tobin's q. In this formulation, the b coefficient measures the capability of total (tangible and intangible) assets to generate extra-rents. The coefficient γ depends on the expected effect of the stock of knowledge on the future economic performance of the firm. In previous studies, K was often computed as an *R&D-based* measure[3] (Griliches and Mairesse, 1984; Jaffe, 1986; Hall, 1993a, 1993b).

According to (9.2), it is possible to say that given b, q increases with both the coefficient γ and the ratio K/A. This means that Tobin's q rises when the firm either fosters the productivity of its stock of knowledge or increases the stock of knowledge itself.

These considerations can be usefully applied to the analysis of the performance of R&D activity in privatized firms.[4] As we know from previous analyses in the book, newly-privatized firms seem to reduce their efforts in

R&D investments after (and in preparation of) the public offer. Consistently with the assumptions that were discussed above, such evidence implies that the firm's stock of knowledge K could progressively decrease after privatization.

Nevertheless, this reduction in R&D efforts should not necessarily lead to a decrease in the value of Tobin's q. According to the considerations expressed above, it might be that the productivity of the R&D activities rises after privatization because the company exploits more effectively its technological capital. As documented in Chapter 4, the significant increase in the number of patents issued and in their relative quality after privatization, which is concurrent with a reduction in the R&D effort, supports this interpretation. Under this hypothesis, the productivity increase of R&D activities (captured by the coefficient γ in expression [9.2]) may partially counterbalance the decrease in the knowledge stock resulting from the reduction in R&D investments, so that the net effect on Tobin's q is not clear.

However, in line with the considerations expressed earlier in the chapter, there can be considerable lags between the changes in the corporate governance structure and those in R&D effectiveness and profitability. Indeed, it is reasonable to think that the productivity of R&D activities gradually progresses over time as the set of values, routines and managerial practices of the organization shift towards private sector standards. With respect to equation (9.2), this implies that the coefficient γ, capturing the sensitivity of market valuation to knowledge assets, may progressively increase over time after privatization. In other words, we should expect that the association between a firm's market valuation and its R&D investments progressively increases and strengthens as time passes from the privatization.

Consistent with previous reasoning, in the following section we shall explore the relationships between privatization, R&D investment behaviour and Tobin's q. With respect to R&D behaviour, we shall refer to the R&D intensity, defined as the ratio of R&D investments to a firm's total sales, because this indicator is consistent with the econometric analysis that was developed in Chapter 4.

Our purpose was to provide preliminary evidence about the relationship between R&D investments and Tobin's q for privatized firms, assuming that their stock market valuation is consistent with equations (9.1) and (9.2). Moreover, we aimed at investigating whether such evidence was consistent with our theoretical claims, in order to identify new and relevant issues that future empirical research on the long-run performance of privatized firms would have to analyse in greater depth.

3.   SAMPLE AND DATA

To examine the effects of privatization on firms' R&D investment behaviour and market value, we first created a data set including R&D expenditures and

Tobin's q information for the sample of privatized companies identified in Chapter 4. This includes 35 companies operating in nine European countries and 11 industries, which were fully or partially privatized through public share offering in the 1980–97 period. Our sample was derived from a larger one presented in the two articles by Megginson and colleagues (Megginson et al. 1994; D'Souza and Megginson, 1999), including 174 companies fully or partially privatized worldwide through public share offering over the same period, following the procedure described in greater detail in Chapter 4. In the end we were able to assemble complete data only for 28 of the 35 initial companies, thus limiting our analysis to six countries (Finland, France, Germany, the Netherlands, Italy and the UK) and ten industrial sectors.

As a second step, we gathered similar data for a set of firms that were publicly traded in the same period, in order to constitute a control group. We followed two main criteria in our matching process. First, each privatized firm had to be matched with a company operating in the same country, in order to take into account possible country-specific effects in the treatment of R&D expenditures (that is, the existence of fiscal incentives or legal differences affecting the capitalization and disclosure of R&D expenditures). Second, wherever possible, an industry-level matching was employed, given that the amount of technological opportunities and the incentives to invest in R&D activities consistently varies across different sectors (Cohen and Levin, 1989).

More precisely, for each privatized firm in our sample we drew a list of all the publicly-traded R&D-active firms in the same country and in the same industry, classified using the two-digit SIC code.[5] We then chose the company whose total sales in the year following the initial public offering (IPO) was most similar to the privatized firm, and retained it if complete data were available for the following years. In some cases, no company met our requirements. This problem was particularly serious in the case of the utilities operating in the electricity, water, gas and telecommunication services industries, since they typically operated as state-owned monopolists prior to privatization and had no counterparts in their industries. In the end, we were able to match 19 privatized firms with private firms, as shown in Table 9.1.

For each firm in both samples we then collected data on the main accounting figures and the market capitalization for the five years after the public offer. At firm level, the available data were R&D expenditures, other key accounting data (total assets, current liabilities, short-term debt, long-term debt, intangible assets, total sales) and market capitalization. The source of accounting figures (except for Italy) was Datastream International, providing a full coverage of British firms and a coverage superior to 75 per cent of the publicly-traded companies from other European countries. Data on R&D expenditures for all the countries were first obtained from Datastream International. However, as the disclosure of annual R&D expenditures is compulsory only for British firms, this information is not always available for other European companies. For firms in these latter countries, therefore, we gathered the data on R&D expenditures from two more databases: Worldscope and Global Vantage. R&D intensity was calculated by dividing the annual R&D investments reported in the profit & loss account by the total net sales of the company.

Table 9.1   Sample firms (privatized versus matched firms)

	Privatized firms			Matched firms		
IPO	Company	Nat.	Industry	Company	Nat.	Industry
1985	British Aerospace	UK	Aerospace/ defence	BBA Group	UK	Motor vehicles
1982	British Amersham	UK	Pharmaceut.	Glaxo	UK	Pharmaceut.
1986	British Gas Distribution	UK	Gas	Burmah Castrol	UK	Oil & gas
1982	British Petroleum	UK	Oil & gas	Shell	UK	Oil & gas
1988	British Steel	UK	Primary metal	Cookson Group	UK	Primary metal
1987	Rolls Royce	UK	Aerospace/ defence	Westland Group	UK	Aerospace/ defence
1986	Elf Aquitaine	FR	Oil & gas	Air Liquide	FR	Chemical
1986	Saint Gobain	FR	Stone, clay & glass	Valeo	FR	Motor vehicles
1987	Alcatel-Alsthom	FR	Electronics & tlc	Schneider	FR	Electrical
1993	Rhône-Poulenc	FR	Pharmaceut.	L'Oréal	FR	Soap/toiletries
1995	Pechiney	FR	Metal products	Fives Lille	FR	Machinery
1995	Usinor Sarcinor	FR	Metal products	Legrand	FR	Electrical
1994	Renault	FR	Motor vehicles	Peugeot	FR	Motor vehicles
1997	Bull	FR	Computers	Compagnie des Signaux	FR	Electronics/tlc
1989	DSM	NE	Chemical	Akzo Nobel	NE	Chemical
1994	Kemira	FI	Chemical	Orion	FI	Pharmaceut.
1994	Outokompu	FI	Primary metal	Partek	FI	Machinery
1995	Eni	IT	Oil & gas	Montedison	IT	Chemical
1988	Volkswagen	DE	Motor vehicles	Ford-Werke	DE	Motor vehicles

Data concerning the firms' market capitalization were obtained from Datastream International for all the countries. The total market value was calculated adding the value of outstanding debt (both short and long term) to market capitalization, as Blundell et al. (1992, 1999) did for similar analyses. Tobin's q, in accordance with the considerations exposed in the previous section, was then computed as the ratio between the total market value of the firm and the book value of its net tangible assets (total net assets minus intangible assets).

Descriptive statistics of R&D intensity, Tobin's q and total sales for both privatized and matched firms from +1 to +5 years after the public offer are reported in Table 9.2. We decided to drop from the time window the actual year of privatization, since accounting and financial figures might be characterized by consistent discontinuities brought by the placement. Also other studies intentionally excluded the year of privatization from their empirical analysis, on the conceptual basis that it includes both the public and the private ownership phase (D'Souza and Megginson, 1999; Megginson et al., 1994). Reported statistics show that privatized firms present a slightly higher R&D intensity and a significantly lower Tobin's q over the whole period. Furthermore, the matched firms show higher means of total sales. In the next section, the patterns of R&D intensity and Tobin's q will be broken down by year and studied in detail.

Table 9.2   Descriptive statistics for privatized and matched firms

	Obs.	Mean	Std deviation	Max	Min
Privatized firms					
R&D intensity	87	0.03472	0.02717	0.00508	0.10549
Tobin's q	87	1.0165	0.4921	0.3390	3.07240
Total sales (thousand millions €)	87	14.7	14.1	0.092	55.58
Matched firms					
R&D intensity	87	0.03338	0.02101	0.00531	0.07908
Tobin's q	87	1.5399	1.2740	0.4826	7.0612
Total sales (thousand millions €)	87	6.953	9.367	0.428	37.8

Sources: Datastream, Global Vantage, Worldscope, Centrale dei Bilanci.

4.   RESULTS

We shall present our empirical results in three stages. First, we shall focus on our sample of privatized companies and provide descriptive evidence on the trends of Tobin's q and of the R&D investment behaviour in the four years following the public offer. Then we shall compare the time series of R&D intensity and Tobin's q for privatized and publicly-traded companies, in order to assess whether significant differences emerge between the two groups. Finally, we shall perform a correlation analysis to look at the association between the two variables in the two different samples and to gauge its evolution over the five-year time window following privatization.

As to the first point, Figure 9.1 shows the evolution of R&D intensity and Tobin's q from the first up to the fourth year following the public offer. To obtain a consistent time series, we considered only the 22 privatized firms for which we had complete data on R&D intensity and Tobin's q over the four years after the IPO.

From the comparison, two different trends for R&D and Tobin's q seem to emerge, particularly during the first two years. First, we notice that the average R&D intensity ratio initially declines after the public offer. The average value of this variable is 0.0265 during the first year after the public offer and 0.024 in the second year (a 9 per cent decrease). This slight decrease is in line with the evidence shown in Chapter 4, where it was highlighted that firms facing privatization tend to redefine their commitment in R&D activities through a restructuring process that typically begins well before the actual state divestiture. Figure 9.1 suggests that restructuring continues throughout the first two years and that the commitment in R&D activities seems to stabilize in the third and fourth years after the public offer.

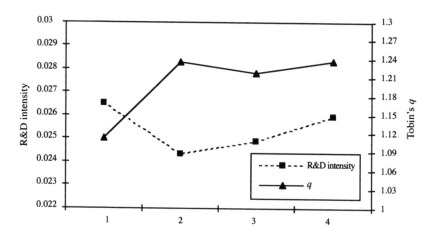

Figure 9.1 R&D intensity and Tobin's q for privatized firms

Turning to Tobin's q, Figure 9.1 shows an increase over the four years after privatization: during the first year after the public offer, the average q is equal to 1.112, whereas, by the end of the fourth year, it has risen to around 1.243. The valuation of privatized firms by the market thus incorporates the positive effects brought by the new ownership and governance structure on the expected profitability. This result is consistent with the literature addressing the financial performance of share issue privatization (Megginson et al., 2000), even though the general focus was on the stock returns rather than on market value. Moreover, as we have already observed with respect to the R&D intensity, the most relevant change in Tobin's q occurs between year 1 and year 2 after the IPO, while afterwards it tends to stabilize.

With regard to the purpose of our study, it is interesting to notice that the pattern of Tobin's q during the first two years clearly diverges from that of R&D intensity. In fact, the annual average of Tobin's q increases by about 11 per cent in the first two years after privatization. Thus, the market valuation of privatized companies does not seem to respond negatively to the decreasing level of R&D activities. On the contrary, the higher value attributed by the market reflects positive expectations that the management may prove better able to generate profits from the firm's tangible and intangible assets, including the R&D capital. Of course, it is not possible to draw any definitive conclusion from the evidence reported in Figure 9.1, since many other factors apart from R&D investments may affect a firm's expected profitability and consequently its market valuation. However, at least intuitively, this observation is consistent with our theoretical considerations about the increase in the productivity of R&D resources (incorporated in coefficient γ in equation [9.2]) after privatization and points out an interesting area that deserves further analysis.

We shall now compare the R&D and Tobin's q behaviour of privatized firms with respect to industry-matched firms. Indeed, it is possible that the observed evolution of R&D intensity and market valuation are not really determined by the new ownership and governance arrangements, but reflect general trends at industry or country level. As to the first variable, the literature on the economics of innovation has clearly stressed that the level and the rate of change of technological opportunities within the industry domain is one of the more plausible predictors of firms' commitment in R&D activity (Cohen and Levin, 1989). In order to account for this influence, in Table 9.3 we compared the time-series behaviour of the average R&D intensity in privatized and industry-matched firms.

We used a one-tailed t-test to statistically compare the differences in the mean values between the two different groups over the different years following the public offer. First, it is interesting to notice that, one year after the public offer, privatized companies tend to invest more in R&D than their publicly-held counterparts. The difference in the R&D intensity value appears to be higher in the first year following the public offer (3.77 per cent versus 3.19 per cent), but this gap tends to shrink, then it disappears in the following years. However, the difference is very small and statistically not significant in each of the four years, as well as over the whole period.

The pattern reported in Table 9.3 is consistent with our theoretical expectations related to the existence of stronger incentives to invest in R&D within public enterprises, partly descending from the objectives of the state as a principal to promote investment levels that are optimal in terms of potential contribution to the social interest, and not only to the private interest. As suggested by Table 9.3, privatization may lead a firm to reduce its R&D investments to levels that are more typical of the private sector. This evidence complements the findings of Chapter 4, where we showed a reduction in the industry-adjusted R&D intensity variable following privatization, using the average R&D intensity at industry level as a control benchmark.

Table 9.3   Average R&D intensity of privatized and matched firms[a]

	IPO + 1	IPO + 2	IPO + 3	IPO + 4	IPO + 5	Total period
Privatized	0.0377	0.0336	0.0338	0.0314	0.0374	0.0347
Matched	0.0319	0.0335	0.0336	0.0332	0.0350	0.0334
Observations	19	19	18	17	14	87
t-test (one-tailed)	−0.619	−0.007	−0.022	0.221	−0.254	−0.363

Note: a) Firms in the privatized and matched samples are listed in Table 9.1.

Sources: Datastream, Global Vantage, Worldscope, Centrale dei Bilanci.

The pattern of Tobin's q in privatized and publicly-held firms, reported in Table 9.4, shows a large difference between the two samples. The one-tailed t-test indicates that this difference is statistically significant at a 5 per cent level over the first three years after privatization. For our research purposes it is interesting to note that the Tobin's q of privatized firms increases, although slightly, over time, while the gap between the two samples monotonically decreases from year +3 to year +5 (from 0.788 to 0.293) Moreover, the difference between the samples is no longer statistically significant at +4 and +5 years after the IPO, supporting the indication that the Tobin's q of privatized firms progressively converges to the level of matched firms.

However, the gap between the two samples is still wide, even five years after privatization. This suggests that, even though it is possible to observe the beginning of the convergence, this process probably takes longer than five years to be completed. Indeed, this preliminary evidence supports the theoretical claim that changes in a firm's economic performance after privatization do not occur instantaneously, requiring instead a certain amount of time to be fully accomplished.

The third step of our analysis consisted in analysing the correlation between R&D intensity and Tobin's q in the two samples. The results reported in Table 9.5 are probably the most potentially interesting for future research. With respect to the publicly-held matched firms, they show that Tobin's q is strongly, positively and significantly (either at the 10 or 5 per cent levels) associated with R&D intensity for all the five years following privatization, consistently with the previously cited literature having found a positive effect of R&D investments on a firm market value.

Table 9.4   Average Tobin's q of privatized and matched firms[a]

	IPO + 1	IPO + 2	IPO + 3	IPO + 4	IPO + 5	Total period
Privatized	0.966	1.028	1.017	1.020	1.064	1.017
Matched	1.463	1.559	1.805	1.442	1.357	1.534
Observations	19	19	18	17	14	87
t-test (one-tailed)	2.037**	1.7215**	1.7949**	1.1247	1.0172	3.4751***

Notes:
a) Firms in the privatized and matched samples are listed in Table 9.1.
** significant at the 5 per cent level for the one-tailed test. *** significant at the 1 per cent level for the one-tailed test.

Sources: Datastream, Global Vantage, Worldscope, Centrale dei Bilanci.

Table 9.5   Correlation between R&D intensity and Tobin's q in privatized and matched firms[a]

	IPO + 1	IPO + 2	IPO + 3	IPO + 4	IPO + 5	Total period
Privatized	0.2374	0.2372	0.1741	0.3701	0.5469**	0.3050***
Observations	19	19	18	17	14	87
Matched	0.406*	0.4762**	0.4194*	0.5169**	0.5429**	0.4458***
Observations	19	19	18	17	14	87

Notes:
a) Firms in the privatized and matched samples are listed in Table 9.1.
*   significant at the 10 per cent level for the one-tailed test. ** significant at the 5 per cent level for the one-tailed test. *** significant at the 1 per cent level.

Sources: Datastream, Global Vantage, Worldscope, Centrale dei Bilanci.

If we turn to privatized firms, we can observe that even if the correlation coefficient is positive, it is lower than the corresponding coefficient of the matched sample and it is not statistically significant for all the first four years following privatization. However, we can also observe that at year +5 the correlation coefficient becomes statistically significant at the 5 per cent level, and its magnitude almost coincides with the magnitude of the correlation coefficient showed for the matched firms for the same year (0.5469 versus 0.5429).

This evidence, though representing neither a conclusion nor a validation, supports the theoretical claim that the market valuation of a firm's R&D activities changes over time after privatization, converging to that of publicly-held companies, and highlights an area that deserves further and more detailed inquiry.

5.   CONCLUSIONS AND FUTURE RESEARCH

In this chapter we discussed the impact of privatization on the economic returns generated by a firm's R&D operations. Even though there exists a broad theoretical and empirical literature on the effects of privatization on the economic performance of the firm, there are, to our knowledge, no contributions studying in depth the specific implications for the effectiveness of the R&D activities.

Research into the economics of innovation and technological change showed that the economic growth of firms, industries and countries is heavily dependent, in the long run, on today's innovation strategies (Griliches, 1979; Romer, 1990). For this reason, understanding the impact of privatization processes on R&D investments and outcomes should be considered as a relevant issue for both researchers and policy makers, given that, in different countries, state-owned enterprises have played a central role in directing and enhancing the development of the national innovation systems, both directly, through their R&D investments and facilities, and indirectly, through their procurement strategies (Nelson, 1993; Katz, 2001).

This question is even more interesting if we consider the evidence of Chapter 4, showing that, although privatized firms seem to significantly reduce their R&D investments after (and in preparation of) the public offer, the number of their patents grows up after controlling for their quality.

We suggested that the literature on innovation and market value, inspired by the seminal contribution of Griliches (1981), can be a useful reference to address these questions. In particular, we showed how Tobin's q can allow us to gauge possible increases in the expected economic pay-offs from R&D investments.

We then provided some preliminary evidence. In order to control for the great variety of contextual variables that generally intervene around privatization and may generate noise around the ownership effect, we adopted a matched-pair research design, similar to other studies aimed at assessing the consequences of privatization (Cragg and Dyck, 1999; Megginson et al. 2000). With reference to our sample of privatized firms, our findings showed that, during the first two years after the public offer, firms reduce the level of R&D investments, while their market valuation, expressed by Tobin's q, rises. Those opposite trends are consistent with our theoretical considerations regarding an increase in the efficiency gains of R&D activity after privatization.

Moreover, the increase in Tobin's q in the years after privatization emerging from our analysis is consistent with the findings of the broad empirical literature on the economic and financial performance of privatized firms (see Megginson and Netter, 2001, for a review) and confirm the positive long-term returns (one, three, five years) earned by the investors in share issue privatization with respect to different benchmarks.

Second, we showed that the first year after the IPO there is a gap between the R&D investments of privatized and matched firms, which tends to disappear from year two onward. The difference in Tobin's q between the samples is more significant and persistent over all the five years after privatization. However, this difference decreases over time, indicating that a convergence process could be taking place.

Third, we worked out a simple correlation analysis between R&D intensity and Tobin's q for both the samples. Our results show that, during the first four years after the IPO, the correlation coefficients are statistically significant only for the firms in the matched sample. At the end of the fifth year after privatization, however, the correlation coefficients are significant for both samples and they almost coincide. Although this evidence is preliminary and requires further inquiry, it highlights that the relationship between market valuation and R&D investments for privatized firms strengthens over time, and suggests that the beneficial effects brought by privatization on innovation activities do not take place overnight, but through a gradual process that can last several years.

These preliminary results encourage new empirical research in this area and highlight some problems that have to be addressed. Of course, many other factors apart from R&D investments may influence the profitability and the valuation (as expressed by Tobin's q) of privatized firms. In particular, the financial literature has long shown that the characteristics of the corporate governance models are significantly related to firm valuation (Morck et al., 1988; Goergen, 1998). The main difficulties for econometric analysis, thus, are related to the problem of simultaneity. In fact, as suggested earlier, the privatization event affects both the firm's market value and its R&D investments. Therefore, we might expect that some of the random elements affecting the dependent variable also influence the independent variable, which consequently would be correlated with the disturbance term.

Finally, we want to comment that, in our analysis, we decided to adopt R&D investments as a measure of the firm's commitment to innovative activities. The effectiveness of this choice could be limited by the fact that R&D investments are an input measure. Further research could adopt alternative innovation measures in the market value model, such as for instance the firm's stock of citation-weighted patents, which has proved to better explain a firm's market value, provided that the patents' relative quality is considered (Hall et al., 2000).

NOTES

1. This claim has been made repeatedly by accounting literature. See Lev and Sougiannis (1996) for a broad discussion.
2. See Chapter 8 for a detailed analysis of the market value equation.

3. This measurement choice is based on the claim that R&D investments generate new tech-
    nological knowledge representing a relevant intangible asset for the firm (Griliches, 1981,
    1990; Hall, 1999a). See discussion in Chapter 2.
4. There already exists a broad empirical literature on the financial and economic perfor-
    mance of privatized firms (see Megginson and Netter, 2001, for a review). Some of
    these analyses also refer to stock-related measures such as Tobin's q (Claessens et al.,
    1997) or stock returns (Megginson et al., 2000; Dewenter and Malatesta, 2001).
    However, these studies are focused on corporate governance and ownership structure
    issues, and do not consider the specific effects of privatization on the economic per-
    formance of R&D activities.
5. The firms were classified by the 1992 SIC code at a quasi two-digit level, mainly accord-
    ing to the previous classification of Hall and Vopel (1996).

10. R&D Financing and Stock Markets

Giancarlo Giudici and Stefano Paleari

1. INTRODUCTION

This chapter discusses how firms may raise capital to finance their R&D activities. It is common belief that efficient financial markets increase the level of venture capital investing, and therefore innovation and employment. Conversely, the lack of capital is often cited as one of the major impediments to innovation.

In this vein, the competitive advantage of US innovative companies during the 1990s over their European counterparts has been explained by a number of determinants, among which the different development of the respective financial markets, and the undynamic state of venture capital and stock exchanges in the European context.

Yet, euphoria for the 'new economy' stocks and the euro's arrival boosted Europe's stock markets, so that in 2000 more companies listed on European stock exchanges than in the US. Much of the merit is due to the birth of the 'new stock markets' established for small but fast-growing firms (the *Neuer Markt* in Germany, the *Nouveau Marché* in France, the *Nuovo Mercato* in Italy, just to mention the largest). At the same time, record levels of private equity investments in growth companies were achieved both in the US and in Europe.

European 'new stock markets' (NMs) provide interesting insights into the relationship between R&D financing and innovation. In fact, it is worth analysing whether the establishment of these new exchanges had any effect on venture capital investments, R&D expenditures and innovation. Moreover, the increasing volatility of stock markets experienced during the 1990s stimulates an analysis of the short-termism and the market myopia affecting, also in the financial markets, the capability of investors to discover the value drivers of innovative firms.

In order to investigate the topics above, we examined the characteristics of a sample of companies listed on the three largest European NMs. In particular, we looked at the equity capital raised at the listing, in relation to the existing assets and their book value.

We showed that European NMs have been essentially 'markets for projects', where young enterprises endowed with few tangible assets can sell their business plans to the market. We posited that, consistent with the results pointed out in the previous chapters, the establishment of NMs contributed to the redirection of research activity, in favour of applied R&D. We highlighted that the listing allowed NM companies to raise a significant amount of new capital, compared with the existing equity resources. We showed that retail investors gave a relevant valuation to intangible capital, by purchasing shares at a price significantly higher than the firms' book value. Therefore, we argue that stock markets (and not private equity investors) acted as the real financiers of NM companies in most cases, thus confuting the traditional belief that professional private equity investors face most of the risk in the life cycle of technology-based companies.

We argue that the stock market turbulence experienced after the 'Internet bubble' might lead investors to select their investments by looking carefully at the long-run value drivers of technology stocks.

The chapter is organized as follows. The topic of innovation and R&D financing is developed in Section 2. The access of innovative firms to stock exchanges is examined in Section 3. Section 4 presents our empirical analysis. Finally, Section 5 presents several concluding remarks.

2. R&D FINANCING AND INNOVATION

Innovation requires R&D investments, and R&D activity needs to be financed. Most of the time, the entrepreneurs' personal savings are not sufficient to cover the investments; therefore, outside finance must be obtained. However, innovation is risky and financiers do not like to engage in risky investments if there are no adequate contractual provisions.

In this section we shall explore the main features characterizing the financing of innovation. In particular, we shall show why traditional sources of capital are inadequate to fund high-tech start-ups and innovative companies, and why private equity, such as venture capital, may better sustain technology-based new enterprises.

After presenting a brief picture of the venture capital industry, we shall highlight how the new paradigms of innovation, based on intangible assets and networks, are challenging the traditional process of firms' evaluation and financing.

2.1 The Relationship between Finance and Innovation

Financial constraints are often considered one of the main impediments to start-ups and high-technology firms seeking to expand and grow (Moore, 1994; Himmelberg and Petersen, 1994; Manigart and Struyf, 1997; Gompers and Lerner, 1999; Giudici and Paleari, 2000a). Most of the time the entrepreneurs' personal wealth is not sufficient to fund new start-ups, nor is managerial experience available. Even if a founder had enough capital, however, he (or she) probably would not be ready to invest all his property into a single project, since, in the case of failure, he would lose everything. Without being offered some kind of insurance, he would prefer not to invest.

Hence, access to finance capital is fundamental for fast-growing innovative firms, in order to sustain capital and R&D expenditures, to follow the growth of the market, and to develop new technologies and intangible resources. Nevertheless, several factors make the cost of capital rather higher for young innovative firms than for mature companies.

Uncertainty, information asymmetry and the risk of failure in developing new technologies are higher than in traditional firms (Binks et al., 1992; Westhead and Storey, 1997). This raises the costs related to external financing, as stated by the agency theory (Jensen and Meckling, 1976) and by the 'pecking order' theory (Donaldson, 1961; Myers, 1984). Potential problems concerning risk and information asymmetry include moral hazard and the adverse selection externalities. Entrepreneurs usually have a superior knowledge of the future prospects of the project to be financed. They can use such knowledge to reduce their effort and maximize their own utility, not the project's value. On the other hand, financiers are usually less able to discriminate between good and bad projects. Moreover, young firms have a short track record and few public documents available to outsiders, which raises the cost of collecting information (Binks and Ennew, 1996).

Debt financing may not be available, because of the high risk and the lack of collateral. However, since interest payments would slow down the expansion of a young firm anyway, a loan is not a good financing instrument for innovative growing firms.

The resort to equity financing provided by closed-end funds and venture capitalists (corporate or business angels) is often the only solution for raising capital from inside entrepreneurs (Sahlman, 1990; Gompers and Lerner, 1999). In fact, young firms are usually too small to be financed through bond or equity issue on capital markets.

Private equity investors negotiate complex contracts and covenants with entrepreneurs so as to mitigate conflicts of interests, to engage in active monitoring and to place valuable managerial competencies at the disposal of growing small firms. Advisory activities by venture capitalists are very important and improve the firm's chance of survival, since entrepreneurs often have no business experience. Baker and Gompers (2001) found that venture capital backing also improves a firm's future in the long run, reducing the failure rate significantly. Venture capitalists' stakes in the equity capital have a relevant image effect, and provide a sort of 'certification effect' on the firm's quality (Megginson and Weiss, 1991).

Venture capital financing allows a separate allocation of cash-flow rights, voting rights, board rights, liquidation rights and other control rights, as the solution to conflicts of interest or agency problems between investors and entrepreneurs (Kaplan and Strömberg, 2001). For example, venture capitalists often purchase a combination of common equity, preferred equity and convertible bonds, and obtain veto rights, so that they can take control of the firm in the event of entrepreneurs' failure or opportunistic behaviour (Cornelli and Yosha, 1998; Hellmann, 1998). Capital is infused at stages corresponding to significant developments in the life of the company, following the business plan objectives (Giudici and Paleari, 2000b). Stage financing limits the venture capitalist's losses in the case of default and represents a threat of abandonment in the short run. Redemption covenants provide the venture capitalists with the means of extracting the original investment from an unsuccessful company, as well as posing a credible threat of withdrawal over the entrepreneur.

Venture capitalists raise finance from outside investors and identify investment opportunities and projects. The returns flow as capital gains upon completion of the project. Seed capital is the first type of financing a newly founded company might want to secure, in order to fund its R&D and commercial expenditures; start-up investments are targeted at companies gearing up to produce and to market their products. Finally, in the expansion stage, the company has to fund growth opportunities, by enlarging its manufacturing and distribution capacity, as well as by engaging in external acquisitions.

Most venture capitalists exit from investments in one of four ways: sale after the company completes an initial public offering (IPO); sale of shares pursuant to an acquisition of the portfolio company; redemption of the venture capitalist's shares pursuant to contractual options; and liquidation, in the case of unsuccessful ventures.

Venture funding is believed to have a positive impact both on creating jobs and boosting capital markets (Black and Gilson, 1998) and on innovation. Hellmann and Puri (2000) highlighted a positive relationship between the market success of innovator firms and the type of financing they obtained (in particular whether they obtain venture capital or not). Kortum and Lerner (2000) estimated that venture capital accounts for 15 per cent of recent industrial innovation in the US. Yet, the presence of efficient exchanges dedicated to start-ups and growth firms is necessary to provide investors with an exit (Schwienbacher, 1999). In fact, Jeng and Wells (2000) showed that a strong IPO market is the main force behind venture capital, especially in later-stage investments.

2.2 Venture Capital Investments

Venture capital is by no means the main source of capital in the economy. In the US, the venture capital industry invested about $137 billion from 1990 to

1999, while the companies listed on the New York Stock Exchange and Nasdaq during the same period raised equity for more than $190 billion and about $300 billion, respectively (NVCA, 2001; Nasdaq, 2001). The difference is even more significant if we take into account the issues of corporate bonds.

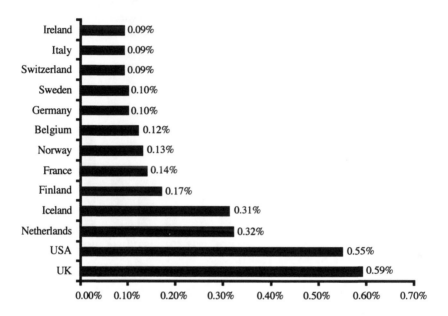

Sources: EVCA (2001) and NVCA (2001).

Figure 10.1 Venture capital investments in the major Western countries, as % of GDP in 1998

While in the US the term 'venture capital' is linked exclusively to equity-related investments in start-ups, or in high-growth companies, European statistics refer to a more general concept of venture capital, which includes any commitment to unlisted companies at any stage, from seed investments to replacements, buy-outs and turn-around operations, the bulk of the activity being later-stage investments. Notwithstanding, in Europe the venture capital industry is even less developed than in the US. From 1990 to 2000 €85 billion were raised by professional private equity investors in Europe. Besides, considering only 1998 and 1999, the companies listed on the major EU exchanges issued equity for more than €200 billion (FIBV, 2001; EVCA, 2001).

Despite its small volumes, however, venture capital helped to create worldwide many successful innovative multinational companies, particularly in high-tech industries. Yet, Figure 10.1 clearly shows that, historically, venture capital activity has been significant only in the US and in the UK, proving rather weak in other major European economies (Germany, France, Italy). This evidence, attributed to several determinants, was often invoked as one of the key distinctions between bank-based versus stock-market-based financial systems (Allen and Gale, 2000). Notwithstanding the scarce relevance of venture capital financing when compared to other sources of finance, the biggest ever private equity investments both in the US and in Europe were made in the later years.

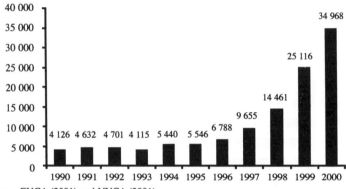

Sources: EVCA (2001) and NVCA (2001).

Figure 10.2   Annual European private equity investments (data in € million)

In 2000, the US private equity industry raised more than $163 billion, a 36 per cent increase from 1999, with venture capital investments accounting for $97 billion (NVCA, 2001). In terms of the amount invested, a record $145 billion was reached, with venture capital funds accounting for almost 72 per cent of the total investments. Technology-related investments totalled $85 billion, up 91 per cent from 1999 (PricewaterhouseCoopers, 2001).

In Europe, the venture capital activity traditionally concerns non-innovative sectors, later development stages or investments without control and monitoring. Yet, 2000 saw the largest amount of money ever invested by European private equity and venture capital firms (EVCA, 2001). The funds invested totalled a record €35 billion in 10 440 companies, with an increase of 39 per cent on the 1999 stock (see Figure 10.2). The funds raised also reached the record amount of €48 billion, a 89 per cent increase on the 1999 (see Figure 10.3). The amount invested in the early stages (seed and start-up) more than doubled to 19 per cent of the total. Expansion investments totalled 37 per cent of the amount, and buy-outs 41 per cent. The capital invested in European high-technology companies totalled €11.5 billion in 2000, up 68 per cent from 1999, albeit seven times lower than the US total (PricewaterhouseCoopers, 2001).

Corporate investors significantly increased their appetite for risky start-ups, doubling their investments from €2.4 billion in 1999 to €4.8 billion in 2000. In summary, €9.2 billion went into pure venture capital stages, up from 76 per cent in 1999.

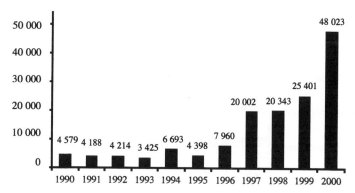

Sources: EVCA (2001).

Figure 10.3   Annual European private equity funds raised (data in € million)

For the first time since 1995, the largest amount of funds raised (24 per cent) came from pension funds, with banks contributing 22 per cent and insurance companies 13 per cent. The UK continued to lead Europe in fund raising with €17.7 billion, and €13.2 billion invested. France followed, with €7.5 billion raised and €5.3 billion invested. Germany came third, with €6.1 billion raised and €4.8 billion invested. Italy was fourth, with €2.9 billion raised and €3.0 billion invested.

The European Venture Capital Association (2001) reported that, over the 1991–95 period, venture-backed European companies experienced exceptional growth rates, outperforming those of the top 500 European companies. On average, sales revenue rose by 35 per cent annually, twice as fast as the top established companies. Staff numbers increased by an average of 15 per cent per year over the same period, but only by 2 per cent for the benchmark top companies. Investments in plants, property and capital equipment grew by an average of 25 per cent annually. In 1995, R&D expenditure represented on average 8.6 per cent of the total sales, compared to 1.3 per cent for the top companies.

That panorama changed radically in 2001. In 2001 the capital invested in technology companies went down astonishingly, with a notable exception, that is, an increase in the life science and health sector (see Figure 10.4). In addition, in 2001 the Internet-related investments marked a downward spiral, declining to the lowest level in two years. In the US the drop-off in non-venture capital equity sources was remarkable: in the second quarter of 2001, venture capitalists contributed 90 per cent of the equity for venture-backed companies, while during the first quarter of 2000 they contributed only 76 per cent of the capital (Venture Economics, 2001).

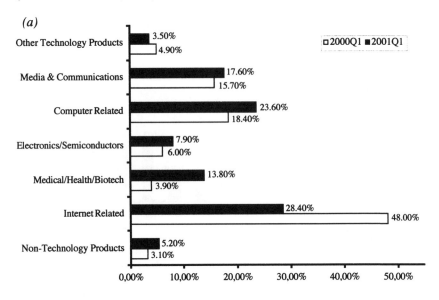

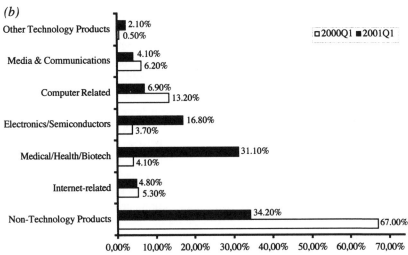

Sources: EVCA (2001), NVCA (2001) and PricewaterhouseCoopers (2001).

Figure 10.4   *Venture capital investments in the US (a) and private equity investments in Europe (b) during the first quarter of 2000 and 2001, by sector*

New equity investments accounted for $10.6 billion during the first quarter of 2001, 61 per cent less than during the same months in 2000. Finance raised totalled $9.7 billion, 68 per cent less than in 2000. In Europe as well, a 60 per cent fall in private equity investments was registered during the first quarter of 2001. Expansion-stage companies received greater attention in 2001 compared to 2000 both in the US and in Europe. Seed and early rounds declined steeply in the US, attracting only 15 per cent of the investments in the second quarter of 2001, while expansion funding grew up to 55 per cent. In Europe, early-stage ventures witnessed a 68 per cent fall by value. Yet, in European countries venture capital investments seem to focus on those sectors, such as technology products and life sciences, where growth opportunities appear to be more promising.

The re-focusing of venture capital investments in 2001, parallel to the swing of the stock exchange performance in industrialized countries, provides new evidence about the strong links between venture financing and stock markets.

Yet, several other determinants affect the private equity market. The institutional environment imposes a number of constraints on how companies and investors interact (La Porta et al., 1997). Different economic systems provide different levels of governance structures and protection to minority shareholders, thus affecting equity investments. Capital gains tax rates, labour market rigidities and the efficiency of bankruptcy procedures also affect venture capital. Active stock markets need to be embedded in an environment where talented managers have broad incentives to become entrepreneurs (Jeng and Wells, 2000).

2.3 The Financing of Innovation in the 'New Economy'

The rapid swings of capital markets prove that a deep rethinking of high-tech activities is going on (Brooking, 1996; Demers and Lev, 2001). The traditional idea of high-tech firms characterized by relevant entry barriers, big laboratories and huge R&D investments is ousted by a new model developed on networks (such as the Internet) and information exchange. Therefore, firms must face an increasingly competitive and dynamic environment, through the development of their 'intellectual capital' (Volderba, 1996), their entry options in emerging markets (Perotti and Rossetto, 2000) and their intangible assets, such as network economies. However, firms' balance sheets fail to account for these investments in a proper manner: many empirical works highlighted that the correlation between stock price and accounting current performance (such as profits and cash flows) has fallen significantly during the last decades (Amir and Lev, 1996; Lev and Zarowin, 1999). The acceleration of advances in technology has called into question the traditional relation between financial variables and equity valuation. As a consequence, the difficulty of evaluating high-tech investments, as well as the difficulty of raising external finance, have been remarked upon.

Several empirical analyses showed that a firm's market value in emerging business (such as the Internet) is poorly correlated with its expected future cash flows (Amir and Lev, 1996; Brooking, 1996; Perotti and Rossetto, 2000).

The growing complexity of innovation activities increases the cost of obtaining the kind of information enabling financiers to verify the accuracy and profitability of firms' investment opportunities. In addition, the problem of pointing out new adequate non-financial measures of value for the 'new economy' stocks arises, since the economy is evolving at such a rapid pace that historical information and accounting data (where existing) are not useful for valuing any emerging business.

3.   THE LISTING OF INNOVATIVE COMPANIES ON THE STOCK EXCHANGE

Stock markets are a primary source of capital for developing companies. Efficient stock markets allow investors to divest their stakes and capitalize their investments; listed firms may raise new capital and improve their efficiency. In this section we consider the costs and benefits of the listing faced by innovative and high-tech firms. We shall examine the listing process as a complex interaction between entrepreneurs, managers, intermediates and the market. Finally we shall focus on the diffusion of 'new stock markets' (NMs) around the world, established for fast-growing, dynamic and innovative companies.

3.1   Costs and Benefits of the Listing on Stock Markets

'Going public is one of capitalism's major sacraments' (*Fortune*, 21 July 1986). Stock markets provide the source for new capital, but they also allow investors to divest their stakes when the firm is mature. The main risk faced by investors and venture capitalists is the risk of not getting their funds back. Thus, a viable exit mechanism is extremely important to the development of venture capital (Jeng and Wells, 2000). First, it provides a financial incentive for equity-compensated managers to expend effort. Second, it gives managers a call option on the control of the firm, since venture capitalists relinquish control at the listing (Black and Gilson, 1998). Third, it allows venture capitalists to recycle both financial and non-financial resources from successful companies to early-stage business.

Initial public offerings allow companies to create the floating capital required by exchange admission rules (Jenkinson and Ljungqvist, 2001; Ritter, 2002). IPOs may have numerous advantages for a company and its entrepreneurs. New equity capital may be raised, and the managers can engage more easily in stock-financed acquisitions and expansions. Yet, the transition from a privately-held to a publicly-traded company imposes substantial and costly changes in the firm's organization. Moreover, before going public, intermediates acting as consultants and underwriters have to be hired. Corporate control considerations are present, too. The contractual right to initiate an IPO ('demand registration right') is commonly discussed between the entrepreneur and the venture capitalists (Halloran et al., 2000). A threat to invoke such an option could be used by the venture capitalist to coerce the entrepreneur into pursuing an efficient business strategy.

The most relevant problem faced by IPO firms is a substantial information asymmetry between insiders (controlling entrepreneurs and managers) and investors about the company value. Analysts frequently use comparable multiples to come up with a preliminary price range to value a firm going public, and rely on forecasts about future accounting figures.

Chapters 1 and 2 showed that innovation activity is characterized by remarkable uncertainty, information asymmetry and investment specificity. Thus, technology-based innovative companies are expected to face several difficulties when going public. The fact that only scant information on R&D and other technology activities is publicly disclosed by innovator firms compounds the information problem of investors when evaluating IPOs. The information asymmetry is more significant, the higher the intensity of a firm's intangible assets, thus affecting financing and the going-public process (Lev, 2000). Maksimovic and Pichler (2001) showed that, in an emerging industry, the timing of external financing and the choice between public and private equity financing depends on the technological risks in the industry. Firms that go public early may gain advantage from beginning full-scale operations before their rivals, but risk being displaced by more efficient rivals during a period of technological change. Moreover, they can provide valuable information to potential competitors.

The remarks above suggest that traditional stock markets are often inadequate to host small but fast-growing firms, the most serious problems being tight listing requirements, high idiosyncratic risk and potential illiquidity. Therefore, many countries established specific stock exchanges for fast-growing and high-tech firms. On the one hand, the listing requirements of these 'new markets' are less severe; on the other hand, several warranties are set to protect investors from insiders' opportunistic behaviour.

The importance of the 'new stock markets' in financing innovative firms became still greater with the advent of the 'new economy' paradigm (Allen and Gale, 1999).

3.2 'New Stock Markets' around the World and in Europe

In the 1990s, Europe was eager to repeat the success of the US high-tech and 'new economy' enterprises. European lateness was blamed on the scarcity of venture capital investments and private equity active investors, and in particular on the absence of high-growth and high-tech segments such as Nasdaq (European Commission, 1994). Paradoxically, as shown in the previous chapters, during the same period market liberalization and privatization caused the investments in R&D to slow down in many sectors. This phenomenon led European countries to play a new role in promoting innovation, by allowing growing firms to enjoy tax relief (Giudici and Paleari, 2002) and, above all, by sustaining the birth of 'new stock markets' for high-growth and high-tech companies. In 1996, referring to the model of Nasdaq, the Easdaq market was founded in Belgium, to host young companies willing to obtain international audience from investors. In the same year, the French *Nouveau Marché* was born, and in 1997 the German *Neuer Markt* was created. In 1999 the London Stock Exchange opened a new specific segment for high-tech firms, TechMark, although a market for small-capitalization firms (Alternative Investment Market, or AIM) was already at work. In 1999 Italy established the *Nuovo Mercato*. In 2000, the Spanish *Nuevo Mercado* opened to high-growth firms. Other 'new' stock markets were then established in the Netherlands (NMAX), in Belgium (Euro-NM Belgium), in Finland (NM List) and in Switzerland (SWX New Market). Outside Europe, Canada, Japan and Hong Kong also instituted new exchanges for high-growth firms (Canadian Venture Exchange, Mothers, and Growth Enterprise Market, respectively).

The major European exchanges agreed to launch the Euro-NM network, grouping the German, French, Italian, Belgian and Dutch 'new stock markets'. However, the Euro-NM initiative failed to establish operating links between the member markets, and the network was disbanded on 31 December 2000, leaving full autonomy to the single NMs. The increasing number of listings on the German, French and Italian markets compared to Easdaq seemed to favour the national market paradigm. Yet, in 2001 Easdaq was taken over by the Nasdaq market, following an aggressive marketing campaign. Moreover, the Dutch, Belgian and French markets merged in the Euronext alliance. The future of the 'new stock markets' in Europe is now fluid: a debate is still going on about what kind of model should be favoured, whether that of a pan-European exchange or one preserving the single national markets.

The basic differences between NMs and the main exchanges concern their listing requirements and their trading system. Generally, NMs' listing requirements are less binding, allowing young but not yet profitable firms to be listed and to issue new capital. Investors' protection is safeguarded through the commitment to regularly disclose information, to ensure research coverage and to lock in inside equity (up to one year). The market trading rules are designed to provide liquidity and firms are often required to appoint a 'specialist' (an intermediate displaying bids on the book).

The listing requirements adopted by European NMs are slightly different across countries. The minimum accounting value of the equity ranges from €1 million (Euro.NM Belgium) to €1.65 million (SWX New Market). Euro.NM Belgium, the SWX New Market and the *Neuer Markt* require a minimum company age equal to three years, while one-year-old companies may list on all the other markets. The Spanish *Nuevo Mercado* is the only one accepting exclusively profitable companies paying dividends. The other markets also list companies with losses, provided they have an ambitious business plan and significant growth opportunities. Easdaq (Nasdaq Europe) requires that the IPO company equity have a book value equal to at least €10 million and a gross income equal to at least €1 million, or a book value equal to at least €20 million, or a market capitalization equal to €20 million, with sales larger than €50 million. The UK Techmark is a segment of the main board; therefore, the listing requirements are not specific, and firms are admitted according to their business activity (for example, information technology and software companies are automatically listed on Techmark).

The capital owned by outsiders must represent 20/25 per cent of the total equity, albeit in some cases exceptions are tolerated. Remarkably, most markets require that at least 50 per cent of the IPO shares be newly issued. This should encourage IPO firms to make new investments and grow.

Since firms going public on the 'new stock markets' are typically young and risky, in most markets insiders have to lock in their equity for up to 12 months. In fact, insiders could engage in opportunistic behaviours, aimed at selling off their shares, when overvalued.

Interestingly, the going-public process is not the same in all the exchanges considered. However, NMs generally adopt the US model, that is, book building with open price. The public offering is reserved for retailers, while institutions are allocated shares on the basis of the book-building process. A price range is contained in the prospectus, while the final offer price is decided after the collection of the institutions' bids. The price range is often set in the light of the accounting data reported by comparable listed firms.

Table 10.1 reports some basic statistics about European 'new stock markets'. A comparison with Nasdaq is also reported. It is apparent that European NMs are still far from the Nasdaq figures. Yet, the German *Neuer Markt* has reached a remarkable market capitalization, which is larger than the other NMs combined, and represents about 5.8 per cent of the German GDP. The Italian *Nuovo Mercato* achieved a significant dimension in a few months. The French *Nouveau Marché* stands out because of the number of listed companies, while the other exchanges have smaller dimensions.

Table 10.1   Statistics for 'new stock markets' around Europe, as at 1 January 2001, and comparison with Nasdaq

Stock market	Country	Market capitalization[a]	Market capitalization /GDP	Listed companies
Neuer Markt	Germany	120 992	5.8%	338
Nuovo Mercato	Italy	25 317	2.1%	40
Nouveau Marché	France	24 280	1.7%	158
Nasdaq Europe (Easdaq)	Belgium	23 900	ns[b]	62
SWX New Market	Switzerland	7 560	2.8%	17
NMAX	Netherlands	894	0.2%	15
Nuevo Mercado	Spain	13 800	2.2%	12
Euro-NM Belgium	Belgium	410	0.2%	16
NM-List	Finland	965	0.7%	11
Nasdaq	USA	3 976 438	41.3%	4 726

Notes:
a) Data in € million.
b) The ratio is not significant, because the majority of the listed companies are not incorporated in Belgium.

4.   THE EMPIRICAL ANALYSIS

In this section we shall explore the relationship between stock markets and R&D activity by analysing a sample of companies listed on the three major European NMs, namely the German *Neuer Markt*, the French *Nouveau Marché* and the Italian *Nuovo Mercato*. We believe that interesting insights on the relationship between R&D financing and innovation may be derived from such an analysis. We shall explore several hypotheses. First, we aim to verify whether the establishment of 'new stock markets' for high-growth firms around Europe had any effect on the financing of innovation, and on the pattern of R&D activity itself. Second, we shall investigate whether financial markets showed any short-termist attitude or myopia in evaluating NM firms and intangible assets, with respect to their growth and innovation opportunities. Then, we shall indicate whether the real financiers of NM companies were the private equity investors or the stock public market. Finally, we shall discuss whether adequate institutional levers will increase the efficiency of NMs in the future.

4.1   Data about the Sample Companies

As at 1 January 2001, 536 companies were listed on the German *Neuer Markt*, on the French *Nouveau Marché*, and on the Italian *Nuovo Mercato*. Table 10.1

highlighted that the *Neuer Markt* is by far the largest market, with respect to both the number of listed companies and market capitalization. The *Nuovo Mercato*, though having a lower number of listed companies, has nevertheless a larger capitalization than its French counterpart.

Figure 10.5 describes the evolution of the number of listed companies on the three NMs, and highlights a rapid growth of the exchanges, when compared to the 'traditional' stock markets for mature firms. Remarkably, the development of NMs coincided in Europe with the process of privatization and market liberalization documented in the previous chapters, as well as with the growth of investments in applied R&D.

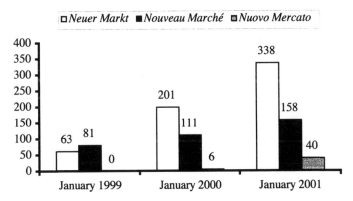

Figure 10.5   Number of companies listed in the stock markets considered in the analysis, 1 January 1999 to 1 January 2001

Table 10.2 reports the number of the foreign companies listed on the three exchanges considered. A significant difference is evident between the German NM and the other two exchanges, these latter listing only few foreign companies. The *Neuer Markt* is significantly populated by foreign companies (11 from Austria, eight from the Netherlands, seven from Israel and six from Switzerland, besides several companies from the UK, Canada, Hungary and Denmark), while the other exchanges are essentially domestic markets.

Table 10.2   Foreign companies listed in the stock markets considered in the analysis, as at 1 January 2001

Stock market	Foreign companies	% of total listed companies
Neuer Markt	47	13.9%
Nouveau Marché	2	1.3%
Nuovo Mercato	1	2.5%

The sample companies are classified in Table 10.3 according to the criteria adopted by the German exchange: (i) 'Information technology' (software and hardware companies), (ii) 'Internet' (portals, e-communities, e-tailers, on-line services, enablers, providers), (iii) 'Electronics & technology' (including technology-based manufacturing firms), (iv) 'Media & entertainment' (including multimedia services), (v) 'Telecommunications', (vi) 'Biotechnology' (including pharmaceuticals), (vii) 'MedTech & health care' and (viii) 'Others'.

Table 10.3   The sample companies, by business activity and stock market

Business activity	Neuer Markt		Nouveau Marché		Nuovo Mercato		All markets	
Information technology	92	(27%)	41	(26%)	13	(33%)	146	(27%)
Internet	68	(20%)	27	(17%)	6	(15%)	101	(19%)
Electronics & technology	69	(20%)	17	(11%)	5	(13%)	91	(17%)
Media & entertainment	42	(12%)	14	(9%)	6	(15%)	62	(11%)
Telecommunications	21	(6%)	18	(11%)	3	(7%)	42	(8%)
Biotechnology	20	(6%)	7	(4%)	3	(7%)	30	(6%)
MedTech & health care	11	(3%)	6	(4%)	0	(0%)	17	(3%)
Others	15	(4%)	28	(18%)	4	(10%)	47	(9%)
Total	338 (100%)		158 (100%)		40 (100%)		536 (100%)	

The largest group is the 'Information technology' segment, followed by the 'Internet' and 'Electronics & technology' segments respectively. 'Media and entertainment' companies are significantly represented. The presence of Internet companies is prominent in the German NM, while the Italian NM lists a relatively large number of 'Information technology' firms. The most diversified exchange seems to be the French stock market.

Table 10.4 reports the companies' mean and median age at their listing, by business activity. The mean age is equal to 11.3 years (12 years in Germany and Italy, eight years in France). Our statistics show that the mean age of European NM companies is significantly lower than the mean age of the companies listed on the main segment of the respective exchanges, where the age ranges, instead, from 35 to 50 years (Giudici and Paleari, 2001).

Not surprisingly, the youngest companies are the 'Internet' firms, while the firms belonging to the 'Electronics and technology' sector are more mature.

Table 10.5 reports the number of NM firms controlled, after their listing, by individuals or companies respectively. The evidence that most of the listed companies are controlled by individual entrepreneurs (with the important exceptions of biotech and health-care companies) characterizes NMs as valuable springboards for talented entrepreneurship.

Table 10.4   The sample companies' age at the listing, by business activity

Business activity	Mean company age (years)	Median company age (years)
Information technology	13.3	13.0
Internet	6.0	5.0
Electronics & technology	15.4	11.0
Media & entertainment	12.0	9.0
Telecommunications	8.5	4.0
Biotechnology	8.2	6.5
MedTech & health care	13.7	9.0
Others	11.6	6.0
Total	11.3	9.0

Table 10.5   The companies' controlling shareholder after the listing, by business activity (sample: 451 listed companies)

Business activity	Controlling shareholder	
	Individual	Company
Information technology	86 (72%)	33 (28%)
Internet	45 (53%)	40 (47%)
Electronics & technology	46 (61%)	30 (39%)
Media & entertainment	33 (61%)	21 (39%)
Telecommunications	24 (63%)	14 (37%)
Biotechnology	11 (48%)	12 (52%)
MedTech & health care	5 (42%)	7 (58%)
Others	20 (45%)	24 (55%)
Total	270 (60%)	181 (40%)

4.2   'Markets for Projects'

The statistics above highlighted the tumultuous growth of NMs in Europe, and seem to challenge the evidence reported by Pagano et al. (1998, 2002). Those authors posited that European exchanges hosted mostly mature and consolidated companies, with no need to finance growth investments, willing to lower their cost of capital and their leverage ratio. In contrast, they showed that technology-based dynamic European firms preferred listing on US exchanges. Thus, it is interesting to focus on the IPO companies, that is, the firms newly listed on NMs after an initial public offering of shares. Those latter companies are absolutely new to the market, and face relevant information asymmetries when going public.

Uncertainty surrounds both the actual value of existing assets, and the value of future growth opportunities to be financed. Therefore, it is worth comparing the amount of the new liquidity collected at the IPO, with the firms' resources.

Table 10.6   *Equity capital raised by the IPO companies listed in the three stock markets considered, up to 1 January 2001*

Capital raised[a]	Neuer Markt	Nouveau Marché	Nuovo Mercato
Total capital raised[a]	11 369	2 210	4 118
(% on 2000 GNP)	0.57%	0.16%	0.36%
mean amount	44.77	17.89	114.39
median value	30.85	10.67	43.78
Capital raised / book value after the listing:			
mean value	86.1%	75.9%	83.8%
median value	88.5%	81.8%	85.2%
Fraction of equity capital sold:			
mean value	24.5%	22.5%	23.7%
median value	25.0%	21.1%	22.1%
Sample companies	219	103	36

Note: a) Data in € million.

The amount of equity capital raised by the sample IPO companies is reported in Table 10.6. Data were recovered for 358 companies. The mean amount of equity capital raised with primary issues is equal to €44.77 million (*Neuer Markt*), €17.89 million (*Nouveau Marché*) and €114.39 million (*Nuovo Mercato*), respectively. Remarkably, the total capital raised on NMs represents a significant fraction of national GDP. In Italy, for example, the amount of capital raised on the *Nuovo Mercato* represents 0.36 per cent of GDP, while total annual expenditures in R&D account for about 1 per cent of domestic wealth. Nevertheless, the comparison with the total domestic expenditures in R&D is only partially informative, as the capital collected at the IPO may also finance other investments.

The difference between the mean and median amount of issued equity highlights that a few companies were able to collect a significant amount of finance from investors. Remarkably, the latter firms went public in 1999 and in the first months of 2000, when the market momentum was particularly favourable.

In all three markets, the amount of the issued capital is significant if compared to the equity accounting value after the listing: on average, it is larger
than 80 per cent of the total amount. This means that the IPO share price is
significantly larger than the book value, and it includes a large premium
over the existing assets, related to growth opportunities and intangible
assets. The marked difference between the fraction of equity capital purchased by IPO investors (on average less than 25 per cent) and the capital
raised, compared to the equity accounting value, is a direct consequence of
the premium paid by the market, and allows inside entrepreneurs to maintain
control over the companies. As a further consequence, the firms' resources
rely heavily on the liquidity collected at the listing, compared to internal
resources. Bertoni and Giudici (2001) analysed the biotech companies
listed on European NMs from 1996 to 2001 and found that, on average,
the equity capital raised at the IPO finances 48 per cent of cash expenses
in the years after the listing, while pre-IPO existing liquidity contributes
only for 4 per cent. Seasoned issues of capital and sales account for 15 per
cent and 33 per cent, respectively. They show that R&D expenses absorb
25 per cent of the cash resources, confirming that IPO proceeds are also
invested in new assets, such as acquisitions, plant and equipment, and
other costs (marketing expenses, labour and services). It is likely that similar
results could be obtained in the other business sectors of NM firms, since the
statistics reported in Table 10.6 appear to be robust, the deviation from
median and mean value being narrow.

Table 10.6 showed that European NMs are essentially 'markets for projects', where entrepreneurs sell ambitious business plans to the public, and
IPO firms are almost entirely financed by the market. In this sense, NMs can
be compared to 'venture capital exchanges', where retailers and commercial
banks play the role of professional investors. The evidence is not consistent
with the common belief that technology-based firms first obtain early
resources from private equity investors, and then go public to finance later-
stage development. In contrast, stock markets played a decisive role in
financing start-up companies. Yet, it is not clear if the evidence (that is, the
onerous premium paid by IPO investors over existing assets) is consistent
with either investors' overoptimism, or the market's buoyancy towards
long-run opportunities. The fact that 45 per cent of the analysed companies
reported losses at the listing, and expected not to realize profits in the short
run, surely confutes the hypothesis of financiers' short-termism.

The preponderance of intangible resources and the lack of positive cash
flow clearly affected the valuation process of NM firms. The uncertainty in
evaluating IPO companies is reflected in Table 10.7, showing the mean
width of the price range reported in the IPO prospectuses. Yet, uncertainty
is particularly intense only for Italian IPOs.

Table 10.7   The width of the offer price range reported in the IPO
prospectuses, by stock market[a]

	Neuer Markt	Nouveau Marché	Nuovo Mercato	All markets
IPO sample companies	294	143	36	520
Mean range width	18.64%	16.95%	46.46%	20.28%
Median value	17.65%	14.84%	30.42%	16.67%
Maximum value	58.82%	114.29%	540.00%	540.00%
Minimum value	5.71%	5.13%	5.26%	5.13%

Note: a) Width is defined as: (max. offer price – min. offer price) / minimum price.

Companies listed on NMs captured the market's attention especially in 1999 and during the first months of 2000, following the 'new economy' euphoria also documented in the US markets by Cooper et al. (2001). Technology-based companies, and above all Internet-stock IPOs, exhibited huge initial returns, and impressive subsequent performance. Giudici and Roosenboom (2001) report that an average IPO on NMs displays a +38.09 per cent first-day return, about three times larger than the first-day return of a typical IPO on the main European stock exchanges. The fact that many of the most welcomed IPO companies reported heavy losses puzzled analysts about the value drivers of NM companies. It has been argued (Hand, 2000; Demers and Lev, 2001) that revenues reported by young technology-based companies are found to be weakly positively priced by financial markets, while selling and marketing expenses are reliably positively priced. Thus, larger losses and expenses create higher market values because they reflect investments in intangible assets. Periodic expenditures on knowledge, customer acquisitions and technology appear to be capitalized as assets by investors.

Yet, after the Nasdaq fall in 2000, NM companies were badly mauled by the change of investors' expectations and sentiment. Indeed, some of them even defaulted because financiers were no longer willing to infuse capital in such distressed companies. There is evidence that, after the bubble burst, the companies' ability to sustain their 'cash burn' emerged as an important value driver, while other previously significant value indicators appeared to have lost importance (Demers and Lev, 2001).

The abnormal volatility of European NMs in 2000 is documented by Table 10.8. The most volatile market was the German *Neuer Markt*, whose market capitalization at the end of 2000 fell eightfold compared to the first months of the same year (fourteenfold if only Internet stocks are considered), disappointing many retail investors.

Table 10.8   *NM volatility in 2000 (ratio between the maximum and minimum stock price of the companies listed, as at 1 January 2001)*

	Neuer Markt	Nouveau Marché	Nuovo Mercato
Listed companies	199	108	6
Mean ratio	8.3	7.3	4.1
Median ratio	5.7	4.8	3.8
Minimum ratio	1.6	1.3	2.5
Maximum ratio	94.2	125.1	6.4

Were IPO subscribers the only ones to complain about their investment? The listing involves several interests. The controlling entrepreneurs, as shown in Table 10.5, hold relevant stakes in their firms after the listing, albeit they often sell a fraction of their shares to the public. Private equity investors and corporate venture capitalists generally trade shares at the IPO as well. Managers and employees are entitled to acquire IPO shares at favourable terms, and may have access to stock option plans. Therefore, it is interesting to find out which category of stakeholders enjoyed the major monetary benefits after the listing.

Table 10.9 reports an analysis conducted by Cassia et al. (2001) on a sample of 38 Italian companies listed on the *Nuovo Mercato*, where the return on investment was computed for the different categories of investors. Interestingly, the rate of return is strongly differentiated and the highest profits were those experienced by controlling entrepreneurs. Assuming a buy-and-hold strategy (that is, not all investors trade share), private equity investors and venture capitalists in many cases reported profits, although there were losses in four cases. Retail investors in most cases were bearing losses.

Table 10.9   *NM investors' rate of return, as at June 2001 (sample: 38 companies listed on the Italian* Nuovo Mercato*)*

Rate of return	Controlling shareholder	Venture capitalist	Managers and staff	Public
Lower than –50%	1	0	0	7
Between –50% and 0%	0	4	1	23
Between 0% and 1 000%	6	9	4	8
Between 1 000% and 10 000%	18	5	9	0
Larger than 10 000%	13	1	1	0

Source: Cassia et al. (2001).

The findings above confirm that NM retail investors, compared to professional private equity financiers, are penalized. They have a lower contractual power over the controlling entrepreneurs and are subject to market turbulence and cycles, although they bear a considerable part of the business risk by providing most of the tangible assets, as documented in Table 10.6.

The results reported in Table 10.9 may be considered as preliminary evidence for a larger survey. Should they be confirmed for all NMs, some questions about stock market efficiency will arise. In particular, while the statistics about venture capitalists' returns are not surprising, and the retail investors' wealth may easily be conditioned by the general market momentum, it is remarkable that controlling shareholders almost always obtain considerable gains from their investments in small, young and risky firms.

5.   CONCLUDING REMARKS

The achievement of NMs in Europe and the progressive integration of financial markets followed the process of privatization and liberalization documented in the previous chapters. The success of European NMs is testified by the impressive number of newly-listed firms and by the significant amount of equity capital raised by IPO companies. Surprisingly, most of the firms listed on NMs were not profitable, raising the following three relevant questions. Was the market rational in pricing NM IPOs? What are the value drivers of NM companies? Should they be financed?

In this chapter we considered a sample of companies listed on the three major European NMs, namely the German *Neuer Markt*, the French *Nouveau Marché* and the Italian *Nuovo Mercato*. We highlighted a positive correlation between the growth of these exchanges and the development of venture capital investments, especially start-ups and technology financing, across Europe.

We underlined that NM companies are far from being later-stage enterprises, willing to finance their expansion. In contrast, we characterized NMs as 'markets for projects', where ambitious business plans are sold to the public. In this sense, NMs do not represent primarily an exit occasion for private equity investors, but a 'public venture capital market' financed by retailers. While the market for venture capital is dominated by 'pressure-resistant' shareholders (David, 1991) such as institutional investors, European NMs still seem to be pervaded by 'pressure-sensitive' retail shareholders. Albeit characterized by risk propensity, NM investors often expect to capitalize significant gains in the short run. Unfortunately, up to now they have been the most penalized financiers, providing most of the tangible assets while bearing the highest risk, compared to their control power over entrepreneurs.

We posited that the establishment of NMs in Europe contributed to the increase of investments in applied R&D, as well as several other determinants pointed out in the preceding chapters. We highlighted that most of the NM firms belong to business sectors (such as the Internet business, computer software, and media) where entry barriers are fairly weak, thus reducing the need for basic research.

We showed that, albeit characterized by a high degree of uncertainty and risk, NM IPOs were positively welcomed by stock markets, which attributed considerable value to their intangible resources, in terms of growth opportunities, innovation capability and capital investments. This value cannot be explained by traditional valuation frameworks based on expected cash flows and profits. Thus, we have to reject the hypothesis of investors' short-termism on financial markets. Yet, we cannot even accept the hypothesis that the market proved fully efficient in pricing NM IPOs.

After a tumultuous growth, European NMs in 2001 were still experiencing a downward correction. Investors focused on growth prospects, but realistic analyses about future profitability were generally neglected. Moreover, there is evidence that entrepreneurs in some cases took advantage of the market euphoria for high-tech stock in 1999 and 2000 in order to raise capital and sell overpriced shares (Bertoni and Giudici, 2001).

We believe that new growing opportunities will be generated in the future by emerging technologies, such as wireless and third-generation mobile platforms, where Europe has a clear lead over the US, as well as by other areas such as life science, security software, optical technology, and interactive television. Yet, we think that stock markets should clearly distinguish between financing the growth of established companies and financing promising (but aleatory) business plans. To this extent, the role of professional investors is fundamental and corporate governance frameworks should be adopted in order to further stimulate the activism of private equity investors. At the same time, underwriters, investors and analysts should be encouraged not to collude. This is not an easy task in bank-based European financial markets, since the actors often belong to the same business group.

PART IV

Conclusions

11. Conclusions and Policy Implications

Mario Calderini, Paola Garrone
and Maurizio Sobrero

1. FINDINGS

The specific contribution of this volume to the debate on the determinants of innovation is, we believe, mainly of an empirical nature. However, in order to define the setting for our empirical effort, different streams of managerial and economic studies needed to be considered, due to the composite set of structures, decisions and events that are deemed to affect a firm's innovation activities. Accordingly, the first part of the volume provides the reader with the systematization of a quite comprehensive theoretical background.

In particular, the literature surveyed by the first three chapters contends that the level of research and development (R&D) investments, their efficiency, and the micro-structure of the innovation process are moulded mainly by three groups of determinants: the corporate governance structure, the degree of product market competition and the corporate combination decisions and patterns. Parts II and III examine the different hypotheses advanced by the surveyed literature.

The reader is referred to the conclusions of each chapter for a synthesis of the main theoretical hypotheses and empirical findings. In these final remarks, we rather single out a restricted number of conceptual predictions, which have been discussed from different perspectives and with different intensity throughout the theoretical surveys. We then move on to summarize the major pieces of evidence that the subsequent chapters, irrespective of their presentation order, have been able to extract from firm and industry data and facts.

First, several aspects of corporate governance that are crucial to innovation are driven by the relationship between ownership and control. All the survey chapters present the claim, made by several studies, that public markets for equity would be relatively less capable than managers of stimulating industrial R&D, and at the same time discuss the adverse hypothesis (that is, efficiency of the financial market). In other words, the discussion of the 'short-termism' perspective unfolds across all the initial chapters.

243

Among the empirical findings presented in the volume, it is the meta-analysis by Oriani and Sobrero (Chapter 8) that more directly tackles the question. The organic representation of available studies shows that financial markets evaluate corporate R&D investments more positively than tangible assets, though the economic value of R&D seems to have been decreasing in recent years. Giudici and Paleari study the performance of European 'new markets' (Chapter 10); in their analysis, they argue that the high-tech stock markets further accommodate the equity propensity towards R&D, emerging as a 'public venture capital market'. Of course, evidence on the market evaluation of firms' innovation activities answers no questions on the quality of R&D investments and their effectiveness as to technical progress, but discharges public stockholders from the accusation of inability to recognize the R&D value.

The analyses by Munari and Sobrero (Chapter 4), and Munari and Oriani (Chapter 9) add a different and complementary kind of evidence. Those studies test whether and how a formerly state-owned company modifies its incentives to innovate and the whole innovation process after the public offer. Chapter 4 shows that the privatization process discourages R&D investments (both in absolute levels and in intensity), but it stimulates inno-vation applications, as testified by a surge in the number of issued patents, even after controlling for their quality. As documented by Chapter 9, the market evaluation of R&D investments is, after the public offer, lower for state-owned enterprises than for their industrial counterparts, even if the gap tends to disappear over the years. This array of stylized facts on privatization and innovation is to some extent strengthened by Calderini and Garrone's analysis of an event that in many cases is temporally related to privatization, that is, the liberalization of retail markets (Chapter 5).

The empirical findings on the effects of privatization, if considered jointly with results on the R&D market value, seem to suggest that the evaluation made by public ownership (that is, by external shareholders) is unequal with respect to different components of the innovation process. It succeeds in appre-ciating R&D in so far as it translates into applications and, thus, stimulates the management to restructure innovation activities at the expense of 'pet' projects, with a productivity gain; however, beneficial longer-term activities might as well be cut. To solve this puzzle, so peculiar to the short-termism debate, the framework needs to be enlarged to comprehend other elements; the following paragraphs illustrate how the works contained in this book have attempted to cope with such an endeavour.

Second, evidence on privatized companies suggests that a critical covariate of the relationship between shareholders and managers is the nature of the principal, as argued by the studies reviewed in Chapter 1. First, large, insti-tutional external stockholders are more competent in evaluating long-term investments, less risk averse, and better able to condition the management. Second, a state as owner is more likely to subsidize basic research and to support it through appropriate control systems and personnel policies. Chapter 3, which surveys several theories on the effects of mergers and acquisitions (M&As) on innovation, also addresses the theme of the nature of principals, though under a different perspective. It leads to the formulation of the hypothesis that the allocation of property rights on the innovation output of research-oriented companies to customer-oriented companies is, under certain conditions, natural but inefficient.

The role of the state as a principal is enlightened by the case studies reported by Munari (Chapter 7). The public offerings of a state-owned enterprise frequently result in scaling down the research facilities, in emphasizing a market-driven approach to the selection of projects, and in radically modifying personnel motivations and attitude towards fundamental research. The ability of concentrated shareholding to sustain innovation activities is not directly addressed, but Giudici and Paleari claim that dispersed, retail shareholders are characterized by expectations of significant short-run gains; in other words, they are unsuitable to finance fundamental research (Chapter 10). Lastly, the evidence on acquisitions in information and communication technology sectors yielded by Calderini, Garrone and Scellato adds some clues to the explanatory power of the principal's type (Chapter 6). The greatest part of the sample is constituted by acquisitions of small, young, and innovative firms by larger organizations, which are frequently better established in the final markets. The aggregate evidence is that, on average, the number of patents applied for by the acquired establishments decreases after the deal; preliminary analysis seems to confirm that the trend is maintained over subsequent years. It is worth emphasizing that both the target and the acquirer are public companies: innovation performances are thus not influenced by a change in the exposure to financial markets. In conclusion, inherently different kinds of principals, such as states, retail investors and large corporations have different incentives and competencies with respect to the upstream phases of the innovation process.

Third, Chapter 2 reviews studies arguing that an increasing degree of product market competition is likely to alter the firm's incentives towards more basic research activities, and to favour R&D investments in applied research and development projects. Our theoretical argument is based on the idea that the relationship between product market competition and the incentive to innovate is shaped by opposing forces, the outcome of which is rather difficult to predict. Following the approach suggested by recent literature on endogenous growth, we grouped these forces into Schumpeterian and Darwinian ones, according to whether they determine a positive or negative relationship between product market competition and innovation. The former group nests around the classical Schumpeterian idea of the monopoly power favouring competition, the latter around the Arrowian intuition of competition stimulating innovation. Our approach to the problem is novel because, instead of elaborating on the classical U-shaped relationship resulting from such opposite forces, we claim that, by separating the problem into two distinct parts, the effect on basic research and the effect on applied/development research, we are able to single out different aspects of the problem. Specifically, we argue that the trade-off between Schumpeterian and Darwinian forces is unbalanced towards the former when dealing with basic research, and towards the latter as far as applied/development research is concerned. The resulting empirical hypothesis (see Chapter 5) is that the effect of an increase in product market competition is ambiguous in terms of the overall R&D intensity, but is quite clear in terms of R&D composition: firms will turn to invest more in applied/development research and less in basic research.

The issue is empirically tackled in Chapter 5, where we demonstrate that a discontinuity in the degree of product market competition in the telecom service market alters the composition of companies' research portfolio, in favour of applied research and to the detriment of basic research.

Finally, the hypothesis that 'managerial myopia' is an inhibiting factor for innovation is a recurring element throughout the studies we surveyed in the first part of the book. It may emerge under different ownership and market structures, and translate into various aspects of the governance decisions and structure, such as the typology of control mechanisms (Chapters 1 and 3) and the poor attention and commitment to long-term projects in the acquisitions led by large, diversified companies (Chapter 3). In particular, a 'championing' culture saves and defends the R&D programmes that are promising according to R&D personnel and chief technical officers, though scarcely understood by external investors and the top management itself. Such an attitude is precisely the most likely victim of many corporate restructuring patterns that characterize modern industries, if managers are unable to convey the value of R&D activities towards internal and external stakeholders. The most recurrent examples are the formalized control systems typical of large and diversified organizations (again, Chapters 1 and 3), the organizational turmoil, risk-aversion and irrational selective attitudes caused by acquisitive events (Chapter 3), or the strategic focus on neck-to-neck competition prevailing in increasingly competitive markets (Chapter 2). Managerial myopia, finally, reflects on R&D organization and personnel behaviour, as suggested by Chapters 1 and 3. R&D departments, teams and personnel are characterized by highly unusual micro-organizational routines and individual motivations that are unlikely to be robust on their own with respect to ownership dispersion and corporate restructuring.

As to managers' short-termist attitudes, the evidence yielded by the preceding chapters is rather spurious. Events such as privatization, liberalization, or

M&As impact simultaneously at different levels of the corporate and business structure, organization and management, thus limiting the opportunity to insulate effects merely inherent to managerial decision making and interventions.

However, evidence on the generalized scaling-down of R&D facilities in formerly state-owned firms noted by Munari (Chapter 7), and on the decreasing patenting activity in acquired business units tested by Calderini, Garrone and Scellato (Chapter 6) allows us not to dismiss the hypothesis of managerial myopia.[1]

2. POLICY IMPLICATIONS

The various empirical results that are presented throughout the book and the lines of arguments that are formulated in support of such results, although not explicitly formulated in a normative perspective, do suggest some relevant issues both for the company's strategy and for technological policy making.

Most of our results can be read compactly in terms of trading off static and dynamic efficiency, or, more precisely, in the classical 'investment versus exploitation' trade-off. As suggested above, one strong motivation for this effort was the shared feeling that policy making has in recent years suffered heavily from a systematic bias towards static efficiency, to the detriment of the dynamic one. As a result, in many key industries competition policy has overwhelmed any serious attempt to bring the innovation-related social welfare into the cost/benefit accounting of new emerging market structures and the related new forms of corporate governance.

The common feature shared by the single chapters of this book, both the theoretical and empirical ones, is precisely the attempt to single out and to quantify not only those new forms of dynamic market failures that are virtually neglected in the policy debate, but also their practical consequences in terms of loss of private and social welfare.

To this purpose, we have been sailing through a number of related but different phenomena, such as privatization, liberalizations and mergers and acquisitions, in order to convince the reader – the manager or the policy maker – that the costs associated with the inaccurate management of these processes are all but negligible.

It is now time to look back at our effort and to build on our results in order to suggest possible implications and lines of intervention. We shall try to detach the set of arguments more appropriately referring to the policy sphere from the one being more genuinely managerial, although in many circumstances the two dimensions of the problem are strictly related.

The policy maker has probably drawn one main conclusion from this reading: the phenomena that have most heavily shaped the new institutional form of crucial European industries share a common feature, that is, they tend to reduce the incentive to engage in in-house private R&D. Therefore, if he/she is willing to give any credit to our findings, he/she is left with two clear objectives for technology policy making: first, to assess whether the decrease in R&D is purely efficiency driven, or conversely, whether it brings in hidden inefficiencies; second, in case the latter holds, to find out how to compensate the inefficient part of such R&D decrease. The answer to the former question is embedded in the discussion of the results presented in almost every single chapter of the book: although the efficiency-driven decrease is certainly an important bit of our story, nevertheless, we cannot exclude and we are strongly in favour of the latter hypothesis, that important dynamic inefficiencies come along with the reshaping of European industries, new institutional settings and corporate structures. Therefore, the policy argument boils down to under-standing which form of intervention is best suited to guarantee an efficient level of technological knowledge production at both industry and company levels.

There are, obviously, two main lines of reasoning that can be followed: on the one side, research policies should be directed to surrogate the decrease in research investment by means of direct public investments; on the other, policies should also be targeted at redirecting companies' incentives towards R&D, or even to directly mitigate the information asymmetries that are the very heart of the market failures outlined all through the previous chapters.

The former option leads us to re-examine the role that the public research system should be asked to play.

It is quite clear that the kind of investments we have been dealing with are characterized, although to a different extent, by a relatively low degree of appropriability, and that they display public-good characteristics. Therefore, one simple option would be that research activities be externalized to the public research system. Three remarks are in order.

First, policy makers, in this very historical circumstance should seriously consider the adequacy of the single national research systems to sustain the extraordinary effort required to inherit the industrial research mission. Doubts can legitimately be cast on the fact that most European countries could confidently assert so.

Second, provided that the national research systems are adequate to do so, policy makers should ask themselves whether the kind of knowledge produced by public research is actually to be considered a perfect substitute for in-house generated knowledge. Of course, if we think of the direct, codified output of research, this latter is certainly a public good that can be indifferently produced in-house or by universities. But, as Pavitt (1991), Rosenberg (1990) and David et al. (1994) prominently documented, the indirect outcomes of research tasks, such as acquiring selection, prospection and absorptive capacity, are as important as the direct ones, if not more. This latter kind of result is highly appropriable, idiosyncratic and not transferable: as such, it is unlikely to be replaced by the public research system. Therefore, even assuming that the public research system can efficiently substitute in-house industrial research, it is debatable whether indirect results can be transferred and internalized by individual firms. The point is that, for firms operating in countries that are not on the frontier of scientific research, this latter output (the indirect results) is far more important than invention as such. The message is, therefore, that it could be risky to rely entirely on the public system to provide the national system of innovation, and particularly private companies, with the appropriate stock of knowledge.

This line of reasoning can be easily applied, on a larger scale, to national technological policies. We address this comment to the countries that are followers in the innovation race and that might, therefore, be tempted to direct their efforts uniquely to the exploitation of technological knowledge created elsewhere, so dismissing their core research capabilities. This strategy is myopic and is likely to lock the national innovation system in an utterly negative trajectory.

Third, as evidenced in Chapter 5, researchers working in public institutions do not seem to have directed their efforts to compensate for the decrease in basic research observed in private companies. We argue that this is the result of a system of incentives that tend to increasingly favour industry-oriented research in academia, to the detriment of fundamental research. On the basis of our results, we can assert that such a structure of incentives is producing an effect that is exactly opposite to what should be sought in terms of social welfare. Public research should be required to compensate the basic research deficit, rather than to amplify the magnitude of the phenomenon. Unfortunately, the new rhetoric of efficiency in European public research is causing dangerous misunderstandings. Words like 'applied' or 'industry oriented' are becoming synonymous with efficiency, while the adjectives 'basic' or 'fundamental' are increasingly associated with the concept of 'useless' research. This is exactly the contrary of what we should do in order to preserve – within Europe, within single countries and within companies – the distinctive capabilities that are needed to be efficient in applied and development activities.

These considerations highlight two major points. First, we should rethink the structure of incentives that is being imposed on public systems through the funding mechanisms, in order to let public researchers invest in the replacing of the missing quota of basic knowledge within the national systems of innovation. Second, when dealing with this kind of market failure, we should not rely entirely on public research systems to produce basic knowledge, but we should also try to preserve the small part of in-house proprietary research that is still carried on in large European companies. This argument leads us to the second of the options sketched above: how to find a way of either influencing companies' incentives or correcting market failures.

This second point is rather delicate, because it involves reconsidering the *trade-off* between the static efficiency benefits associated with competition and the dynamic inefficiencies associated with high degrees of market turmoil and industry dynamics. Of course, the idea that the social benefits of competition should be traded off against the reduction in the stock of knowledge that is available to the industry should not lead anyone to conclude that industrial dynamics should be somehow limited. Nevertheless, it seems strange that, among the numerous regulatory actions designed to limit the negative effects of different sources of market failures, no regulatory effort has been produced in relation to innovation-related market failures.

The question is, therefore, how to preserve a critical mass of basic and applied knowledge within large European companies without losing the beneficial effects of competition, that is, without limiting industrial dynamics. In our view, there are two main lines of intervention. First, by providing direct support to industrial basic and mission-oriented research; second, by improving the accountability of R&D expenses.

As far as direct support is concerned, the obvious objection is, of course, why companies should be funded (either by means of direct funding or through fiscal credits) to do what they normally are expected to do for their own convenience. This argument is actually very strong, since the non-public nature of research results that we have been describing all through the book makes the spillover-related free-riding problem almost irrelevant in this context.

In response to the previous objection, sponsors of fiscal credits to support R&D argue that these latter should be applied only to incremental expenses, that is, to the part of research exceeding the activities that companies would perform anyway. However, the application of incremental fiscal incentives for research in the new competitive scenario characterizing many industries presents severe problems, especially over the transitory period. At present, the distribution of investments in research is extremely skewed. Historically, large European companies, especially in formerly regulated sectors, have invested considerable resources in research, whereas the new entrants have, so far, invested very little in research (especially in its more fundamental component), or in most cases nothing. Obviously, such an uneven starting point may create severe difficulties in the application of incremental fiscal credits, favouring the new entrants which might, with little effort, gain very large incremental benefits, so damaging the larger companies, which would be required to produce extraordinary incremental efforts.

Moreover, a well-known kind of moral hazard holds in this contest: companies might use both direct funding and fiscal credits rather arbitrarily. In fact, the actual allocation of direct funding to research activities, or the nature itself of research activities yielding fiscal credits is hardly observable; it might be impossible to verify, *ex post*, that public support was expressly directed to research tasks. The risk is that the resources made available by public support are directed to development and commercial activities, thus amplifying the companies' tendency to favour the short-term dimension in their investment decisions.

Finally, when designing effective science and technology policies, two characteristics of inventive activities should be taken into account: first, that new basic principles, fundamental knowledge and scientific breakthroughs are usually obtained in scientific fields rather far from those normally being covered by research labs. Second, the number of corporate research labs in the world that are really at the frontier of scientific research and that can reasonably be expected to produce new knowledge is restricted to a very few cases. Therefore, policies should be directed not so much to foster inventive activity as such, because this would produce inefficient efforts in the vast majority of companies. Rather, policies should concentrate on the *kind* of output that companies are really aiming at, when they decide to do research with their own money. First, in-house basic research facilities are a fringe benefit that, when offered to researchers on the job market, allow the smartest and most productive ones to be selected and recruited. Second, in-house research is normally a very efficient way to train researchers. Third, scientific knowledge is not available on the shelf at no cost; companies must have some in-house capabilities in order to plug in to the university research centres that make new knowledge available. Fourth, basic research capabilities are essential to making right decisions about the new directions of applied research, for being acquainted with scientific paradigms should allow companies to be efficient in exploring the frontiers of knowledge and in selecting the most promising ideas. Fifth, the potential applications and the new directions of applied research are usually unintentional products of basic research activities. Finally, performing in-house research normally yields high returns in terms of reputation.

The common feature of all the different elements making in-house research economically valuable is the possibility of linking up to the scientific community and the opportunity of exploiting the positive externalities that may be derived from that. In our view, it is in this direction that public support should be targeted. The most direct way to accomplish this task is the definition of flexible contractual arrangements, in universities and in private companies that would allow private and public researchers to share their time between public institutions and companies. Furthermore, public incentives should be expressly directed to support the exchanges between public and private institutions, and more in general to foster the participation of companies' research staff in the scientific community. Therefore, fiscal credits should be based on the output rather than on the input (expenses) of R&D activities.

The second direction of intervention suggested above is the improvement of R&D accountability. The review of short-termism that is presented in Chapter 2 and thoroughly discussed in many other parts of the book is complemented by the evidence presented in Chapters 8 and 9, where longitudinal approaches to investors' evaluations of firms' expenditures on R&D show positive dynamic market reactions. Such reactions, however, when observed more closely, are still extremely varied and often discount signalling effects, rather than a precise evaluation of accounting figures related to R&D expenses and projects. It is therefore not yet clear to what extent markets are currently able to discriminate different types of innovative investments based on financial figures alone. Indeed, as pointed out by a growing number of accounting scholars, current accounting standards are no longer adequate to give a full account of the multifaceted, uncertain, unpredictable and knowledge-intensive nature of basic, mission-oriented and even applied research projects, and of their long-term economic value. Therefore, accounting information about a firm's R&D spending is generally of little help. First, firms may find it difficult to identify what really counts as an R&D cost. The R&D spending is generally aggregated in one single item, which conveys little information about the real nature of the costs. More importantly, in many countries the local accounting principles require a firm to deduct all its R&D expenditure as a current expense against income, although the benefits derived from such expenses are typically long-lived and should be more appropriately treated as a capital expenditure. Such information deficit tends to make shareholders short-sighted and, as a consequence, to bias managers' incentives towards short-term objectives.

The issue is twofold. On the one hand, the increasing blurring of country barriers with respect to the market of the financial instruments targeted to support innovative projects requires a specific effort towards the harmonization of sometimes quite diverse norms and accounting principles, both between and within geographical areas. This is true in particular for the EU area, where several national discrepancies in the accounting principles regulating the R&D expenses, as well as different definitions of what can or cannot be considered 'R&D activity' for fiscal purposes still coexist.

On the other hand, it is also very important that national policy makers turn their attention to innovating the classification and the accounting schemes of intangible assets, both improving the accounting treatment of R&D expenses and devising new ways to measure innovation performances. This issue is at the core of the international debate concerning the accountability of intangible investments and their role in determining firms' performance and value. While this is certainly, from a policy perspective, a means and not an end, unfortunately such an important issue has been neglected by policy makers, and put aside as if it were a technical issue, mainly of interest to the Certified Public Accountants (CPA) communities of the different countries. Yet, as the role of intangibles in gaining competitive advantage has recently been breaking down the barriers of the accounting department within firms, and reaching the offices of CEOs and top executives, we believe that it is of the foremost importance, especially for European governments, to raise the level of the debate of this issue. Empirical studies of the economic implications of R&D investments have steadily grown in the last ten years, mostly using US data and resources deriving from the pioneering effort started in the 1980s by Zvi Griliches to build reliable statistics in this field. The need to review R&D accountability was strongly advocated in the works by Baruch Lev and colleagues (Lev and Sougiannis, 1996, 1999; Lev, 2001). We believe that the improvement of the accounting standards, practices, principles and indicators related to R&D activities and the intangible part of their output is a similarly crucial area of action for policy makers.

We hasten to say that the merit of this effort is to take innovation back to the very heart of the debate on corporate governance, market structure and innovation, broadening the traditional R&D-intensity perspective. Policy guidelines should be inspired by the consideration that only a balanced profile of long- and short-term research investments will guarantee crucial industries and the national systems of innovation an appropriate rate of technological progress. The issue is crucial to policy makers; the negative effects will become manifest, by definition, in the medium/long term, when it might be far too late to implement policies aimed at mitigating the effects of a collapse in the industries' knowledge base.

NOTE

1. More precisely, the reported stylized facts are consistent with two concurrent explanations. First, managers behave in an opportunistic fashion, and are either unable or unwilling to sponsor promising yet risky (or long-term) R&D activities; this may also occur due to co-ordination failures between managers across different corporate levels and units. Second, key researchers and technical managers leave (or plan to leave) the company due to a radical change in the principal's nature, as during privatization and acquisition programmes, or in the amount of resources available to fundamental research, as after public offer of state-owned companies.

Bibliography

Abernathy, W.J. and Clark, K.B. (1985), 'Innovation: Mapping the Winds of Creative Destruction', *Research Policy*, **14** (1), 3–22.

Aboody, D. and Lev, B. (2000), 'Information Asymmetry, R&D and Insider Gains', *Journal of Finance*, **55** (6), 2747–66.

Aghion, P., Bloom, N., Blundell, R., Griffith, R. and Howitt, P. (2002), 'Competition and Innovation: An Inverted U Relationship', IFS Working Paper 02/04, Institute for Fiscal Studies, London, UK.

Aghion, P. and Howitt, P. (1998), *Endogenous Growth Theory*, Cambridge, USA: MIT Press.

Aghion, P. and Tirole, J. (1998) 'The Management of Innovation', *Quarterly Journal of Economics*, **109**, 1185–209.

Ahuja, G. and Katila, R. (2001), 'Technological Acquisitions and the Innovation Performance of Acquiring Firms: A Longitudinal Study', *Strategic Management Journal*, **22**, 197–220.

Allen, F. and Gale, D. (1999), 'Diversity of Opinions and Financing of New Technologies', *Journal of Financial Intermediation*, **8** (1), 68–89.

Allen, F. and Gale, D. (2000), *Comparing Financial Systems*, Cambridge, USA: MIT Press.

Amir, E. and Lev, B. (1996), 'Value-relevance of Nonfinancial Information: The Wireless Communications Industry', *Journal of Accounting and Economics*, **22** (1–3), 3–30.

Amit, R. and Livnat, J. (1988), 'Diversification and the Risk–Return Trade-off', *Academy of Management Journal*, **31**, 154–65.

Anand, B. and Galetovic, A. (2000), 'Weak Property Rights and Holdup in R&D', *Journal of Economics and Management Strategy*, **9** (4), 615–42.

Ancona, D. and Caldwell, D. (1992), 'Demography and Design: Predictors of New Product Team Performance', *Organization Science*, **3** (3), 321–41.

Andrade, G., Mitchell, M. and Stafford, E. (2001), 'New Evidence and Perspectives on Mergers', *Journal of Economics Perspectives*, **15** (2), 103–20.

Archibugi, D. and Pianta, M. (1992), *The Technological Specialisation of Advanced Countries*, Boston, USA: Kluwer Academic Publishers.

Argote, L., Beckman, S. L. and Epple, D. (1990), 'The Persistence and Transfer of Learning in Industrial Settings', *Management Science*, **36** (2), 140–54.

Arora, A. and Gambardella, A. (1991), 'Complementarity and External Linkage: The Strategies of the Large Firms in Biotechnology', *Journal of Industrial Economics*, **37** (4), 361–79.

Arora, A. and Merges, R. (2000), 'Property Rights, Firm Boundaries and R&D Inputs', Working Paper, H. John Heinz III School of Public Policy and Management, Carnegie Mellon University, Pittsburgh, USA.

Arrow, K. (1962), 'Economic Welfare and the Allocation of Resources for Invention', in R.R. Nelson (ed.), *The Rate and Direction of Inventive Activity*, Princeton, USA: Princeton University Press.

Badaracco, J.J. (1991), *The Knowledge Link*, Boston, USA: Harvard Business School Press.

Bajo, E., Bigelli, M. and Sandri, S. (1998), 'The Stock Market Reaction to Investment Decisions: Evidence from Italy', *Journal of Management and Governance*, **2** (1), 1–16.

Baker, M. and Gompers, P.A. (2001), 'The Determinants of Board Structure at the Initial Public Offering', Working Paper, Harvard University, Cambridge, USA.

Baysinger, B.D. and Hoskisson, R.E. (1989), 'Diversification Strategy and R&D Intensity in Large Multiproduct Firms', *Academy of Management Journal*, **32** (2), 205–14; 310–32.

Baysinger, B.D. and Hoskisson, R.E. (1990), 'The Composition of Boards of Directors and Strategic Control', *Academy of Management Review*, **15** (1), 72–88.

Baysinger, B.D., Kosnik, R.D. and Turk, T.A. (1991), 'Effects of Board and Ownership Structure on Corporate R&D Strategy', *Academy of Management Journal*, **34**, 205–14.

Belcher, A. (1996), 'R&D Disclosure: Theory and Practice', in A. Belcher, J. Hassard and S. Procter (eds), *R&D Decisions. Strategy, Policy and Disclosure*, London, UK: Routledge.

Berk, J.B., Green, R.C. and Naik, V. (1999), 'Optimal Investment, Growth Options, and Security Returns', *Journal of Finance*, **54** (5), 1553–607.

Berle, A. and Means, G. (1932), *The Modern Corporation and Private Property*, New York, USA: World Inc. (It. transl. 1966, *Società per Azioni e Proprietà Privata*, Torino, Italy: Einaudi).

Berndt, E. (1990), 'The Impact of Corporate Restructuring on Industrial Research and Development: Comments and Discussion', *Brookings Papers on Economic Activity: Microeconomics*, 125–9.

Bertoni, F. and Giudici, G. (2001), 'The Good, the Bad and the Ugly... Everyone Wants to Join the *Nuovo Mercato*', Séminaire *Introductions en Bourse*, Université Paris XII, Paris, France, 29 March.

Bertoni, F., Giudici, G. and Randone, P.A. (2002), 'Stock Markets Funding for Biotech Pharmaceutical Companies: Nasdaq vs. European New Markets',

Workshop *The Post-entry Performance of Firms: Technology, Growth, and Survival*, University of Bologna, Bologna, Italy, 22–23November.

Beuzit, P. (2000), 'La Recherche au Cœur de la Stratégie de la Firme: l'Example de Renault', *Le Journal de l'Ecole de Paris*, **22**.

Bha, R. and Dumontier, P. (2001), 'R&D Intensity and Corporate Financial Policy: Some International Evidence', *Journal of Business Finance and Accounting*, **28** (5).

Bharadwaj, A.S., Bharadwaj, S.G. and Konsynski, B.R. (1999), 'Information Technology Effects on Firm Performance as Measured by Tobin's q', *Management Science*, **45** (7), 1008–24.

Bijker, W.E., Hughes, T.P. and Pinch, T. (eds) (1987), *The Social Construction of Technological Systems*, Cambridge, USA: MIT Press.

Binks, M. and Ennew, C. (1996), 'Growing Firms and the Credit Constraint', *Small Business Economics*, **8**, 17–25.

Binks, M., Ennew, C. and Reed, C. (1992), 'Information Asymmetries and the Provision of Finance to Small Firms', *International Small Business Journal*, **11** (1), 35–46.

Bizjack, J.M., Brickley, J.A. and Coles, J.L. (1993), 'Stock-based Incentive Compensation and Investment Behaviour', *Journal of Accounting and Economics*, **16**, 349–72.

Black, B. and Gilson, R. (1998), 'Venture Capital and the Structure of Capital Markets: Banks versus Stock Markets', *Journal of Financial Economics*, **47** (3), 243–77.

Bloningen, B.A. and Taylor, C.T. (2000), 'R&D Intensity and Acquisitions in High-technology Industries: Evidence from the US Electronic and Electric Equipment Industries', *Journal of Industrial Economics*, **48** (1), 47–70.

Bloom, N. and Van Reenen, J. (2000), 'Real Options, Patents, Productivity and Market Value: Evidence from a Panel of British Firms', IFS Working Paper 00/21, Institute for Fiscal Studies, London, UK.

Blundell, R., Bond, S., Devereux, M. and Schiantarelli, F. (1992), 'Investment and Tobin's q', *Journal of Econometrics*, **51** (1–2), 233–57.

Blundell, R., Griffith, R. and Van Reenen, J. (1995), 'Dynamic Count Data Models of Technological Innovation', *Economic Journal*, **105**, 333–44.

Blundell, R., Griffith, R. and Van Reenen, J. (1999), 'Market Share, Market Value and Innovation in a Panel of British Manufacturing Firms', *Review of Economic Studies*, **66** (3), 529–54.

Bommer, M. and Jalajas, D.S. (1999), 'The Threat of Organizational Downsizing on the Innovative Propensity of R&D Professionals', *R&D Management*, **29** (1), 27–34; 47–70.

Bond, S. and Cummins, J. (2000), 'The Stock Market and Investment in the New Economy: Some Tangible Facts and Intangible Fictions', in *NBER Research Meeting on Economic Fluctuations and Growth*, 22 July,

National Bureau of Economic Research, Cambridge, USA.

Boycko, M., Shleifer, A. and Vishny, R.W. (1996), 'A Theory of Privatization', *Economic Journal*, **106**, 309–19.

Bozeman, B. and Loveless, S. (1987), 'Sector Context and Performance. A Comparison of Industrial and Government Research Units', *Administration and Society*, **19** (2), 197–235.

Breitzman, A., Thomas, P. and Cheney, M. (2000), 'Technological Power-house or Diluted Competence: Techniques for Assessing Mergers via Patent Analysis', Paper presented at the Competitive Technical Intelligence 2000 Conference, San Francisco, USA.

Brooking, A. (1996), *Intellectual Capital: Core Assets for the Third Millennium Enterprise*, London, UK: Thomson Business Press.

Buchanan, J.M. (1972), *Theory of Public Choice*, Ann Arbor, USA: University of Michigan Press.

Burgelman, R.A. (1984), 'Managing the Internal Corporate Venturing Process', *Sloan Management Review*, **25** (2), 33–48.

Burgelman, R.A. (1986), 'Managing Corporate Entrepreneurship: New Struc-tures for Implementing Technological Innovation', in M. Horwitch (ed.), *Technology in the Modern Corporation*, New York, USA: Pergamon Press.

Burt, R. (1992), *Structural Holes: The Social Structure of Competition*, Cambridge, USA: Harvard University Press.

Business Week (1994), 'Can America Afford the Transistor Today?', *Business Week*, 7 March.

Business Week (1995), 'Blue-sky Research Comes Down to Earth', *Business Week*, 3 July.

Business Week (1999), 'An Ivory Tower that Spins Pure Gold', *Business Week*, 19 April.

Bussolati, C., Malerba, F. and Torrisi, S. (1996), *L'Evoluzione dell'Industria ad Alta Tecnologia in Italia. Entrata Tempestiva, Declino e Opportunità di Recupero*, Bologna, Italy: Il Mulino.

Calderini, M. (2001), 'Competition, Learning and the Composition of R&D Activities', PhD Thesis, University of Manchester, UK.

Calderini, M. and Garrone, P. (2000), 'Non-linear Dynamic Effects in the Composition of R&D', *Quaderni di Economia*, no. 3/2000, Turin, Italy: Polytechnic University of Turin.

Calderini, M. and Garrone, P. (2001), 'Liberalisation, Industry Turmoil and the Balance of R&D Activities', *Information Economics and Policy*, **13** (2), 199–230.

Candoy-Seske, R. and Palmer, A.R. (1988), *Techniques of Privatization of State Owned Enterprises: Inventory of Country Experience and Reference Materials*, Washington, DC, USA: World Bank.

Capron, L., Dussuage, P. and Mitchell, W. (1998), 'Resource Redeployment

Following Horizontal Acquisitions in Europe and North America, 1988–1992', *Strategic Management Journal*, **19** (7), 631–61.

Carpenter, M.A. and Westphal, J.D. (2001), 'The Strategic Context of External Network Ties: Examining the Impact of Director Appointments on Board Involvement in Strategic Decision Making', *Academy of Management Journal*, **44** (4), 639–61.

Cartwright, S. and Cooper, C.L. (1993), 'The Role of Cultural Compatibility in Successful Organisational Marriage', *Academy of Management Executive*, **7** (2), 57–70.

Cassia, L., D'Adamo, M. and Paleari, S. (2001), 'I Veri Guadagni nelle Offerte Pubbliche Iniziali: Azionisti di Controllo, Venture Capitalist, Manager e Investitori Individuali al Nuovo Mercato', *AF Analisi Finanziaria*, **43** (3), 48–74.

Cawkell, A.E. (1977), 'Understanding Science by Analysing its Literature', in E. Garfield (ed.), *Essays of an Information Scientist*, Vol. 2, Philadelphia, USA: ISI Press.

Centre National d'Etudes des Télécommunications (CNET) (1995), 'Le CNET et Son Histoire', France Télécom Technical Mementos, National Centre for Telecommunication Studies, Lannion, France.

Chakrabarti, A.K. (1990), 'Organizational Factors in Post-acquisition Performance', *IEEE Transactions on Engineering Management*, **37** (4), 259–68.

Chan, L.K., Lakonishock, J. and Sougiannis, T. (1999), 'The Stock Market Valuation of Research and Development Expenditures', NBER Working Paper no. 7223, National Bureau of Economic Research, Cambridge, USA.

Chan, S.H., Kensinger, J.W., Keown, A.J. and Martin, J.D. (1997), 'Do Strategic Alliances Create Value?', *Journal of Financial Economics*, **46** (2), 199–221.

Chan, S.H., Martin, J.D. and Kensinger, J.W. (1990), 'Corporate Research and Development Expenditures and Share Value', *Journal of Financial Economics*, **26**, 255–76.

Chandler, A.D. (1962), *Strategy and Structure: Chapters in the History of the Industrial Enterprise*, Cambridge, USA: MIT Press.

Chauvin, K.W. and Hirschey, M. (1993), 'Advertising, R&D Expenditures and the Market Value of the Firm', *Financial Management*, **22** (4), 128–40.

Chesnais, F. (1993), 'The French National System of Innovation', in R.R. Nelson (ed.), *National Innovation Systems. A Comparative Analysis*, New York, USA: Oxford University Press.

Cho, M.H. (1998), 'Ownership Structure, Investment, and the Corporate Value: An Empirical Analysis', *Journal of Financial Economics*, **47**, 103–21.

Claessens, S., Djankov, S. and Pohl, G. (1997), 'Ownership Structure and Corporate Performance: Evidence from the Czech Republic', World Bank, Occasional Papers Series, Washington, DC, USA: World Bank.

Clark, K.B. (1987), 'Investment in New Technology and Competitive Advantage', in D.J. Teece (ed.), *The Competitive Challenge. Strategies for Industrial Innovation and Renewal*, Cambridge, USA: Ballinger.

Cockburn, I. and Griliches, Z. (1988), 'Industry Effects and Appropriability Measures in the Stock Market's Valuation of R&D and Patents', *American Economic Review*, **78** (2), 419–23.

Cohen, W.M. (1995), 'Empirical Studies of Innovative Activity', in P. Stoneman (ed.), *Handbook of the Economics of Innovation and Technological Change*, Oxford, UK: Basil Blackwell.

Cohen, W.M. and Levin, R.C. (1989), 'Empirical Studies of Innovation and Market Structure', in R. Schmalensee and R. Willig (eds), *Handbook of Industrial Organization*, Amsterdam, The Netherlands: North-Holland.

Cohen, W.M. and Levinthal, D.A. (1989), 'Innovation and Learning: The Two Faces of R&D', *Economic Journal*, **99**, 569–96.

Cohen, W.M. and Levinthal, D.A. (1990), 'Absorptive Capacity: A New Perspective on Learning and Innovation', *Administrative Science Quarterly*, **36** (1), 128–52.

Collison, D., Grinyer, D. and Russel, A. (1993), *Management's Economic Decisions and Financial Reporting*, London, UK: ICAEW.

Colvin, G. (1998), 'Stop Whining about Wall Street', *The Fortune Magazine* 2 February, 153–59.

Connolly, R.A., Hirsch, B.T. and Hirschey, M. (1986), 'Union Rent Seeking, Intangible Capital, and Market Value of the Firm', *Review of Economics and Statistics*, **68** (4), 567–77.

Connolly, R.A. and Hirschey, M. (1988), 'Market Value and Patents: A Bayesian Approach', *Economics Letters*, **27**, 83–7.

Connolly, R.A. and Hirschey, M. (1990), 'Firm Size and R&D Effectiveness', *Economics Letters,* **32**, 277–81.

Cooper, M., Dimitrov, O. and Rau, P.R. (2001), 'A Rose.com by Any Other N', *Journal of Finance*, **56** (6).

Cornelli, F. and Yosha, O. (1998), 'Stage Financing and the Role of Convertible Debt', Institute of Finance and Accounting (IFA) Working Paper no. 253, London Business School, London, UK.

Cowan, A.L. (1988), 'The Trench Warriors', *The New York Times*, Section 3, 29 May, 1, 5.

Cragg, M.I. and Dyck, A.I.J. (1999), 'Management Control and Privatization in the United Kingdom', *RAND Journal of Economics*, **30** (3), 475–97.

Cuervo, A. and Villalonga, B. (2000), 'Explaining the Variance in the Performance Effects of Privatization', *Academy of Management Review*, **25**, 581–91.

D'Souza, J. and Megginson, W.L. (1999), 'The Financial and Operating Performance of Privatized Firms during the 1990s', *Journal of Finance*, **54**, 1397–438.

Daily, C.M. and Dalton, D.R. (1992), 'The Relationship between Governance Structure and Corporate Performance in Entrepreneurial Firms', *Journal of Business Venturing*, **7** (5), 375–7.

Daily, C.M., Johnson, J.L., Ellstrand, A.E. and Dalton, D.R. (1998), 'Meta-analytic Reviews of Board Composition, Leadership Structure, and Financial Performance', *Strategic Management Journal*, **19** (3), 269–85.

Das, S., Sen, P.K. and Sengupta, S. (1998), 'Impact of Strategic Alliances on Firm Valuation', *Academy of Management Journal*, **41** (1), 27–41.

Dasgupta, P. and David, P.A. (1994), 'Toward a New Economics of Science', *Research Policy*, **23**, 487–521.

Dasgupta, P. and Stiglitz, J. (1980), 'Industrial Structure and the Nature of Innovative Activity', *Economic Journal*, **90**, 266–93.

David, P.A. (1991), 'Reputation and Agency in the Historical Emergence of the Institutions of Open Science', Working Paper, Stanford University, Stanford, USA.

David, P.A., Mowery, D.C. and Steinmueller, W.E. (1994), 'Analysing the Economic Payoffs from Basic Research', in D.C. Mowery (ed.), *Science and Technology Policy in Interdependent Economies*, Norwell, USA: Kluwer Academic Publishers.

Davies, A. (1991), 'Strategic Planning for the Board', *Long Range Planning*, **24** (2), 94–101.

De Alessi, L. (1987), 'Property Rights and Privatization', *Proceedings of the American Academy of Political Science*, **36**, 24–35.

de Bandt, J. (1998), 'Privatization in an Industrial Policy Perspective: The Case of France', in D. Parker (ed.), *Privatization in the European Union. Theory and Policy Perspectives*, New York, USA: Routledge.

Demers, E. and Lev, B. (2001), 'A Rude Awakening: Internet Shakedut in 2000', *Review of Accounting Studies*, **6** (2–3 June–September), 331–59.

Demsetz, H. and Lehn, K. (1985), 'The Structure of Corporate Ownership: Theory and Consequences', *Journal of Political Economy*, **93**, 1155–77.

Dewenter, K.L. and Malatesta, P.H. (2001), 'State-owned and Privately-owned Firms: An Empirical Analysis of Profitability, Leverage and Labor Intensity', *American Economic Review*, **91**, 320–34.

Dixit, A.K. and Pindyck, R.S. (1994), *Investment under Uncertainty*, Princeton, USA: Princeton University Press.

Donaldson, G. (1961), *Corporate Debt Capacity: A Study of Corporate Debt Policy and the Determination of Corporate Debt Capacity*, Boston, USA: Harvard Business School, Research Division.

Doukas, J. and Switzer, L. (1992), 'The Stock Market's Valuation of R&D Spending and Market Concentration', *Journal of Economics and Business*, **44** (2), 95–114.

Dyck, A.I.J. (1999), 'Privatization and Corporate Governance: Principles,

Evidence and Future Challenges', HBS Working Paper, Harvard Business School, Boston, USA.

Eisenhardt, K.M. (1985), 'Control: Organizational and Economic Approaches', *Management Science*, **31**, 134–49.

Eisenhardt, K.M. (1989), 'Agency Theory: An Assessment and Review', *Academy of Management Review*, **14** (1), 57–75.

Emmert, M.A. and Crow, M.M. (1988), 'Public, Private and Hybrid Organizations: An Empirical Examination of the Role of Publicness', *Administration and Society*, **20** (2), 216–44.

Encaoua, D., Laisney, F., Hall, B.H. and Mairesse, J. (eds) (2000), *Economics and Econometrics of Innovation*, Amsterdam, The Netherlands: Kluwer Academic Publishers.

Ernst, H. and Witt, J. (2000), 'The Influence of Corporate Acquisitions on the Behaviour of Key Inventors', *R&D Management*, **30** (2), 105–20.

European Commission (1994), *Research into the Financing of New Technology-based Firms (NTBFs)*, Paris, France: European Commission.

EVCA (2001), *EVCA Annual Survey of Pan-European Private Equity and Venture Capital*, Zaventem, Belgium: European Venture Capital Association.

Fama, E.F. (1970), 'Efficient Capital Markets: A Review of Theory and Empirical Work', *Journal of Finance*, **25** (2), 383–417.

Fama, E.F. (1991), 'Efficient Capital Markets: II', *Journal of Finance*, **46** (5), 1575–617.

Fama, E.F. and Jensen, M.C. (1983), 'Separation of Ownership and Control', *Journal of Law and Economics*, **26** (2), 301–26.

Fama, E.F. and Jensen, M.C. (1985), 'Organizational Forms and Investment Decisions', *Journal of Financial Economics*, **14** (1), 101–19.

Farnham, D. and Horton, S. (1989), 'Managing Private and Public Organizations', in D. Farnham and S. Horton (eds), *Managing the New Public Service*, Basingstoke, UK: Macmillan.

Fazzari, S., Hubbard, G. and Peterson, B. (1988), 'Financing Constraints and Corporate Investment', *Brookings Papers on Economic Activities*, **1**, 141–206.

Fédération Internationale des Bourses de Valeurs (FIBV) (2001), *Annual Statistics*, Paris, France: International Federation of Stock Exchanges.

Fisher, F.M. and McGowan, J.J. (1983), 'On the Misuse of Accounting Rates of Return to Infer Monopoly Profits', *American Economic Review*, **73** (1), 82–97.

Forbes, D.P. and Milliken, F.J. (1999), 'Cognition and Corporate Governance: Understanding Boards of Directors as Strategic Decision-making Groups', *Academy of Management Review*, **24** (3), 489–505.

Franks, J.R. and Mayer, C.P. (1996), 'Corporate Control: A Synthesis of the International Evidence', in J.C. Coffee, R.J. Gilson and L. Lowestein (eds), *Relational Investing*, New York, USA: Oxford University Press.

Fransman, M. (1994a), 'AT&T, BT and NTT: A Comparison of Vision, Strategy and Competence', *Telecommunication Policy*, **18**, 137–53.

Fransman, M. (1994b), 'AT&T, BT and NTT: The Role of R&D', *Telecommunication Policy*, **18**, 295–305.

Frydman, R., Hessel, M.P. and Rapaczynski, A. (1998), 'Why Ownership Matters? Entrepreneurship and Restructuring of Enterprises in Central Europe', Columbia Law-Econ Working Paper no. 172, New York, USA.

Galal, A.L., Jones, L., Tandon, P. and Vogelsang, I. (1994), *Welfare Consequences of Selling Public Enterprises*, Oxford, UK: Oxford University Press.

Galbani, A. and Paris, L. (1994), 'La Ricerca nel Settore Elettrico', in G. Zanetti (ed.), *Storia dell'Industria Elettrica in Italia*, Bari, Italy: Laterza.

Gambardella, A. and Torrisi, S. (1999), 'The Market Value of Knowledge and Inter-firm Linkages: A Preliminary Investigation', II Workshop of the Dynacom TSER Project, 27–30 May, Paris, France.

Garvey, G., Grant, S. and King, S. (1996), 'Myopic Corporate Behaviour with Optimal Management Incentives', *Journal of Industrial Economics*, **47**, 230–49.

Geroski, P. (1995), *Market Structure, Corporate Performance and Innovative Activity*, Oxford, UK: Oxford University Press.

Ghemawat, P. (1991), *Commitment: The Dynamic of Strategy*, New York, USA: Free Press.

Giudici, G. and Paleari, S. (2000a), 'The Provision of Finance to Innovation: A Survey Conducted among Italian Technology-based Small Firms', *Small Business Economics Journal*, **14**, 37–53.

Giudici, G. and Paleari, S. (2000b), 'The Optimal Staging of Venture Capital Financing when Entrepreneurs Extract Private Benefits from their Firm', *Enterprise and Innovation Management Studies*, **1** (2), 153–74.

Giudici, G. and Paleari, S. (2001), 'What Drives the Initial Market Performance of Italian IPOs? An Empirical Investigation of Underpricing and Price Support', Working Paper, Polytechnic University of Milan, Milan, Italy.

Giudici, G. and Paleari, S. (2002), 'Should Firms Going Public Enjoy Tax Benefits? The Italian Experience in the '90s', *European Financial Management*, forthcoming.

Giudici, G. and Roosenboom, P.J. (2001), 'Pricing Initial Public Offerings on "New" European Stock Markets', Working Paper, University of Bergamo, Bergamo, Italy, and Erasmus University, Rotterdam, The Netherlands.

Godin, B. (1996), 'Research and the Practice of Publications in Industries', *Research Policy*, **25**, 587–606.

Goergen, M. (1998), *Corporate Governance and Financial Performance. A Study of German and UK Initial Public Offerings*, Cheltenham, UK and Northampton, USA: Edward Elgar.

Gompers, P.A. and Lerner, J. (1999), *The Venture Capital Cycle*, Boston, USA: MIT Press.

Gompers, P.A. and Metrick, A. (2001), 'Institutional Investor and Equity Prices', *Quarterly Journal of Economics*, **116** (1), 229–59.

Goodman, P.S., Ravlin, E., Schminke, M. (1987), 'Understanding Groups in Organizations', *Research in Organizational Behavior*, **9**, 1–71.

Granovetter, M.S. (1973), 'The Strength of Weak Ties', *American Journal of Sociology*, **78** (6), 1360–79.

Graves, S.B. (1988), 'Institutional Ownership and Corporate R&D in the Computer Industry', *Academy of Management Journal*, **31**, 417–27.

Green, J.P., Stark, A.W. and Thomas, H.M. (1996), 'UK Evidence on the Market Valuation of Research and Development Expenditures', *Journal of Business Finance and Accounting*, **23** (2), 191–216.

Greene, W.H. (1996), *Econometric Analysis*, New York, USA: Prentice-Hall International.

Griliches, Z. (1979), 'Issues in Assessing the Contribution of Research and Development to Productivity Growth', *Bell Journal of Economics*, **10**, 92–116.

Griliches, Z. (1981), 'Market Value, R&D and Patents', *Economics Letters*, **7** (2), 183–7.

Griliches, Z. (1990), 'Patents Statistics as Economic Indicators: A Survey', *Journal of Economic Literature*, **28**, 1661–707.

Griliches, Z. (1995), 'R&D and Productivity: Econometric Results and Measurement Issues', in P. Stoneman (ed.), *Handbook of the Economics of Innovation and Technological Change*, Oxford, UK: Basil Blackwell.

Griliches, Z. and Mairesse, J. (1984), 'Productivity and R&D at the Firm Level', in Z. Griliches (ed.), *R&D, Patents, and Productivity*, Chicago, USA: University of Chicago Press and NBER.

Griliches, Z., Pakes, A. and Hall, B.H. (1987), 'The Value of Patents as Indicators of Inventive Activity', in P. Dasgupta and P. Stoneman (eds), *Economic Policy and Technological Performance*, Cambridge, UK: Cambridge University Press.

Gros Pietro, G.M., Reviglio, E. and Torrisi, A. (2001), *Assetti Proprietari e Mercati Finanziari Europei*, Bologna, Italy: Il Mulino.

Grossman, S. and Hart, O. (1986), 'The Costs and Benefits of Ownership, a Theory of Lateral and Vertical Integration', *Journal of Political Economy*, **94**, 691–719.

Gulati, R. and Westphal, J.D. (1999), 'Cooperative or Controlling? The Effects of CEO–Board Relations and the Content of Interlocks on the Formation of Joint Ventures', *Administrative Science Quarterly*, **44** (3), 473–506.

Hagedoorn, J. and Duysters, G. (2002a), 'External Sources of Innovative Capabilities: The Preference for Strategic Alliances or M&A', *Journal of Management Studies*, **39** (2), 167–88.

Hagedoorn, J. and Duysters, G. (2002b), 'The Effects of Mergers and Acquisitions on the Technological Performance of Companies in a High-tech Environment', *Technology Analysis and Strategic Management*, **14** (1), 67–85.

Hall, B.H. (1988), 'The Effects of Take-over Activity on Corporate Research and Development', in A.J. Auerback (ed.), *Corporate Takeovers: Causes and Consequences*, Chicago, USA: University of Chicago Press.

Hall, B.H. (1990a), 'The Impact of Corporate Restructuring on Industrial Research and Development', *Brookings Papers on Economic Activity: Microeconomics*, 85–153.

Hall, B.H. (1990b), 'The Manufacturing Sector Masterfile: 1959–1987', NBER Working Paper, National Bureau of Economic Research, Cambridge, USA.

Hall, B.H. (1993a), 'The Stock Market's Valuation of R&D Investment during the 1980s', *American Economic Review*, **83** (2), 259–64.

Hall, B.H. (1993b), 'Industrial Research during the 1980s: Did the Rate of Return Fall?', *Brookings Papers on Economic Activity: Microeconomics* (2), 289–343.

Hall, B.H. (1994), 'Corporate Restructuring and Investment Horizons in the United States, 1976–1987', *Business History Review*, **68** (1), 110–23.

Hall, B.H. (1999a), 'Innovation and Market Value', NBER Working Paper, National Bureau of Economic Research, Cambridge, USA.

Hall, B. H. (1999b), 'Mergers and R&D Revisited', Paper prepared for the Quasi-experimental Methods Symposium, Econometrics Laboratory, UC Berkeley, 3–7 August, http://emlab.berkeley.edu/users/bhhall/ (October 2001).

Hall, B.H., Griliches, Z. and Hausman, J.A. (1986), 'Patents and R&D: Is There a Lag?', *International Economic Review*, **27** (2), 265–83.

Hall, B.H., Jaffe, A.B. and Trajtenberg, M. (2000), 'Market Value and Patent Citations: A First Look', NBER Working Paper, National Bureau of Economic Research, Cambridge, USA.

Hall, B.H. and Kim, D. (2000), 'Valuing Intangible Assets: The Stock Market Value of R&D Revised', Working Paper, University of California at Berkeley and Harvard University, Berkeley and Cambridge, USA.

Hall, B.H. and Vopel, K. (1996), 'Innovation, Market Share and Market Value', Working Paper, University of California at Berkeley and University of Mannheim, Berkeley and Mannheim, USA.

Halloran, M.J., Benton, L.F., Gunderson, R.V., Del Calvo, J. and Kintner, T.W. (2000), *Venture Capital and Public Offering Negotiation*, Gaithersburg, USA: Aspen Law & Business.

Hand, J.R.M. (2000), 'Profits, Losses and the Non-linear Pricing of Internet Stocks', Working Paper, Kenan-Flagler Business School, University of North Carolina at Chapel Hill, USA.

Hannan, M.T. and Freeman, J. (1984), 'Structural Inertia and Organizational Change', *American Sociological Review*, **49**, 149–64.

Hansen, G.S. and Hill, C.W.L. (1991), 'Are Institutional Investors Myopic? A Time Series Study of Four Technology-driven Industries', *Strategic Management Journal*, **12**, 1–16.

Harrison, J. (1994), 'LBOs Slash R&D: So What?', *Academy of Management Executive*, **8** (2), 83–4.

Hart, O. (1995), 'Corporate Governance: Some Theory and Implications', *Economic Journal,* **105**, 678–89.

Haunschild, P.R. (1993), 'Interorganizational Imitation: The Impact of Interlocks on Corporate Acquisition Activity', *Administrative Science Quarterly*, **38**, 564–84.

Hausman, J., Hall, B.H. and Griliches, Z. (1984), 'Econometric Model for Count Data with an Application to the Patents–R&D Relationship', *Econometrica*, **52** (4), 265–83.

Hayes, R.H. and Abernathy, W.J. (1980), 'Managing Our Way to Economic Decline', *Harvard Business Review*, **58** (4), 67–77.

Hayes, R.H. and Garvin, D.A. (1982), 'Managing as if Tomorrow Mattered', *Harvard Business Review*, **60** (3), 70–71.

Hedges, L.V. and Olkin, I. (1985), *Statistical Methods for Meta-analysis*, New York, USA: Academic Press.

Heiner, R.A. (1983), 'The Origin of Predictable Behavior', *American Economic Review*, **73** (4), 560–96.

Hellmann, T. (1998), 'The Allocation of Control Rights in Venture Capital Contracts', *RAND Journal of Economics*, **29** (1), 57–76.

Hellmann, T. and Puri, M. (2000), 'The Interaction between Product Market and Financing Strategy: The Role of Venture Capital', *Review of Financial Studies*, **13** (4), 959–84.

Henderson, R. (2000), 'Drug Industry Mergers Won't Necessarily Benefit R&D', *Research Technology Management*, **43** (10–15), 32–59.

Henderson, R. and Cockburn, I. (1996), 'Scale, Scope and Spillovers: The Determinants of Research Productivity in the Pharmaceutical Industry', *RAND Journal of Economics*, **27** (1), 32–59.

Henderson, R., Jaffe, A.B. and Trajtenberg, M. (1998), 'Universities as a Source of Commercial Technology: A Detailed Analysis of University Patenting, 1965–1988', *Review of Economics and Statistics*, **80** (1), 119–27.

Hicks, D. (1995), 'Tacit Competencies and Corporate Management of the Public–Private Character of Knowledge', *Industrial and Corporate Change*, **4**, 375–84.

Hicks, D., Isard, P. and Martin, B. (1996), 'A Morphology of Japanese and European Corporate Research Networks', *Research Policy*, **25**, 359–78.

Hill, C.W. and Snell, S.A. (1988), 'External Control, Corporate Strategy and Firm Performance in Research-intensive Industries', *Strategic Management Journal*, **32** (1), 25–46.

Hill, C.W. and Snell, S.A. (1989), 'Effects of Ownership Structure and Control on Corporate Productivity', *Academy of Management Journal*, **32** (1), 25–46.

Himmelberg, C.P. and Petersen, B.C. (1994), 'R&D and Internal Finance: A Panel Study of Small Firms in High-tech Industries', *Review of Economics and Statistics*, **76**, 38–51.

Hirschey, M. (1982), 'Intangible Capital Aspects of Advertising and R&D Expenditures', *Journal of Industrial Economics*, **30**, 375–90.

Hitt, M.A., Hoskisson, R.E., Ireland, R.D. and Harrison, J.S. (1991), 'Effects of Acquisitions on R&D Inputs and Outputs', *Academy of Management Journal*, **34** (3), 639–706.

Hitt, M A., Hoskisson, R.E., Johnson, R.A. and Moesel, D.D. (1996), 'The Market for Corporate Control and Firm Innovation', *Academy of Management Journal*, **38** (5), 1084–119.

Holmstrom, B. (1989), 'Agency Costs and Innovation', *Journal of Economic Behavior and Organization*, **12** (3), 305–28.

Holmstrom, B. and Kaplan, S. (2001), 'Corporate Governance and Merger Activity in the United States: Making Sense of the 1980s and 1990s', *Journal of Economic Perspectives*, **15** (2), 121–44.

Holmstrom, B. and Ricart i Costa, J. (1986), 'Managerial Incentives and Capital Management', *Quarterly Journal of Economics*, **101**, 835–60.

Hoskisson, R.E. and Hitt, M.A. (1988), 'Strategic Control Systems and Relative R&D Investments in Large Multiproduct Firms', *Strategic Management Journal*, **9**, 605–21.

Hoskisson, R.E. and Johnson, R.A. (1992), 'Corporate Restructuring and Strategic Change: The Effect on Diversification Strategy and R&D Intensity', *Strategic Management Journal*, **13** (8), 625–34.

Huchzermeier, A. and Loch, C.H. (2001), 'Project Management under Risk: Using the Real Options Approach to Evaluate Flexibility in R&D', *Management Science*, **47** (1), 85–101.

Hunter, J.E. and Schmidt, F.L. (1990), *Methods for Meta-analysis: Correcting Errors and Bias in Research Findings*, Newbury Park, USA: Sage.

Hunter, J.E., Schmidt, F.L. and Jackson, G.B. (1982), *Meta-analysis: Cumulating Research Findings across Studies*, Beverly Hills, USA: Sage.

Inkpen, A., Sundaram, A. and Rockwood, K. (2000), 'Cross-border Acquisitions of US Technology Assets', *California Management Review*, **42** (3), 50–71.

IRI (1993–1999), *R&D Trends Forecast for 1993–1999*, Washington, DC, USA: Industrial Research Institute, http://www.onlinejournal.net/iri/RTM/ (November 2000).

Jacobs, M.T. (1991), *Short-term America: The Causes and Cures of Our Business Myopia*, Boston, USA: Harvard Business School Press.

Jacobs, M.T. (1998), 'How US Financial Regulations Reduce the Time Horizons for US Investment', CATO Regulation, http:\\www.cato.org. (January 2000).

Jaffe, A.B. (1986), 'Technological Opportunity and Spillovers of R&D: Evidence from Firms' Patents, Profits and Market Value', *American Economic Review*, **76** (5), 984–1001.

Jaffe, A.B. (2000), 'The US Patent System in Transition: Policy Innovation and the Innovation Process', *Research Policy*, **29** (4), 531–77.

Jaffe, A.B. and Lerner, J. (1999), 'Privatizing R&D: Policy Patent and the Commercialization of National Laboratories Technologies', NBER Working Paper n. 7064, National Bureau of Economic Research, Cambridge, USA.

Jaffe, A.B. and Trajtenberg, M. (1999), 'International Knowledge Flows: Evidence from Patent Citations', *Economics of Innovation and New Technology*, **8** (1), 105–36.

Jaffe, A.B., Trajtenberg, M. and Fogarty, M.S. (2000), 'The Meaning of Patent Citations: Report on the NBER/Case-Western Reserve Survey of Patentees', NBER Working Paper, National Bureau of Economic Research, Cambridge, USA.

Jagle, A.J. (1999), 'Shareholder Value, Real Options, and Innovation in Technology-intensive Companies', *R&D Management*, **29** (3), 271–87.

James, A. and Barker, K. (2000), 'Comparing Technology Management Issues in Mergers and Acquisitions and Joint Ventures', in James, A. and Barker, K., *Technology Strategy and Strategic Alliances – Selected Papers from the 1998 R&D Management Conference*, 53–66.

James, A., Georghiou, L. and Metcalfe, J.S. (1998), 'Integrating Technology into Merger and Acquisition Decision-making', *Technovation*, **18** (8–9), 563–73.

Jarrel, G.A., Lehn, K. and Marr, W. (1985), 'Institutional Ownership, Tender Offers and Long Term Investments', Working Paper, Office of the Chief Economist, Securities and Exchange Commission, Washington, DC, USA.

Jeng, L.A. and Wells, P.C. (2000), 'The Determinants of Venture Capital Funding: Evidence Across Countries', *Journal of Corporate Finance*, **6** (3), 241–89.

Jenkinson, T. and Ljungqvist, A. (2001), *Going Public: The Theory and Evidence on How Companies Raise Equity Finance*, Oxford, UK: Oxford University Press.

Jensen, M.C. (1978), 'Some Anomalous Evidence Regarding Market Efficiency', *Journal of Financial Economics*, **6** (2–3), 95–101.

Jensen, M.C. (1986), 'The Takeover Controversy: Analysis and Evidence', *Midland Corporate Finance Journal*, **4** (Summer), 6–32.

Jensen, M.C. (1993), 'The Modern Industrial Revolution, Exit, and the Failure of Internal Control Systems', *Journal of Finance*, **48** (July), 831–80.

Jensen, M.C. and Meckling, W.H. (1976), 'Theory of the Firm: Managerial Behavior, Agency Costs and Ownership Structure', *Journal of Financial Economics*, **3**, 305–60.

Johnson, G., Smith, S. and Codling, B. (2000), 'Microprocesses of Institutional Change in the Context of Privatization', *Academy of Management Review*, **25**, 572–80.

Johnson, J.L., Daily, C.M. and Ellstrand, A.E. (1996) 'Boards of Directors: A Review and Research Agenda', *Journal of Management*, **22** (3), 409–39.

Johnson, R.A., Hoskisson, R.E. and Hitt, M.A. (1993), 'Board of Directors' Involvement in Restructuring: The Effects of Boards versus Managerial Control Characteristics', *Strategic Management Journal*, **14**, 33–50.

Kahneman, D. and Tversky, A. (1979), 'Prospect Theory: An Analysis of Decision under Risk', *Econometrica*, **47**, 262–91.

Kamien, M.I., Muller, E. and Zang, I. (1992), 'Research Joint Ventures and R&D Cartels', *American Economic Review*, **82** (5), 1293–306.

Kamien, M.I. and Schwartz, N.L. (1982), *Market Structure and Innovation*, Cambridge, USA: Cambridge University Press.

Kaplan, S.N. and Strömberg, P. (2001), 'Financial Contracting Theory Meets the Real World: An Empirical Analysis of Venture Capital Contracts', NBER Working Paper no. 7660, National Bureau of Economic Research, Cambridge, USA.

Karim, S. and Mitchell, W. (2000), 'Path-dependent and Path-breaking Change: Reconfiguring Business Resources Following Acquisitions in the US Medical Sector, 1978–1995', *Strategic Management Journal*, **21**, 1061–81.

Katz, R. (2001), 'Structural Reforms and Technological Behavior. The Sources and Nature of Technological Change in Latin America in the 1990s', *Research Policy*, **30**, 1–19.

Katz, R. and Allen, T. J. (1982), 'Investigating the Not Invented Here (NIH) Syndrome: A Look at the Performance, Tenure, and Communication Patterns of 50 R&D Project Groups', *R&D Management*, **12** (1), 7–19.

Keasey, K., Thompson, S. and Wright, M. (1997), *Corporate Governance: Economic, Management and Financial Issue*, Oxford, UK: Oxford University Press.

Keck, S.L. and Tushman, M.L. (1993), 'Environmental and Organizational Context and Executive Team', *Academy of Management Journal*, **36** (6), 1314–45.

Kenward, N. (1993), 'The Embers of Energy Research', *Director*, **46** (7), 25–6.

Kochnar, R. and David, P. (1996), 'Institutional Investors and Firm Innovation, a Test of Competing Hypotheses, *Strategic Management Journal*, **17**, 73–84.

Kogut, B. and Zander, U. (1992), 'Knowledge of the Firm, Combinative Capabilities, and the Replication of Technology', *Organization Science*, **3** (3), 383–95.

Kortum, S. and Lerner, J. (2000), 'Assessing the Contribution of Venture Capital to Innovation', *RAND Journal of Economics*, **31**, 674–92.

Kosnik, R.D. (1990), 'Effects of Board Demography and Directors' Incentives on Corporate Green-mail Decisions', *Academy of Management Journal*, **33**, 129–50.

KPMG (1995), *TRANSACC. Transnational Accounting*, London, UK: Macmillan.

La Porta, R. and Lopez de Silanes, F. (1999), 'The Benefits of Privatization: Evidence from Mexico', *Quarterly Journal of Economics* (November), 1193–242.

La Porta, R., Lopez de Silanes, F., Shleifer, A. and Vishny, R.W. (1997), 'Legal Determinants of External Finance', *Journal of Finance*, **52** (3), 1131–50.

Laffont, J. and Tirole, J. (1993), 'Privatization and Incentives', in J. Laffont and J. Tirole, *The Theory of Incentives in Procurement and Regulation*, Cambridge, USA: MIT Press.

Lane, P.J. and Lubatkin, M. (1998), 'Relative Absorptive Capacity and Interorganizational Learning', *Strategic Management Journal*, **19** (5), 461–77.

Laverty, K.J. (1996), 'Economic Short-termism: The Debate, the Unresolved Issues, and the Implications for Management Practice and Research', *Academy of Management Review*, **21**, 825–39.

Lawrence, B.S. (1997), 'The Black Box of Organizational Demography', *Organization Science*, **8** (1), 1–22.

Leonard-Barton, D. (1992), 'Core Capabilities and Core Rigidities: A Paradox in Managing New Product Development', *Strategic Management Journal*, **13** (Summer Special Issue), 111–25.

Lev, B. (1999), 'R&D and Capital Markets', *Journal of Applied Corporate Finance*, **11** (Winter), 21–35.

Lev, B. (2000), 'New Accounting for a New Economy', Working Paper, Stern Business School, New York, USA.

Lev, B. (2001), *Intangible: Management, Measurement, and Reporting*, Washington, DC, USA: Brookings Institution Press.

Lev, B. and Sougiannis, T. (1996), 'The Capitalization, Amortization and Market Relevance of R&D', *Journal of Accounting and Economics*, **21**, 107–38.

Lev, B. and Sougiannis, T. (1999), 'Penetrating the Book-to-market Black Box: The R&D Effect', *Journal of Business Finance and Accounting*, **26** (3–4), 419–49.

Lev, B. and Zarowin, P. (1999), 'The Boundaries of Financial Reporting and How to Extend Them', *Journal of Accounting Research* (Autumn), 353–85.

Lichtenberg, F.L. and Siegel, D. (1990), 'The Effects of Leveraged Buyouts on Productivity and Related Aspects of Firm Behaviour', *Journal of Financial Economics*, **26** (2), 165–94.

Lindenberg, E.B. and Ross, S.A. (1981), 'Tobin's q Ratio and Industrial Organization', *Journal of Business*, **54** (1), 1–32.

Loescher, S.M. (1984), 'Bureaucratic Measurement, Shuttling Stock Shares, and Shortened Time Horizons: Implications for Economic Growth', *Quarterly Review of Economics and Business*, **24** (Winter), 8–23.

Long, W.F. and Ravenscraft, D.J. (1993), 'LBOs, Debt and R&D Intensity', *Strategic Management Journal*, **14**, 119–35.

Lustgarten, S. and Thomadakis, S. (1987), 'Mobility Barriers and Tobin's q', *Journal of Business*, **60** (4), 519–37.

Mahoney, J., Sundaramurthy, C. and Mahoney, J.T. (1997), 'The Effects of Corporate Antitakeover Provisions on Long-term Investment: Empirical Evidence', *Managerial and Decision Economics*, **18**, 349–65.

Maksimovic, V. and Pichler, P. (2001), 'Technological Innovation and Initial Public Offerings', *Review of Financial Studies*, **14** (2), 459–94.

Malerba, F. (1993), 'The National System of Innovation in Italy', in R.R. Nelson (ed.), *National Innovation Systems. A Comparative Analysis*, Oxford, UK: Oxford University Press.

Manigart, S. and Struyf, C. (1997), 'Financing High-technology Start-up in Belgium: An Explorative Study', *Small Business Economics*, **9**, 125–35.

Mannix, E.A. and Lowestein, G.F. (1994), 'The Effects of Interfirm Mobility and Individual versus Group Decision Making on Managerial Time Horizons', *Organisational Behaviour and Human Decision Processes*, **59**, 371–90.

Mansfield, E., Rapoport, J., Romeo, A., Wagner, S. and Beardsley, J. (1977), 'Social and Private Rates of Return from Industrial Innovations', *Quarterly Journal of Economics*, **91**, 221–40.

Markides, C.C. (1992), 'Consequences of Corporate Refocusing: *ex-ante* Evidence', *Academy of Management Journal*, **35**, 398–412.

Maruseth, P.B. and Verspagen, B. (1998), 'Knowledge Spillover in Europe and its Consequences for Systems of Innovation', Draft, ECIS Eindhoven University of Technology, Eindhoven, The Netherlands.

Maskell, P. and Malmberg, A. (1999), 'Localised Learning and Industrial Competitiveness', *Cambridge Journal of Economics*, **23** (2), 167–86.

McConnell, J.J. and Muscarella, C.J. (1985), 'Corporate Capital Expenditure Decisions and the Market Value of the Firm', *Journal of Financial Economics*, **14** (3), 399–422.

McEvily, S.K. and Chakravarthy, B. (1999), 'Resource Context and the Returns to Investments in R&D', *Academy of Management Best Paper Proceedings*, Briarcliff Manor, USA: Academy of Management.

McGrath, R.G. (1997), 'A Real-options Logic for Initiating Technology Positioning Investments', *Academy of Management Review*, **22** (4), 974–96.

Megginson, W.L., Nash, R C., Netter, J.M. and Schwartz, A.L. (2000), 'The

Long-run Return to Investors in Share Issue Privatization', *Financial Management*, **29** (1), 67–77.

Megginson, W.L., Nash, R.C. and Van Rendenborgh, M. (1994), 'The Financial and Operating Performance of Newly-privatized Firms: An International Empirical Analysis', *Journal of Finance*, **49**, 403–53.

Megginson, W.L. and Netter, J.M. (2001), 'From State to Market: A Survey of Empirical Studies on Privatization', *Journal of Economic Literature*, **39** (2), 321–89.

Megginson, W.L. and Weiss, K.A. (1991), 'Venture Capitalist Certification in Initial Public Offerings', *Journal of Finance*, **46**, 879–903.

Meschi, M. (1997) 'Analytical Perspectives on Mergers and Acquisitions. A Survey', Working Paper no. 5/97, in *CIBS Research Papers in International Business*, Centre for International Business Studies, South Bank University, London, UK.

Meulbroek, L., Mitchell, M. and Mulherin, J. (1990), 'Shark Repellants and Managerial Myopia: An Empirical Test', *Journal of Political Economy*, **98** (5), 1108–17.

Miles, D. (1993), 'Testing for Short Termism in the UK Stock Market', *Economic Journal*, **103**, 1379–96.

Mizruchi, M.S. (1996), 'What do Interlocks Do? An Analysis, Critique and Assessment of Research on Interlocking Directorates', *Annual Review of Sociology*, **22**, 271–99.

Mohanram, P. and Nanda, A. (1996), 'When do Joint Ventures Create Value?', *Academy of Management Best Papers Proceedings*, Briarcliff Manor, USA: Academy of Management.

Montgomery, C.A. and Wernerfelt, B. (1988), 'Diversification, Ricardian Rents and Tobin's q', *RAND Journal of Economics*, **19** (4), 623–32.

Moore, B. (1994), 'Financial Constraint to the Growth and Development of Small High-technology Firms', in A. Hughes and D. Storey (eds), *Finance and the Small Firms*, London, UK: Routledge.

Morck, R., Shleifer, R. and Vishny, R.W. (1988), 'Characteristics of Targets of Hostile and Friendly Takeovers', in A.J. Auerbach (ed.), *Corporate Takeovers: Causes and Consequences*, Chicago, USA: University of Chicago Press.

Morris, D. (1999), 'The Stock Market and Short Termism', in D. Morris (ed.), *The British Economic Performance*, London, UK: Routledge.

Munari, F. (2002), 'The Effects of Privatization on Corporate R&D Units. Evidence from Italy and France', *R&D Management*, **33** (3), 223–232.

Munari, F., Roberts, E.B. and Sobrero, M. (2002), 'Privatization Processes and the Redefinition of Corporate R&D Boundaries', *Research Policy*, **31** (1), 31–53.

Myers, S.C. (1977), 'Determinants of Corporate Borrowing', *Journal of Financial Economics*, **5** (2), 147–75.

Myers, S.C. (1984), 'The Capital Structure Puzzle', *Journal of Finance*, **39**, 572–92.

Narayanan, M.P. (1985), 'Managerial Incentives for Short-term Results', *Journal of Finance*, **40**, 1469–84.

NASDAQ (2001), *Nasdaq-Amex Fact Book and Company Directory*, New York, USA: Nasdaq-Amex Market Group.

Nelson, R.R. (1959), 'The Simple Economics of Basic Scientific Research', *Journal of Political Economy*, **67** (3), 297–306.

Nelson, R.R. (1993), *National Innovation Systems. A Comparative Analysis*, Oxford, UK: Oxford University Press.

Nelson, R.R. and Winter, S.G. (1982), *An Evolutionary Theory of Economic Change*, Cambridge, USA: Belknap Press of Harvard University Press.

Nickell, S. (1996), 'Competition and Corporate Performance', *Journal of Political Economy*, **104**, 724–46.

Niskanen, W.A.J. (1971), *Bureaucracy and Representative Government*, Chicago, USA: Aldine.

Nonaka, I. and Takeuchi, H. (1995), *The Knowledge-creating Company*, New York, USA: Oxford University Press.

NVCA (2001), *2001 Venture Capital Yearbook*, New York, USA: National Venture Capital Association.

O'Reilly, C.A., Caldwell, D.F. and Barnett, W.P. (1989), 'Work Group Demography, Social Integration and Turnover', *Administrative Science Quarterly*, **34**, 21–37.

Odlyzko, A. (1995), 'The Decline of Unfettered Research', Draft, Digital Technology Center, University of Minnesota, Minneapolis, USA, http://www.dtc.umn.edu/~odlyzko/doc/decline.txt. (January 2002).

Office of Technology Assessment and Forecast (OTAF) (1998), *Concordance between the 1972 Standard Industrial Code (SIC) Classification System and the US Patent Classification (USPC) System as it Existed on 31 December 1997*, Washington, DC, USA: United States Department of Commerce, Patent and Trademark Office.

Organization for Economic Cooperation and Development (OECD) Report (1998), *Measuring the ICT Sector,* Paris, France: OECD Publications.

Organization for Economic Cooperation and Development (OECD) (ed.) (1999a), *Research and Development in Industry*, Paris, France: OECD Publications.

Organization for Economic Cooperation and Development (OECD) (ed.) (1999b), *STAN Industrial Database*, Paris, France: OECD Publications.

Oriani, R. (2002), 'Il Valore della Conoscenza Tecnologica dell'Impresa. Un'Analisi nella Prospettiva della Teoria delle Opzioni Reali', Unpublished Doctoral Thesis, University of Bologna, Bologna, Italy.

Ouchi, W.G. (1979), 'A Conceptual Framework for the Design of Organizational Control Mechanisms', *Management Science*, **25** (9), 833.

Pagano, M., Panetta, F. and Zingales, L. (1998), 'Why do Companies Go Public? An Empirical Analysis', *Journal of Finance*, **53**, 27–64.

Pagano, M., Röell, A. and Zechner, J. (2002), 'The Geography of Equity Listing: Why do European Companies List Abroad?', *Journal of Finance*, **57** (6).

Pakes, A. (1985), 'On Patents, R&D and the Stock Market Rate of Return', *Journal of Political Economy*, **93** (2), 390–409.

Palley, T. (1997), 'Managerial Turnover and the Theory of Short Termism', *Journal of Economic Behaviour and Organisation*, **32**, 547–57.

Palmer, D.A. (1993), 'Late Adoption of the Multidivisional Form by Large US Corporations: Institutional, Political and Economic Accounts', *Administrative Science Quarterly*, **38** (1), 100–132.

Parker, D. (ed.), (1998), *Privatization in the European Union. Theory and Policy Perspectives*, New York, USA: Routledge.

Pavitt, K. (1991), 'What Makes Basic Research Economically Useful?', *Research Policy*, **20**, 547–57.

Payson, S. and Jankowski, J. (2000), *Sixth Year of Unprecedented R&D Growth Expected in 2000*, Arlington, USA: National Science Foundation.

Pelz, D. and Andrews, F.M. (1966), *Scientists in Organizations*, New York, USA: Wiley.

Perotti, E. and Rossetto, S. (2000), 'The Pricing of Internet Stocks: Portals as Platforms of Entry Options', Working Paper, University of Amsterdam, Amsterdam, The Netherlands.

Pfeffer, J. (1983), 'Organizational Demography', *Research in Organizational Behavior*, **5**, 1–37.

Pollak, M. (1989), *Corporate Mergers Implicated in Slowed-down Industrial R&D Spending*, Washington, DC, USA: National Science Foundation.

Porter, M.E. (1992), 'Capital Disadvantage: America's Failing Capital Investment System', *Harvard Business Review*, **70** (5), 65–82.

Powell, W.W. and Di Maggio, P. (1991), *The New Institutionalism in Organization Analysis*, Chicago, USA and London, UK: University of Chicago Press.

PricewaterhouseCoopers (2001), *Money for Growth – Technology Investment Report 2000, UK*, New York, USA: PricewaterhouseCoopers.

Ramamurti, R. (2000), 'A Multilevel Model of Privatisation in Emerging Economies', *Academy of Management Review*, **25** (3), 525–50.

Rao, P.M. (2000), 'The Changing Structure of Corporate R&D in US Telecommunications: Is Software Taking the Helm?', *Telecommunications Policy*, **23** (1), 265–89.

Rappa, M.A. and Debackere, K. (1992), 'Technological Communities and the Diffusion of Knowledge', *R&D Management*, **22** (3), 209–20.

Ravenscraft, D.J. and Scherer, F.M. (1987), *Mergers, Sell-offs, and Economic Efficiency*, Washington, DC, USA: Brookings Institute.

Ritter, J.R. (2002), 'Investment Banking and Securities Issuance', in M. Harris, R. Stulz and G. Constantinides (eds), *Handbook of the Economics of Finance*, Amsterdam, The Netherlands: North-Holland.

Roberts, E.B. (1995), 'Benchmarking the Strategic Management of Technology-I', *Research and Technology Management* (January–February), 44–56.

Roberts, E.B. (2001), 'Benchmarking Global Strategic Management of Technology', *Research and Technology Management*, **44**, 25–6.

Romer, P. (1990), 'Endogenous Technological Change', *Journal of Political Economy*, **97**, 71–102.

Rosenberg, N. (1990), 'Why do Firms Do Basic Research (with Their Own Money)?', *Research Policy*, **19**, 165–74.

Rosenberg, N. (1994), *Exploring the Black Box*, Cambridge, UK: Cambridge University Press.

Rosenbloom, R.S. and Spencer, W.J. (1996), *Engines of Innovation: US Industrial Research at the End of an Era*, Boston, USA: Harvard Business School Press.

Rosenthal, R. (1991), *Meta-analytic Procedures for Social Research*, London, UK: Sage.

Rudge, A.W. (1990), 'Clifford Paterson Lecture: Organization and Management of R&D in a Privatized British Telecom', *Science and Public Affairs*, **4**, 155–64.

Rumelt, R.P. (1987), 'Theory, Strategy and Entrepreneurship', in D. Teece (ed.), *The Competitive Challenge*, New York, USA: Harper & Row.

Sahlman, W. (1990), 'The Structure and Governance of Venture Capital Organizations', *Journal of Financial Economics*, **27**, 473–521.

Salter, A.J. and Martin, B. (2001), 'The Economic Benefits of Publicly Funded Basic Research: A Critical Review', *Research Policy*, **30** (3), 509.

Scherer, F.M. (1965), 'Firm Size, Market Structure, Opportunity and the Output of Patented Inventions', *American Economic Review*, **55** (5), 1095–125.

Scherer, F.M. (1967), 'Market Structure and the Employment of Scientists and Engineers', *American Economic Review*, **57**, 524–31.

Schrader, S. (1991), 'Informal Technology Transfer between Firms: Cooperation through Information Trading', *Research Policy*, **20**, 153–70.

Schumpeter, J. (1942), *Capitalism, Socialism and Democracy*, New York, USA: Harper & Brothers.

Schwienbacher, A. (1999), 'Innovation and Venture Capital Exits', Working Paper, Center for Research in Finance and Management, University of Namur, Namur, Belgium.

Shleifer, A. and Vishny, R.W. (1986), 'Large Shareholders and Corporate Control', *Journal of Political Economy*, **94** (3), 461–89.

Simon, H.A. (1957), *Administrative Behavior*, New York, USA: Macmillan (It. transl. 1979, *Il Comportamento Amministrativo*, Bologna, Italy: Il Mulino).

Singh, H. and Zollo, M. (1998), 'The Impact of Knowledge Codification, Experience Trajectories and Integration Strategies on the Performance of Corporate Acquisitions', Working Paper Series, 98–02, The Wharton Financial Institutions Center, University of Pennsylvania, Philadelphia, USA.

Siniscalco, D., Bortolotti, B., Fantini, M. and Vitalini, S. (1999), *Privatizzazioni Difficili*, Bologna, Italy: Il Mulino.

Stein, J.C. (1988), 'Takeover Threats and Managerial Myopia', *Journal of Political Economy*, **96**, 61–80.

Stein, J.C. (1989), 'Efficient Capital Markets, Inefficient Firms: A Model of Myopic Corporate Behavior', *Quarterly Journal of Economics*, **104** (4), 655–69.

Stern, S. (1999a), 'Do Scientists Pay to Be Scientists?', NBER Working Paper no. 7410, National Bureau of Economic Research, Cambridge, USA.

Stern, S. (1999b), 'The Intangibles Research Project', New York University, New York, USA, http:\\www.stern.nyu.edu (March 2000).

Stern, S., Porter, M.E. and Furman, J.L. (2000), 'The Determinants of National Innovation Capacity', NBER Working Paper no. 7876, National Bureau of Economic Research, Cambridge, USA.

Stuart, T.E. and Podolny, J.M. (1996), 'Local Search and the Evolution of Technological Capabilities', *Strategic Management Journal*, **17** (Summer Special Issue), 21–38.

Sutton, J. (1991), *Sunk Costs and Market Structure*, Cambridge, USA: MIT Press.

Sutton, J (1998), *Technology and Market Structure*, Cambridge, USA: MIT Press.

Symeonides, G. (1996), 'Innovation, Firm Size and Market Structure: Schumpeterian Hypotheses and Some New Themes', OECD Working Paper no. 161, Paris, France: OECD Publications.

Tanenbau, W. (2001), 'Patent, Copyright and Domain Name Intellectual Property Due Diligence for Mergers and Acquisitions', *Law Journal-web document,* http://www.ljextra.com/practice/mergers (April 2002).

Tassey, G. (1999), 'Trends in the US Economy: Strategies and Policy Implications', in *NIST Briefing Note*, Gaithersburg, USA: National Institute of Standards and Technology, http://www.nist.gov/director/prog-ofc/report99-2.pdf (March 2000).

Tijssen, R. and Van Wijk, E. (1999), 'In Search of the European Paradox: An International Comparison of Europe's Scientific Performance and Knowledge Flows in Information and Communication Technologies Research', *Research Policy*, **28**, 522–3.

Toivanen, O. and Stoneman, P. (1998), 'Dynamics of R&D and Investments: UK Evidence', *Economics Letters*, **58** (1), 119–26.

Trajtenberg, M. (1990), 'A Penny for your Quotes: Patent Citations and the Value of Innovations', *RAND Journal of Economics*, **21** (1), 172–87.

Tushman, M.L. and Romanelli, E. (1985), 'Inertia, Environments, and Strategic Choice: A Quasi-Experimental Design for Comparative-longitudinal Research', *Management Science*, **32** (5), 608–22.

Ueda, M. (1997), 'Expertise and Finance: Mergers Motivated by Technological Change', Working Paper Series, Department of Economics and Business, University Pompeu Fabre, Barcelona, Spain, http://www.econ.upf.es/cgi-bin/authpapers (November 2000).

USPTO (1998): see OTAF (1998).

Valery, N. (1999) 'Adopting Orphans', *The Economist*, **350**, 20 February.

Vanhaverbeke, W. and Duysters, G. (1997), 'A Longitudinal Analysis of the Choice between Technology-based Strategic Alliances and Acquisitions in High-tech Industries: The Case of the ASIC Industry', NIBOR/RM/97/07 Working Paper, Netherlands Institute of Business Organization and Strategy Research, Maastricht, The Netherlands, http://www.unimaas.nl/document/fdewb.htm (April 2002).

Venture Economics (2001), *2000 Year-in-Review*, Arlington, USA: Venture Economics.

Vermeulen, F. and Barkema, H. (2001), 'Learning through Acquisitions', *Academy of Management Journal*, **44** (3), 457–76.

Vickers, J. and Yarrow, G. (1988), *Privatization: An Economic Analysis*, Cambridge, USA: MIT Press.

Volderba, H.W. (1996), 'Toward the Flexible Form: How to Remain Vital in Hypercompetitive Environments', *Organization Science*, **7** (4), 359–74.

Walsh, J.P. and Seward, J.K. (1990), 'On the Efficiency of Internal and External Corporate Control Mechanisms', *Academy of Management Review*, **15** (3), 421–58.

Wang, K., Chua, W. and Megginson, W.L. (2001), 'Signal Power of Technological and Financial Variables in Venture Capital', Vol. Draft, Price College of Business, University of Oklahoma, Norman, USA.

Westhead, P. and Storey, D.J. (1997), 'Financial Constraints on the Growth of High-tech Small Firms in the UK', *Applied Financial Economics*, **7**, 197–201.

Westphal, J.D. and Zajac, E.J. (1997), 'Defections from the Inner Circle: Social Exchange, Reciprocity, and the Diffusion of Board Independence in US Corporations', *Administrative Science Quarterly*, **42** (1), 161–84.

Wiersema, M.F. and Bantel, K.A. (1992), 'Top Management Team Demography and Corporate Strategic Change', *Academy of Management Journal*, **3** (1), 9–30.

Williamson, O.E. (1988), 'Corporate Finance and Corporate Governance', *Journal of Finance*, **48**, 267–91.

Woolridge, J.R. and Snow, C.C. (1990), 'Stock Market Reaction to Strategic Investment Decisions', *Strategic Management Journal*, **11** (5), 353–63.

Zahra, S.A. (1996), 'Governance, Ownership, and Corporate Entrepreneurship: The Moderating Impact of Industry Technological Opportunities', *Academy of Management Journal*, **39**, 1713–35.

Zahra, S.A., Ireland, D., Gutierrez, I. and Hitt, M.A. (2000), 'Privatization and Entrepreneurial Transformation: Emerging Issues and a Future Research Agenda', *Academy of Management Review*, **25**, 509–27.

Zahra, S.A. and Pearce, J.A., II (1989) 'Boards of Directors and Corporate Financial Performance', *Journal of Management*, **15** (2), 291–335.

Zander, U. and Kogut, B. (1995), 'Knowledge and the Speed of the Transfer and Imitation of Organizational Capabilities: An Empirical Test', *Organization Science*, **6** (1), 76–92.

Index